F1

Get the Most out of Excel!

The Ultimate Excel Tip Help Guide ™

F1 Get the Most out of Excel!

The Ultimate Excel Tip Help Guide

Written by: Joseph Rubin, CPA

Published by: Limelight Media Inc.
              10680 W Pico Blvd # 270
              Los Angeles, CA USA 90064
              sales@limelightmediainc.com
              www.limelightmediainc.com

Distributed by: Limelight Media Inc.

First printing: May 2004
              Printed in the State of India

Library of Congress Control Number (LCCN):
2004092192

ISBN: 0-9746368-2-7

Trademarks:

About The Author

Joseph Rubin, CPA, principal of **www.exceltip.com** (a leading Excel Web site) is the author of the very successful books:

+ ***Financial Statements.xls***
+ ***Mr Excel On Excel***

Joseph Rubin has over 25 years of financial experience in the accounting industry. He has served as CFO, Controller and has run his own CPA practice for years.

Joseph Rubin, CPA, is an independent consultant specializing in the development of applications using Microsoft Excel for the financial industry and has instructed thousands of professionals on Microsoft Excel.

Contact the author — jrubin@exceltip.com

This book is dedicated to my family, my wife, and my three children.

Special thanks to:

> *Ido Ben Horin*

> *Chris Tobin*

Joseph Rubin

How This Book Is Organized

To help you find and read the tip you need, the book has been divided to eight parts, with each part divided to categories.

Part 1 — What's New in Excel 2002 & 2003?

This part is dedicated to the new features in Excel 2002 & Excel 2003.

Part 2 — Working Inside

This part contains tips that will help you with the very basic techniques, including: Selecting, Navigating, Custom Keyboard Shortcuts, Copying & Pasting, Editing, Validating, Find, Find & Replace, Formatting (including Cell Formatting, Numbers Formatting, Euro, Conditional Formatting), and Style.

Part 3 — Excel Environment

This part contains tips that will help you get Information (Watch Window), add Comments, Picture, work with Smart Tags, handle the window (Hide, Protect Cells, Task Pane), Menus & Toolbars, Sheet (Insert, Coloring, Copying, Moving, Sorting, Protecting, Hiding), and Workbook (Opening, Closing, Saving, Recover, Path, Protecting, Password, Template).

Part 4 — Text, Dates, Times

This part contains tips that will help you work with Text (Combining, Extracting, Separating, Formulas), Import Text Files (Reverse Text, Formatting, Minus), Update Internet Data, Work with Dates (Entering, Formatting, Formulas, Validating), and Times (Entering, Formulas, Converting).

Part 5 — Summing & Counting

This part contains tips that will help you use the Calculating and Summing (Fast, Summing Rounding Numbers), as well as various options Excel offers, the SUMIF Formula, the Counting (Formulas, COUNTIF) technique, and the Euro Currency Add-In.

Part 6 — Formulas

This part contains tips that will help you work with Formulas, use the defined Name, Formulas (Entering, Editing, Nesting, Absolute & Relative, Array, Custom Function, Paste Values, Protecting, Formatting, Auditing, Errors, Links), use Lookup Formulas & Power Techniques (Vlookup, Index, Match, Sumif, Offset, Combo Box).

Part 7 — Printing & Mailing

This part contains tips that will help you Print (Page Setup, Watermark, Numbering, Path, Troubleshooting, Objects, Custom Views, Report Manager, and Custom Report Manager) and Mail (Workbook Size).

Part 8 — Lists, Analyzing Data

This part (which is the largest part) contains tips that will help you use List Objects, Sort Technique, Format Lists, Filter, add Subtotals to lists, Group & Outlines reports, Consolidate lists, Compare Lists, and analyze data using the PivotTables.

How to Find the Subject You Want

Φ By looking at the Bookmark page (which is the first page of the book), in the Part where the subject is included.

Φ By finding the Tip number or the page number in the Table of Contents (see page ix).

Φ By finding the subject in the Index. Be aware that the numbers in the Index are Tip numbers, not page numbers (see page 809).

How to Use a Tip Page

At the top-right corner of each Tip page, you will find:

Φ The Tip number (for Tips that spread over more than one page, see the page number for the Tip in the Tip box).

Φ The *Category* the Tip belongs to.

Φ The *Excel Version* the Tip belongs to.

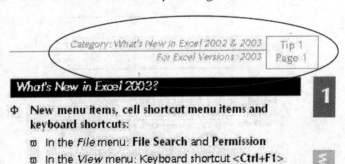

Category: What's New in Excel 2002 & 2003 — Tip 1 / Page 1
For Excel Versions: 2003

What's New in Excel 2003?

Φ **New menu items, cell shortcut menu items and keyboard shortcuts:**

ϖ In the *File* menu: **File Search** and **Permission**

ϖ In the *View* menu: Keyboard shortcut **<Ctrl+F1>** that make the **Task Pane** visible (to hide it press < Ctrl+F1>its toggle).

The Book's Left-Side Pages

This is your page — you may add *Notes*, *My Tips/Shortcuts*, references, and more.

For additional help, we've added *Related Tips/Shortcuts* as recommendations.

Tip 4	*F1 — Get the Most out of Excel!*
Notes:	
My Tips/ Shortcuts:	
Related Tips/ Shortcuts:	*Tip 9: Moving the Cell Pointer Around a Selected Range*
	Tip 12: Selecting Cells from Any Cell to the Last Cell in the Sheet's Used Range
	To select the first cell, press <Ctrl+Home>. To select the last cell, press <Ctrl+End>.

www.exceltip.com

What's New in Excel 2002 & Excel 2003 Tips List

Table of Contents at a Glance

Table of Contents

Navigating

Custom Keyboard Shortcuts

Copying & Pasting

Editing

Part 3 — Excel Environment 163

Information

Comments

Windows

Menus & Toolbars

Part 4 — Text, Dates, Times........................ 299

Text

Summing

SUMIF Formula

Counting

Euro Currency Tools Add-In

Part 6 — Formulas 443

Names

Mailing

Part 8 — Lists, Analyzing Data....................623

List Objects

Sorting

Formatting Lists

Filtering

Subtotals

PivotTables

Part 1 — What's New in Excel 2002 & 2003?

1

What's New in Excel 2002 & 2003

Speech

Notes:

_____

_____

_____

_____

_____

_____

**My Tips/
Shortcuts:**

_____

_____

_____

_____

_____

_____

**Related
Tips:**   *What's New in Excel 2002 & Excel 2003,
           Tips List, see page ix.*

_____

_____

What's New in Excel 2003?

✦ **New menu items, cell shortcut menu items and keyboard shortcuts:**

❖ In the *File* menu: **File Search** and **Permission**

❖ In the *View* menu: Keyboard shortcut **<Ctrl+F1>** makes the **Task Pane** visible. To hide it, press **<Ctrl+F1>**(its toggle).

❖ In the *Tools* menu: **Research** along with keyboard shortcut **<Alt+Click>**.

❖ In the *Data* menu: **List** along with keyboard shortcut **<Ctrl+L>** and **XML**.

❖ In the *Window* menu: **Compare Side by Side**.

❖ In the *Help* menu: **Contact Us** and **Check for Updates**.

❖ In the cell shortcut menu: **Create List** and **Lookup**.

❖ New keyboard shortcuts: **<Ctrl+A>** to select **List/Current Region**; **<Ctrl+A+A>** to select all cells in the sheet (for more details, see *Tip #8*).

For more details about the new additions, see *page ix*.

✦ **Expanded Task Panes** (for more details, see *Tip #92*)

Task Panes were new features in **Excel 2002**, and have been expanded in **Excel 2003**. There are now 11 **Task Panes**, with the new ones being:

❖ **Getting Started**

❖ **Help**

❖ **Research**

❖ **Template Help**

❖ **Shared Workspace**

❖ **Document Updates**

❖ **XML Source**

continued...

Notes:

_____

_____

_____

_____

_____

_____

_____

_____

_____

_____

**My Tips/
Shortcuts:**

_____

_____

_____

_____

_____

_____

_____

_____

_____

www.exceltip.com

What's New in Excel 2003? (cont.)

1

W hat's New in Excel 2002 & 2003

✦ **Sort Ascending/Sort Descending when using AutoFilter**

For more details, see *Tip #262*.

	Invoice Number ▾	Date ▾	Customer Name ▾	Market ▾	Quantity ▾	Income ▾
1						
2	1012	12/15/2002	Sort Ascending	Europe	178	1,775.00
3	1004	04/15/2002	Sort Descending	Europe	185	1,854.00
4	1011	11/15/2002	(All)	Europe	199	1,985.00
5	1001	01/15/2002	(Top 10...)	Europe	252	2,523.00
6	1003	03/15/2002	(Custom...)	N.America	665	6,652.00
7	1029	05/15/2002	Amazon	N.America	685	6,851.00
8	1010	15/15/2002	eBay	Africa	741	7,412.00
9	1013	01/15/2003	ExcelTip	Europe	965	9,652.00
10	1005	05/15/2002	Ford	Africa	966	9,658.00
11	1020	09/15/2003	GM	Europe	989	9,885.00
12	1025	01/15/2004	Intel	N.America	998	9,981.00
13	1009	09/15/2002	Microsoft	Europe	999	9,985.00
14	1021	15/4/2012	Toyota (Blanks) (NonBlanks) ExcelTip	N.America	1,156	11,557.00

✦ **Expanded Subtotal Function Options**

The **Subtotal** function has the following new options:

❖ Two new statistical functions: **VAR** and **VARP**.

❖ The **Subtotal** function returns values from hidden cells (when using **AutoFilter**, **Subtotals** and **Consolidate Using Links** techniques) in two formats, either including hidden values or ignoring them.

For more details, see *Tip #263*.

Function_num (includes hidden values)	Function_num (ignores hidden values)	Function
1	101	AVERAGE
2	102	COUNT
3	103	COUNTA
4	104	MAX
5	105	MIN
6	106	PRODUCT
7	107	STDEV
8	108	STDEVP
9	109	SUM
10	110	VAR
11	111	VARP

continued...

Notes:

**My Tips/
Shortcuts:**

What's New in Excel 2003? (cont.)

✦ **XML Support**

You may import and export XML data in any schema.
XML support allows you to:

❖ Expose your data to external processes in a business-centric XML vocabulary.

❖ Organize and work with workbooks and data in ways that were previously impossible or very difficult. By using your XML schemas, you can now identify and extract specific pieces of business data from ordinary business documents.

❖ Attach a custom XML schema to any workbook by using the XML Source task pane to map cells to elements of the schema. Once you have mapped the XML elements to your sheet, you can seamlessly import and export XML data into and out of the mapped cells.

To use XML, select **XML** from the *Data* menu.

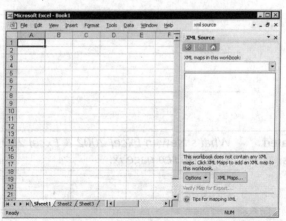

Notes:

_____

_____

_____

_____

_____

_____

**My Tips/
Shortcuts:**

_____

_____

_____

_____

_____

_____

**Related
Tips:**   *What's New in Excel 2002 & Excel 2003,
Tips List, see page ix.*

_____

_____

What's New in Excel 2002/2003: Menu, Cell Shortcut Menu and Keyboard Shortcuts

1

✦ *File* **Menu:**

 ❖ **Excel 2002: Search**, and a new **Search** icon on the regular **Standard** toolbar.

 ❖ **Excel 2003: File Search**. The **File Search** icon does not appear on the **Standard** toolbar, but can be added from the **Tools** category in **Commands** tab of the *Customize* dialog box.

 ❖ **Excel 2003: Permission**. For more details, go to www.microsoft.com and search for *IRM — Information Rights Management*.

✦ *View* **Menu:**

 ❖ **Excel 2002: Task Pane**

 ❖ **Excel 2003: Task Pane** and the new keyboard shortcut **<Ctrl+F1>**(see *Tip #92*)

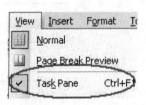

continued...

Notes:

_____

_____

_____

_____

_____

_____

**My Tips/
Shortcuts:**

_____

_____

_____

_____

_____

_____

_____

_____

_____

What's New in Excel 2002/2003: Menu, Cell Shortcut Menu and Keyboard Shortcuts (cont.)

1

W hat's New in Excel 2002 & 2003

✦ *Insert* **Menu:**

❖ **Excel 2002 & 2003: Symbol** (see *Tip #56*)

❖ **Excel 2002 & 2003: Diagram**

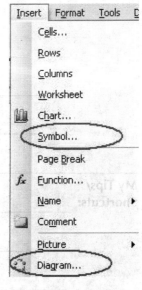

✦ *Tools* **Menu:**

❖ **Excel 2003: Research** and the new keyboard shortcut **<Alt+Click>**.

❖ **Excel 2002 & Excel 2003: Error Checking** (see *Tip #218*)

❖ **Excel 2002 & Excel 2003: Speech** (see *Tip #3*)

❖ **Excel 2002 & Excel 2003: Euro Conversion** (see *Tip #186*)

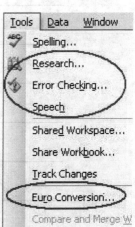

continued...

11

Notes:

_____

_____

_____

_____

_____

_____

**My Tips/
Shortcuts:**

_____

_____

_____

_____

_____

_____

_____

_____

_____

_____

What's New in Excel 2002/2003: Menu, Cell Shortcut Menu and Keyboard Shortcuts (cont.)

1

✦ *Data* **Menu:**
   ❖ **Excel 2003: List** and the new keyboard shortcut **<Ctrl+L>** (see *Tip #252*)
   ❖ **Excel 2003: XML** (see *Tip #1*).

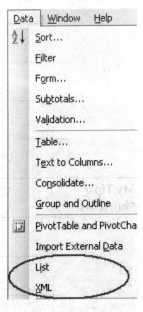

✦ *Window* **Menu:**
   ❖ **Excel 2003: Compare Side by Side**. This new feature improves the **Arrange** menu item.

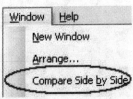

✦ *Help* **Menu:**
   ❖ **Excel 2003: Contact Us**
   ❖ **Excel 2003: Check for Updates** (connects to the Web for Microsoft Office updates).

continued...

W hat's New in Excel 2002 & 2003

Notes:

_____

_____

_____

_____

_____

_____

_____

_____

**My Tips/
Shortcuts:**

_____

_____

_____

_____

_____

_____

_____

_____

_____

_____

What's New in Excel 2002/2003: Menu, Cell Shortcut Menu and Keyboard Shortcuts (cont.)

1

W hat's New in Excel 2002 & 2003

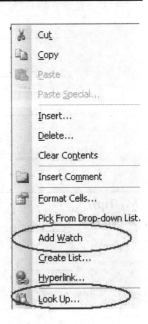

+ **Cell Right-Click Shortcut Menu, Keyboard Shortcut <Shift+F10>:**
  + **Excel 2002 & 2003: Add Watch** (see *Tip #71*)
  + **Excel 2003: Create List** (see the *Data* menu, above, and see *Tip #252*)
  + **Excel 2003: Lookup** (see **Research** in the *Tools* menu above (Why is it a different name? I have no answer!)

Notes:

_____

_____

_____

_____

_____

**My Tips/
Shortcuts:**

_____

_____

_____

_____

_____

_____

_____

_____

_____

_____

Let Excel Read Text for You

➤ **To let Excel read text for you:**
1. Select a range of cells.
2. From the *Tools* menu, select **Speech** and then **Show Text To Speech Toolbar**.
3. Click the leftmost icon, **Speak Cells**, or click **Speak On Enter** (the rightmost icon) to listen upon selecting the cell.

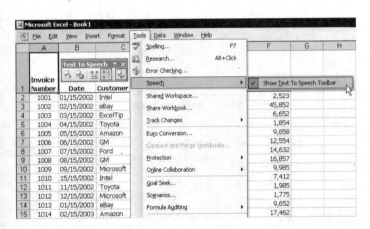

Part 2 — Working Inside

2

Selecting

Navigating

Custom Keyboard Shortcuts

Copying & Pasting

Editing

Formatting

Styles

Notes:

**My Tips/
Shortcuts:**

Related Tips/ Shortcuts:	*Tip 9: Moving the Cell Pointer Around a Selected Range*
	Tip 12: Selecting Cells from Any Cell to the Last Cell in the Sheet's Used Range
	To select the first cell, press **<Ctrl+Home>**.
	To select the last cell, press **<Ctrl+End>**.

Moving to the Last (or First) Cell in a Range

Using keyboard shortcuts

➤ **To move to the last (or first) cell in a range:**

✦ Vertically from top to bottom, press **\<Ctrl+Down Arrow\>**.

✦ Vertically from bottom to top, press **\<Ctrl+Up Arrow\>**.

✦ Horizontally from left to right, press **\<Ctrl+Right Arrow\>**.

✦ Horizontally from right to left, press **\<Ctrl+Left Arrow\>**.

Using the mouse

✦ Double-click one edge of the selected cell when the mouse image changes to four directional arrows.

Microsoft Excel - Book1

	File	Edit	View	Insert	Format	Tools	Data	Window	Help

	A	B	C	D	E	F	G
1	1	2	3	4	5	6	7
2	2	4	6	8	10	12	14
3	3	6	9	12	15	18	21
4	4	8	12	16	20	24	28
5	5	10	15	20	25	30	35
6	6	12	18	24	30	36	42
7	7	14	21	28	35	42	49
8	8	16	24	32	40	48	56
9	9	18	27	36	45	54	63
10	10	20	30	40	50	60	70

Notes:

**My Tips/
Shortcuts:**

Related Tips:	*Tip 6: Quickly Selecting a Range of Cells*
	Tip 7: Selecting a Range of Non-Adjacent Cells
	Tip 8: Selecting the Current Region/List

Selecting Cells in Horizontal or Vertical Ranges

Using keyboard shortcuts

➤ **To select a range of cells:**
  ✦ Vertically from top to bottom, press **<Ctrl+Shift+Down Arrow>**.
  ✦ Vertically from bottom to top, press **<Ctrl+Shift+Up Arrow>**.
  ✦ Horizontally from left to right, press **<Ctrl+Shift+Right Arrow>**.
  ✦ Horizontally from right to left, press **<Ctrl+Shift+Left Arrow>**.

➤ **To select cells one after another:**
  ✦ Press **<Shift+ Arrow>**.

Using the mouse

✦ Select a cell in a range, press the **<Shift>** key and double-click the edge of the selected cell when the mouse image changes to four directional arrows.

	A	B	C	D	E	F	G
1	1	2	3	4	5	6	7
2	2	4	6	8	10	12	14
3	3	6	9	12	15	18	21
4	4	8	12	16	20	24	28
5	5	10	15	20	25	30	35
6	6	12	18	24	30	36	42
7	7	14	21	28	35	42	49
8	8	16	24	32	40	48	56
9	9	18	27	36	45	54	63
10	10	20	30	40	50	60	70
11							

Microsoft Excel - Book1

File Edit View Insert Format Tools Data Window Help

Notes:

**My Tips/
Shortcuts:**

| **Related
Tips /
Shortcuts:** | *Tip 7: Selecting a Range of Non-Adjacent Cells* |
| | *Tip 8: Selecting the Current Region/List* |

To select the **Current Region/List**, press **<Ctrl+Shift+*>** (in **Excel 2003**, press this or **<Ctrl+A>**).

Quickly Selecting a Range of Cells

➢ **To quickly select a range of cells:**

✦ **Option One:** Select the first cell, press **<Shift>**, select another cell and then click the mouse.

✦ **Option Two:** Select the first cell, type the address of the last cell in the **Name** box, and then press **<Shift+Enter>**.

Microsoft Excel - Book1						
File	Edit	View	Insert	Format	Tools	Data	Window	Help
D10	▼	*fx*				
	A	B	C	D	E	F
1						
2						
3						
4						
5						
6						
7						
8						
9						
10				⊕		
11						
12						

Notes:

_____

_____

_____

_____

_____

_____

**My Tips/
Shortcuts:**

_____

_____

_____

_____

_____

_____

**Related
Tips:**

Tip 8: Selecting the Current Region/List

Tip 10: Selecting Special Cells

*Tip 12: Selecting Cells from Any Cell to the
Last Cell in the Sheet's Used Area*

Selecting a Range of Non-Adjacent Cells

➢ **To select a range of non-adjacent cells:**

1. Select cell **A1**, and press **<Ctrl+Shift+Down Arrow>**.

2. Continue holding down **<Ctrl>**, and select another range.

3. Select additional ranges while continuing to press **<Ctrl>**.

2

	A	B	C	D	E	F	G
1	1	2	3	4	5	6	7
2	2	4	6	8	10	12	14
3	3	6	9	12	15	18	21
4	4	8	12	16	20	24	28
5	5	10	15	20	25	30	35
6	6	12	18	24	30	36	42
7	7	14	21	28	35	42	49
8	8	16	24	32	40	48	56
9	9	18	27	36	45	54	63
10	10	20	30	40	50	60	70
11	11	22	33	44	55	66	77
12	12	24	36	48	60	72	84
13	13	26	39	52	65	78	91

Microsoft Excel - Book1

File   Edit   View   Insert   Format   Tools   Data   Window   Help

Notes:

_____

_____

_____

_____

_____

_____

_____

**My Tips/
Shortcuts:**

_____

_____

_____

_____

_____

_____

**Related
Tips:**

Tip 10: Selecting Special Cells

*Tip 12: Selecting Cells from Any Cell to the
Last Cell in the Sheet's Used Range*

Tip 14: Selecting All Sheet Cells

Selecting the Current Region/List

 Using keyboard shortcuts

The **Current Region/List** is a range of cells containing data bounded by blank rows and columns.

➢ **To select the Current Region/List:**

✦ Select a cell inside the **Current Region/List** range and press **<Ctrl+Shift+*>** (when using the * on the numeric keypad, press **<Ctrl+*>**).

✦ **New keyboard shortcut in Excel 2003:** Select a cell inside the **Current Region/List** and press **<Ctrl+A>** (you can still use **<Ctrl+Shift+*>**) (see Tip #1).

	A	B	C	D	E	F	G
1	1	2	3	4	5		7
2	2	4	6	8	10		14
3	3	6	9	12	15		21
4	4	8	12	16	20		28
5	5	10	15	20	25		35
6	6	12	18	24	30		42
7	7	14	21	28	35		49
8	8	16	24	32	40		56
9	9	18	27	36	45		63
10	10	20	30	40	50		70
11	11	22	33	44	55		77
12	12	24	36	48	60		84
13							84
14	14	28	42	56	70		84
15	15	30	45	60	75		105
16	16	32	48	64	80		112
17	17	34	51	68	85		119

Microsoft Excel - Book1

File　Edit　View　Insert　Format　Tools　Data　Window　Help

Notes:

_____

_____

_____

_____

_____

**My Tips/
Shortcuts:**

_____

_____

_____

_____

_____

_____

Related Tips:	*Tip 4: Moving to the Last (or First) Cell in a Range*
	Tip 6: Quickly Selecting a Range of Cells
	Tip 13: Moving Between Unprotected Cells in a Protected Sheet

Moving the Cell Pointer Around a Selected Range

Using keyboard shortcuts

✦ **For fast typing in a border area, select a range of cells. The borders of the selected range are clearly defined:**

❖ To move vertically downward within the selected range, press **<Enter>**.

❖ To move vertically upward, press **<Shift+Enter>**.

❖ To move horizontally to the right, press **<Tab>**.

❖ To move horizontally to the left, press **<Shift+Tab>**.

❖ To move from one corner to the other corner of the range, press **<Ctrl+.>** (**<Ctrl>** and a period).

	A	B	C	D	E	F	G
1	1	2	3	4	5	6	
2	2	4	6	8	10	12	
3	3	6	9	12	15	18	
4	4	8	12	16	20	24	
5	5	10	15	20	25	30	
6	6	12	18	24	30	36	
7	7	14	21	28	35	42	
8	8	16	24	32	40	48	
9	9	18	27	36	45	54	
10	10	20	30	40	50	60	
11							
12							

Microsoft Excel - Book1

File Edit View Insert Format Tools Data Window Help

Notes:

_____

_____

_____

_____

_____

_____

**My Tips/
Shortcuts:**

_____

_____

_____

_____

_____

**Related
Tips:**   _Tip 5: Selecting Cells in Horizontal or
Vertical Ranges_

Tip 6: Quickly Selecting a Range of Cells

_Tip 7: Selecting a Range of Non-Adjacent
Cells_

Selecting Special Cells

Selecting special cells in a sheet, for example, cells containing Constants, Formulas, blank cells, and more (see the *Go To Special* dialog box) enables you to copy, move, delete, color, fill, or protect these cells.

➤ **To select special cells:**

1. Press **<F5>**, or from the *Edit* menu, select Go To.
2. In the *Go To* dialog box, click **Special**.
3. Select one of the option buttons, and click **OK**.

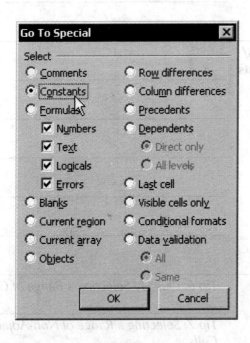

Notes:

_____

_____

_____

_____

_____

_____

**My Tips/
Shortcuts:**

_____

_____

_____

_____

_____

_____

_____

Related Tips:	Tip 6: Quickly Selecting a Range of Cells
	Tip 7: Selecting a Range of Non-Adjacent Cells
	Tip 86: Hiding/Unhiding a Row(s) or Column(s)

Selecting a Column(s) or Row(s) Using Keyboard Shortcuts

Using keyboard shortcuts

✦ To select a column(s), select a cell or several cells in a sheet, and press **<Ctrl+Spacebar>**.

✦ To select a row(s), select a cell or several cells in a sheet, and press **<Shift+Spacebar>**.

✦ To continue selecting columns or rows, press **<Shift+Arrow>** keys.

2

Selecting

	A	B	C	D	E	F	G
1	1	2	3	4	5	6	
2	2	4	6	8	10	12	
3	3	6	9	12	15	18	
4	4	8	12	16	20	24	
5	5	10	15	20	25	30	
6	6	12	18	24	30	36	
7	7	14	21	28	35	42	
8	8	16	24	32	40	48	
9	9	18	27	36	45	54	
10	10	20	30	40	50	60	
11							

Microsoft Excel - Book1

File   Edit   View   Insert   Format   Tools   Data   Window   Help

Related Tips: Tip 9: Selecting Cells in Horizontal or Vertical Ranges

Tip 8: Selecting the Current Region (List)

Tip 10: Selecting All Sheet Cells

Notes:

_____

_____

_____

_____

_____

_____

My Tips/
Shortcuts:

_____

_____

_____

_____

_____

_____

Related	*Tip 5: Selecting Cells in Horizontal or*
Tips:	*Vertical Ranges*
	Tip 8: Selecting the Current Region/List
	Tip 14: Selecting All Sheet Cells

Selecting Cells from Any Cell to the Last Cell in the Sheet's Used Range

Using keyboard shortcuts

The keyboard shortcuts **<Ctrl+Shift+End>** and **<Ctrl+Shift+Home>** enable the quick selection of cells either down to the last cell of the sheet's **Used Range** or to the first cell (**A1**), respectively.

Example:

To clear the cell content from cell **A7** to the last cell in the sheet's **Used Range** (cell **G13** in this example):

1. Select cell **A7**.
2. Press **<Ctrl+Shift+End>**.
3. Press **<Delete>**.

	A	B	C	D	E	F	G
1	1	2	3	4	5	6	
2	2	4	6	8	10	12	
3	3	6	9	12	15	18	
4	4	8	12	16	20	24	
5	5	10	15	20	25	30	
6	6	12	18	24	30	36	
7	7	14	21	28	35	42	
8	8	16	24	32	40	48	
9	9	18	27	36	45	54	
10	10	20	30	40	50	60	
11							
12							
13							
14							

Microsoft Excel - Book1

File   Edit   View   Insert   Format   Tools   Data   Window   Help

Notes:

**My Tips/
Shortcuts:**

Related Tips:	*Tip 107: Protecting the Sheet or the Cells in the Sheet*
	Tip 109: Limiting the Movement in a Protected Sheet
	Tip 110: Limiting the Movement in an Unprotected Sheet

Moving Between Unprotected Cells in a Protected Sheet

Using keyboard shortcuts

Press **<Tab>** to move between unprotected cells in a protected sheet.

Example:

In the screenshot below, the colored cells (containing formulas) are protected. Press **<Tab>** to move between unprotected cells (the uncolored cells).

	A	B	C	D
1				
2	December 31, 2003 ▼			
3				
4	XYZ Corporation Inc.			
5	BALANCE SHEET			
6				
7			December 31	
8		Notes	2003	2002
9	ASSETS			
10				
11	**Current Assets**			
12	Cash	5	301,124	318,697
13	Accounts Receivable	7	1,653,558	1,538,494
14	Inventories	8	546,173	520,133
15	Prepaid Expenses	9	13,552	23,659
16	Total Current Assets		2,514,407	2,400,982
17				
18	**Property and Equipment (at Cost)**	10		
19	Land & Building		674,019	677,191
20	Machinery and Equipment		386,140	326,052
21	Furniture and Fixtures		59,410	47,906
22	Total Property and Equipment		1,119,569	1,051,150
23	Less: Accumulated Depreciation		(478,852)	(419,540)
24	Net Book Value		640,717	631,610
25				
26	**Other Assets**			
27	Investment in Revenue Bond	11	364,321	300,260
28	Patents, Trademarks and Goodwill	12	52,250	52,500
29	Total Other Assets		416,571	352,760
30				
31	TOTAL ASSETS		3,571,695	3,385,352

Microsoft Excel - Financial Statements
File Edit View Insert Format Tools Data Window Help

Notes:

_____

_____

_____

_____

_____

_____

**My Tips/
Shortcuts:**

_____

_____

_____

_____

_____

_____

Related Tips:	*Tip 5: Selecting Cells in Horizontal or Vertical Ranges*
	Tip 7: Selecting a Range of Non-Adjacent Cells
	Tip 8: Selecting the Current Region/List

Selecting All Sheet Cells

Using keyboard shortcuts

✦ **To select the sheet cells**: In **Excel 97**, **2000** and **2002**, press **<Ctrl+A>**.

✦ In **Excel 2003**, select a cell in a blank range area and press **<Ctrl+A>**. When selecting a cell in the **Current Region/List** range area, press **<Ctrl+A+A>**.

For more on this keyboard shortcut, *see Tip #1.*

A note to Excel developers:

When selecting the **Current Region** in **Excel 2003** using **<Ctrl+A>**, the active cell remains the same; however, by pressing the **<Ctrl+Shift+*>** keyboard shortcut, the active cell is the first cell in the selected range.

Using the mouse

Click **Select All** at the top-left corner of the sheet.

	A	B	C	D	E	F	G
1	1	2	3	4	5	6	7
2	2	4	6	8	10	12	14
3	3	6	9	12	15	18	21
4	4	8	12	16	20	24	28
5	5	10	15	20	25	30	35
6	6	12	18	24	30	36	42
7	7	14	21	28	35	42	49
8	8	16	24	32	40	48	56
9	9	18	27	36	45	54	63
10	10	20	30	40	50	60	70
11							
12							

Notes:

My Tips/ Shortcuts:

Related Tips:	Tip 187: Range Name Syntax
	Tip 188: Defining a Range Name
	Tip 213: Moving Between Precedent and Dependent Cells

2

Quickly Selecting a Range in the Workbook

The best way to select a cell or range of cells in either the current or any other sheet in the workbook is by selecting the **Name** defined for that range from the **Name Box** dropdown list to the left of the **Formula Bar**.

The **Name Box** contains a list of the **Names** assigned to the cell addresses. Selecting a **Name** is the same as selecting the address of a cell or range of cells in the active workbook.

For more details on *Defining a Range Name*, see *Tip #188*.

	B	C	D	E	F	G
Dollar	2	3	4	5	6	7
Euro	4	6	8	10	12	14
NetCashFlow	6	9	12	15	18	21
NetIncome						
4	4	8	12	16	20	24	28
5	5	10	15	20	25	30	35
6	6	12	18	24	30	36	42
7	7	14	21	28	35	42	49
8	8	16	24	32	40	48	56
9	9	18	27	36	45	54	63
10	10	20	30	40	50	60	70
11						

Notes:

_____

_____

_____

_____

_____

_____

_____

My Tips/
Shortcuts:

_____

_____

_____

_____

_____

_____

Related Tips:	*Tip 17: Selecting a Sheet from a Sorted Sheets List*
	Tip 102: Coloring Sheet Tabs
	Tip 104: Sorting Sheets in Ascending Order

Selecting a Sheet in the Workbook

Using keyboard shortcuts

+ To move to the next sheet in the workbook, press **<Ctrl+Page Down>**.

+ To move to the previous sheet in the workbook, press **<Ctrl+Page Up>**.

Using the mouse

+ To the left of the sheet tabs in the horizontal **Scroll Bar** are four small arrows.

  1. Place the mouse pointer over one of the arrows and right-click.

  2. From the shortcut menu, select a sheet from the list of sheet names.

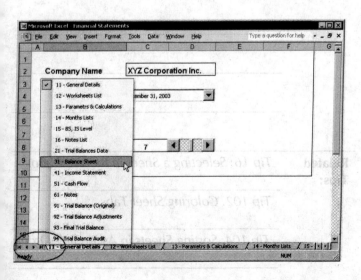

Notes:

My Tips/ Shortcuts:

Selecting a Sheet from a Sorted Sheets List

➢ **To select a sheet from a list of sheets sorted in ascending order, install the ChooseSheet.xla Add-in:**

1. Download the **ChooseSheet.xla** add-in from the ExcelTip.com Web site: www.exceltip.com.

2. Save the downloaded **ChooseSheet.xla** file in any folder.

3. From the *Tools* menu, select **Add-Ins**, and then click **Browse**.

4. Locate and select the **ChooseSheet.xla** file and click **OK**.

5. From the Add-ins available, check the **ChooseSheet.xla** box, and then click **OK**.

6. To select a sheet from the sorted sheets list, click the new **Choose Sheet** icon (number 7 in the **Regular** toolbar).

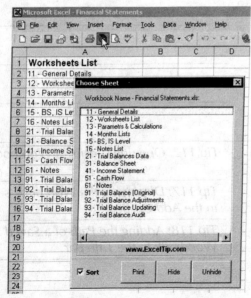

47

Notes:

**My Tips/
Shortcuts:**

Moving Between Open Workbooks

Using keyboard shortcuts

✦ The keyboard shortcut for moving to the next open workbook is either **<Ctrl+Tab>** or **<Ctrl+F6>**.

✦ To move to the previous open workbook, press **<Ctrl+Shift+Tab>**.

✦ Press **<Alt+W>** to open the *Window* menu, and then the workbook index number.

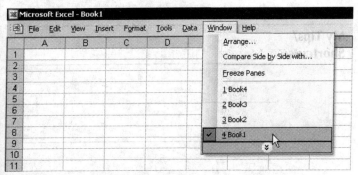

Using the mouse

✦ From the *Window* menu, select a workbook from the list of open workbooks.

Related   Tip 85: Making a Cell the First Cell in the
Tip: Active Window

Tip 20: Pasting Values

2

Notes:

My Tips/
Shortcuts:

| **Related** | Tip 85: Making a Cell the First Cell in the |
| **Tips:** | Active Window |

Tip 203: Pasting Values

Adding a Custom Keyboard Shortcut

Using keyboard shortcuts

To add a custom keyboard shortcut, add, save and store a VBA code line. It is recommended that general custom keyboard shortcuts be saved in the **Personal Macro Workbook**. This workbook is created the first time you record and store a macro, and remains hidden when Excel is opened.

➢ **To create the Personal Macro Workbook while storing a new keyboard shortcut:**

   1. From the *Tools* menu, select **Macro**, and then **Record New Macro**.

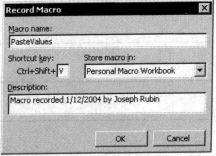

   2. In the **Macro** name box, insert a name for the macro (no spaces are allowed between characters).

   3. In the **Shortcut key** box, press **<Shift+ V>**.

   4. Choose **Personal Macro Workbook** from the **Store macro in** dropdown list, and click **OK**.

   5. Record anything you like and then stop recording

by pressing the **Stop Recording** icon.

continued...

Notes:

My Tips/ Shortcuts:

Adding a Custom Keyboard Shortcut (cont.)

6. Open the **VBE** (Visual Basic Editor) by pressing **<Alt+F11>**.

7. Double-click **Module1** under **VBAProject (PERSONAL.XLS)**.

8. In the **PasteValues** macro, replace the lines recorded with:

   Selection.Formula = Selection.Value

   This code converts a selected cell's formula to its current value.

9. Click **Save**.

10. Press **<Alt+F4>** to close and then reopen Excel.

11. To determine if **PERSONAL.XLS** is open, select **Unhide** from the *Windows* menu.

12. To check the keyboard shortcut, select cells containing formulas, and press **<Ctrl+Shift+V>**.

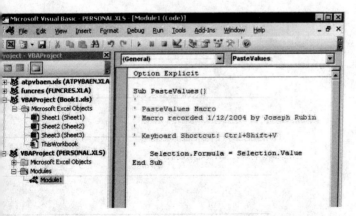

continued...

Notes:

**My Tips/
Shortcuts:**

Adding a Custom Keyboard Shortcut (cont.)

➤ **To add/change a keyboard shortcut:**

1. In Excel, press **<Alt+F8>** to open the *Macro* dialog box.
2. Select the macro from **Macro name** list.
3. Click **Options**.
4. In the *Macro Options* dialog box, change or add the **Shortcut key** and click **OK**.

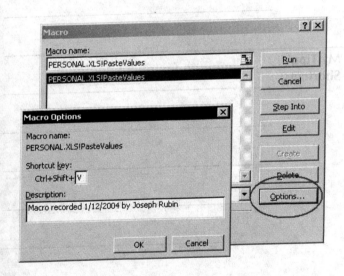

2

Custom Keyboard Shortcuts

55

Notes:

**My Tips/
Shortcuts:**

**Related
Tips:**   *Tip 21: Fast Copying & Pasting in Adjacent
Cells*

*Tip 22: Fast Copying & Pasting Right or
Down in a List*

*Tip 23: Copying & Pasting Cell Content to
Thousands of Cells*

Copying, Cutting and Pasting (Moving)

Using keyboard shortcuts

✦ To copy, press **<Ctrl+C>**.

✦ To cut, press **<Ctrl+X>**.

✦ To paste, with the option of repeating the operation (if copying), press **<Ctrl+V>**.

✦ To paste, without the option of repeating the operation (if copying), press **<Enter>**.

Using the mouse

➢ **To copy a cell(s), row(s), column(s), or sheet:**

1. Select a cell(s), row(s), column(s), or sheet tab.

2. Press **<Ctrl>** and hold the mouse over the selection border, while left-clicking and moving the object to a new location.

   OR

   Press **<F8>** to lock the **<Ctrl>** key (the letters **EXT** appear in the Status Bar), while left-clicking and moving the object to a new location.

3. Release both the **<Ctrl>** key and the mouse.

   OR

   Press **<F8>** again to unlock the **<Ctrl>** key.

➢ **To move (cut and paste) a cell(s), row(s), column(s), or sheet:**

1. Select the object.

2. Hold the mouse over the selection border, left-click and move the object to a new location.

3. Release the mouse.

Notes:

_____

_____

_____

_____

_____

**My Tips/
Shortcuts:**

_____

_____

_____

Related Tips:	*Tip 20: Copying, Cutting and Pasting (Moving)*
	Tip 22: Fast Copying & Pasting Right or Down in a List
	Tip 23: Copying & Pasting Cell Content to Thousands of Cells

Fast Copying & Pasting in Adjacent Cells

Using the mouse

➤ **To copy quickly by double-clicking:**

1. Select cell **B1**.
2. Place the mouse on the handle in the bottom right-hand corner of the cell.
3. Double-click when the mouse pointer changes into a plus symbol. Excel copies the constants or formulas in the cell down the length of column B.

2

Microsoft Excel - Book1						
File Edit View Insert Format Tools Data Window Help						
B1	▼	ƒx =A1				
	A	B	C	D	E	F
1	1	1				
2	2					
3	3					
4	4					
5	5					
6	6					
7	7					
8	8					
9	9					
10	10					

Copying & Pasting

Notes:

**My Tips/
Shortcuts:**

| **Related
Tips:**	Tip 23: Copying & Pasting Cell Content to Thousands of Cells
	Tip 24: Pasting Multiple Copied Ranges Using the Clipboard
	Tip 25: Inserting a Copied Cell(s) Without Overwriting Existing Data

Fast Copying & Pasting Right or Down in a List

➢ **To copy to the right or down:**
  ✦ **To the right:** Select a range of cells to the right and press **<Ctrl+R>** (see the screenshots).
  ✦ **Down:** Select the cells in the row(s) under the list and press **<Ctrl+D>**.

2

Before:

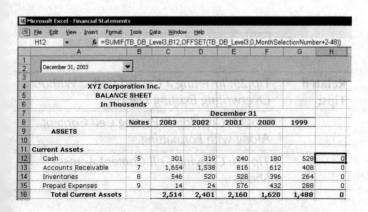

After:

Notes:

**My Tips/
Shortcuts:**

Related Tips:	*Tip 25: Inserting a Copied Cell(s) Without Overwriting Existing Data*
	Tip 27: Copying & Pasting Cell Content Along with Formatting
	Tip 28: Copying Cell Content Across Sheets

Copying & Pasting Cell Content to Thousands of Cells

➢ **To copy & paste cell content to thousands of cells:**
1. Select and copy cell **A1**.
2. Type a cell address in the **Name box**, for this example, type **A5000**.
3. Press **<Shift+Enter>** to select the cells from **A1:A5000**.
4. To paste, press **<Enter>**.

	A	B	C	D	E	F
1	ExcelTip					
2						
3						
4						
5						
6						
7						
8						
9						

Microsoft Excel - Book1
File Edit View Insert Format Tools Data Window Help
A5000

Related Tips: Tip 27: Copying & Pasting Cell Content Along with Formatting.

Tip 28: Copying Cell Content Across Sheets.

Tip 29: Copying/Moving a Cell(s) Between Sheets/Workbooks.

Notes:

My Tips/
Shortcuts:

Related	*Tip 27: Copying & Pasting Cell Content*
Tips:	*Along with Formatting*
	Tip 28: Copying Cell Content Across
	Sheets
	Tip 29: Copying/Moving a Cell(s) Between
	Sheets/Workbooks

Pasting Multiple Copied Ranges Using the Clipboard

✦ In **Excel 2000**, the **Clipboard** holds up to 12 copied
  ranges. To make the **Clipboard** toolbar visible:

  ❖ Press **<Ctrl+C+C>**

     OR

     From the *View*
     menu, select
     Toolbars and then
     Clipboard.

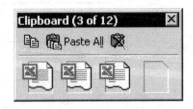

✦ In **Excel 2002** and **Excel 2003**, use the keyboard
  shortcut **<Ctrl+C+C>** to open the *Task Pane* dialog
  box, which contains the copied ranges (up to 24) that
  have been saved to memory.

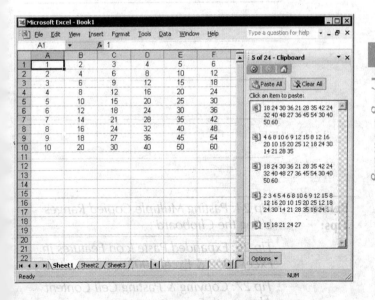

Notes:

_____

_____

_____

_____

_____

_____

_____

**My Tips/
Shortcuts:**

_____

_____

_____

_____

_____

_____

Related Tips:	*Tip 24: Pasting Multiple Copied Ranges Using the Clipboard*
	Tip 26: Expanded Paste Icon Features in Excel 2002 & Excel 2003
	Tip 27: Copying & Pasting Cell Content Along with Formatting

Inserting a Copied Cell(s) Without Overwriting Existing Data

Using keyboard shortcuts

➢ **To copy & paste a cell(s) containing data without overwriting existing data using only a keyboard shortcut:**

1. Copy a cell(s) containing data.
2. Select a cell inside the range of cells that should not be overwritten.

3. Press **<Ctrl++>** (plus sign) to open the *Insert* dialog box.

4. Select **Shift cells right** or **Shift cells down**, and click **OK**.

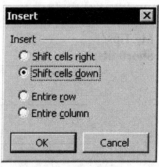

Using the mouse

➢ **To copy & paste a cell(s) without overwriting existing data, using both a keyboard shortcut and the mouse:**

1. Select a cell(s) that contains the data to be copied.
2. Hold the **<Ctrl+Shift>** keys, move the mouse over the selection border, and when the cursor changes to a small cross, drag the cell(s) to a new location and paste it.
3. Notice the gray line bar that follows the mouse. Position it in the new location and release the mouse.

Notes:

_____

_____

_____

_____

_____

_____

My Tips/
Shortcuts:

_____

_____

_____

_____

_____

_____

Related Tips:	*Tip 23: Copying & Pasting Cell Content to Thousands of Cells*
	Tip 24: Pasting Multiple Copied Ranges Using the Clipboard
	Tip 25: Inserting a Copied Cell(s) Without Overwriting Existing Data

Expanded Paste Icon Features in Excel 2002 & Excel 2003

Excel 2002 & **Excel 2003** have expanded **Paste** icon features.

Access the following tasks by clicking the arrow to the right of the icon:

✦ Paste **Formulas**

✦ Paste **Values**

✦ Paste **No Borders**

✦ **Transpose**

✦ **Paste Link**

✦ Open the *Paste Special* dialog box.

Notes:

_____

_____

_____

_____

_____

_____

**My Tips/
Shortcuts:**

_____

_____

_____

_____

_____

_____

Related Tips:	*Tip 24: Pasting Multiple Copied Ranges Using the Clipboard*
	Tip 25: Inserting a Copied Cell(s) Without Overwriting Existing Data
	Tip 28: Copying Cell Content Across Sheets

Copying & Pasting Cell Content Along with Formatting

Excel 2002 & **Excel 2003** have expanded **Paste Special** features, enabling you to copy and paste formulas/values and paste them along with their formatting.

2

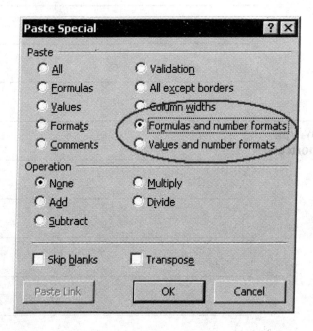

Notes:

_____

_____

_____

_____

_____

_____

_____

_____

**My Tips/
Shortcuts:**

_____

_____

_____

_____

_____

_____

_____

Related Tips:	Tip 21: Fast Copying & Pasting in Adjacent Cells
	Tip 27: Copying & Pasting Cell Content Along with Formatting
	Tip 105: Grouping/Ungrouping Sheets

Copying Cell Content Across Sheets

➤ **To fill across sheets (that is, copy information from selected cells to all sheets in the workbook), simultaneously:**

1. Select a range of cells to copy.

2. Right-click the sheet tab, and from the shortcut menu, select **Select All Sheets**.

3. From the *Edit* menu, select **Fill** and then **Across Worksheets**.

4. In the *Fill Across Worksheets* dialog box, check one of the three option buttons and click **OK**.

5. To remove sheet groupings, select the sheet tab, hold **<Shift>** and then click.

   OR

   Right-click the sheet tab and select **Ungroup Sheets** from the shortcut menu.

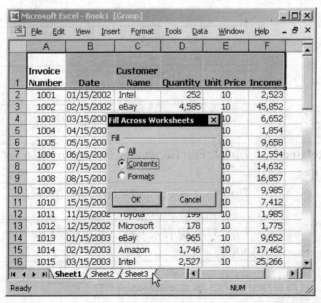

Notes:

**My Tips/
Shortcuts:**

Related Tips:	*Tip 21: Fast Copying & Pasting in Adjacent Cells*
	Tip 105: Grouping /Ungrouping Sheets
	Tip 231: Copying Page Setup to Other Sheets

Copying/Moving a Cell(s) Between Sheets/Workbooks

Using keyboard shortcuts

➢ **To copy and paste cells to another sheet:**
   1. Select a range of cells that contains data.
   2. Press and hold **<Ctrl+Alt>** and drag the data from the corner of the selection area to a new location in another sheet.

➢ **To move cells to another sheet:**
   1. Select a range of cells that contains data.
   2. Press and hold **<Alt>** and drag the data from the corner of the selection area to a new location in another sheet.

➢ **To copy/move cells to another workbook:**
   1. From the *Windows* menu, choose **Arrange**.

   2. Select any of the **Arrange Windows** options and click **OK**.

      In **Excel 2003**, use **Compare Side by Side** to arrange the windows.

   3. Select a range of cells that contains data.
   4. Press and hold **<Ctrl+Alt>** (to copy) or **<Alt>** (to move) and drag the cells to a new locations in a sheet in another workbook.

Copying & Pasting

Notes:

_____

_____

_____

_____

_____

My Tips/
Shortcuts:

_____

_____

_____

_____

_____

Related Tips:	*Tip 31: Quickly Entering Text into Cells from a List of Previous Entries or a Validation list*
	Tip 32: Preventing Duplicates While Entering Data
	Tip 33: Validating Number Entries

Preventing Moving to the Next Cell After Typing

Using keyboard shortcuts

➤ **To prevent moving to the next cell after typing:**

✦ Press **<Ctrl+ Enter>** (instead of **<Enter>**).

   OR

   Deselect the **Move selection after Enter Direction** checkbox, as described below.

➤ **To change the move selection after pressing <Enter>:**

1. From the *Tools* menu, select **Options** and then the **Edit** tab.

2. From the **Move selection after Enter Direction** dropdown list, select the desired direction.

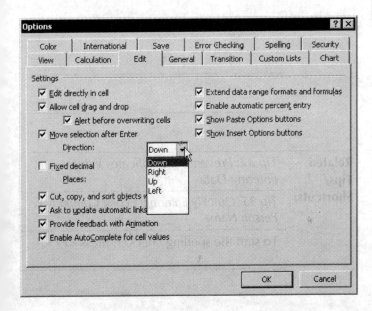

Notes:

_____

_____

_____

_____

_____

_____

My Tips/
Shortcuts:

_____

_____

_____

_____

_____

_____

Related Tips/ Shortcuts:	*Tip 32: Preventing Duplicates While Entering Data*
	Tip 35: Quickly Entering a Long Company or Person Name
	To start the spelling checker, press **<F7>**.

Quickly Entering Text into Cells from a List of Previous Entries or a Validation List

➢ **To select from a list of previous text entries or from a Validation list** (to add **Validation** list, see *Tip #229, page 2*):

1. Select the empty cell under the last filled cell.

2. Press **<Shift+F10>** or right-click and then select **Pick from Drop-down List** from the shortcut menu.

   OR

   Press **<Alt+ Down Arrow>**.

Notes:

_____

_____

_____

_____

_____

_____

_____

**My Tips/
Shortcuts:**

_____

_____

_____

_____

_____

_____

_____

Related Tips:	*Tip 33: Validating Number Entries*
	Tip 34: Validating Text Entries
	Tip 35: Quickly Entering a Long Company or Person Name

Preventing Duplicates While Entering Data

➢ **To prevent duplicates while entering data:**

1. Select a range of cells, for example, **A2:A20**.
2. From the *Data* menu, select **Validation**.
3. Select the **Settings** tab.
4. From the **Allow** dropdown list, select **Custom**.
5. In the **Formula** box, enter the following formula:

   =COUNTIF($A$2:$A$20,A2)=1

6. Select the **Error Alert** tab.
7. In the **Title** box, enter **Duplicate Entry**.
8. In the **Error message** box, enter "**The value you entered already appears in the list above**".
9. Click **OK**.

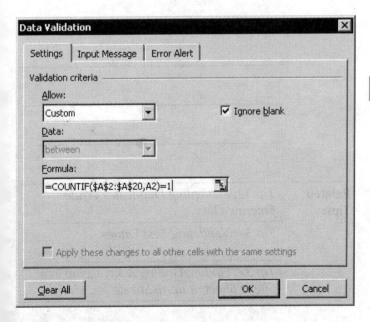

Notes:

**My Tips/
Shortcuts:**

**Related
Tips:**

*Tip 32: Preventing Duplicates While
Entering Data*

Tip 34: Validating Text Entries

*Tip 37: Finding/Finding & Replacing in a
Single Sheet or in All Sheets*

Validating Number Entries

➢ **To validate number entries:**

1. Select the range of cells.

2. From the *Data* menu, select **Validation**.

3. Select the **Settings** tab.

4. From the **Allow** dropdown list, select **Whole number** (or **Decimal**).

5. From the **Data** dropdown list, select **Between**.

6. In the **Minimum** box, enter the required lower limit, for example, **1000**.

7. In the **Maximum** box, enter the required upper limit, for example, **9999**.

8. Click **OK**.

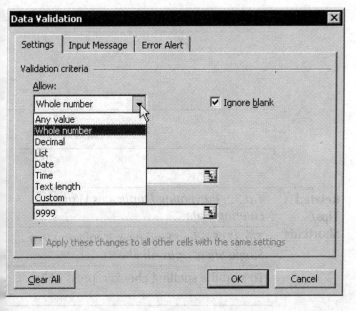

Notes:

_____

_____

_____

_____

_____

_____

_____

**My Tips/
Shortcuts:**

_____

_____

_____

_____

_____

_____

Related Tips/ Shortcuts:	*Tip 32: Preventing Duplicates While Entering Data*
	Tip 37: Finding/Finding & Replacing in a Single Sheet or in All Sheets
	To start the spelling checker, press **<F7>**.

Validating Text Entries

➢ **To validate text entries:**

1. Select the range of cells.
2. From the *Data* menu, select **Validation**.
3. Select the **Settings** tab.
4. From the **Allow** dropdown list, select **Custom**.
5. In the **Formula** box, enter the following formula:

   =IsText (A1)

   where **A1** is the first cell in the range.
6. Click **OK**.

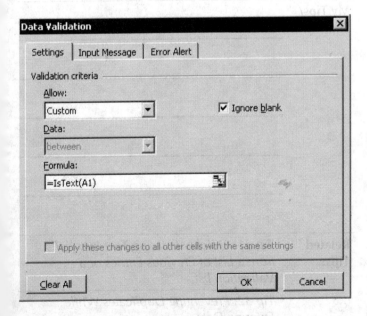

Notes:

_____

_____

_____

_____

_____

**My Tips/
Shortcuts:**

_____

_____

_____

_____

_____

_____

_____

**Related
Tips:**

*Tip 31: Quickly Entering Text into Cells
from a List of Previous Entries or a
Validation list*

*Tip 32: Preventing Duplicates While
Entering Data*

Tip 33: Validating Number Entries

Quickly Entering a Long Company or Person Name

➢ **To replace short text with long text or a sentence, use the AutoCorrect feature:**

1. From the *Tools* menu, select **AutoCorrect**.
2. In the **Replace** box, type **ipg**, and in the **With** box, type **Independent Publishers Group**.
3. Click **OK**.
4. Enter the text **ipg** into any cell and press **<Enter>**. The text **Independent Publishers Group** immediately appears in the cell.

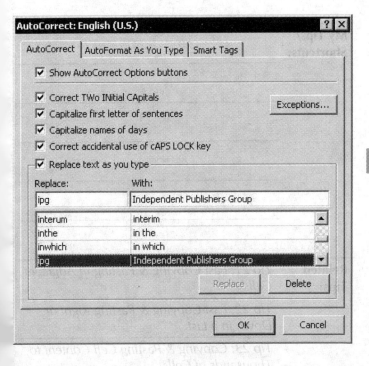

87

Notes:

**My Tips/
Shortcuts:**

**Related
Tips:**

*Tip 21: Fast Copying & Pasting in Adjacent
Cells*

*Tip 22: Fast Copying & Pasting Right or
Down in a List*

*Tip 23: Copying & Pasting Cell Content to
Thousands of Cells*

Transposing Cells

➤ **To transpose cells:**

1. Copy a range of cells (see range **A1:A6** below).

2. Select a cell.

3. Press
   <Shift I F10>.

   OR

   From the
   shortcut menu,
   select **Paste
   Special**.

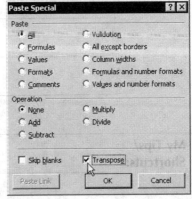

4. Select the **Transpose** checkbox, and click **OK**. The
   list is now presented in horizontal cells.

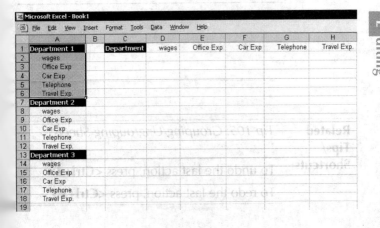

Notes:

**My Tips/
Shortcuts:**

**Related
Tips/
Shortcuts:**
Tip 105: Grouping/Ungrouping Sheets

To undo the last action, press **<Ctrl+Z>**.

To redo the last action, press **<Ctrl+Y>**.

Finding/Finding & Replacing in a Single Sheet or in All Sheets

➢ **To search and replace in one sheet:**
   ✦ To search for text, use the keyboard shortcut **<Ctrl+F>** or select **Find** from the *Edit* menu.
   ✦ To search for and replace text, use the keyboard shortcut **<Ctrl+H>** or select **Replace** from the *Edit* menu.

➢ **To find & replace all sheets in the workbook:**
   1. From the sheet tab's shortcut menu, select **Select All Sheets**.
   2. Press **<Ctrl+F>** to find or **<Ctrl+H>** to find and replace. (Note: **<Ctrl+F>** works only for a single sheet in **Excel 97**). In **Excel 2002**, choose **Sheet** or **Workbook** from the **Within** dropdown list (see the screenshot below).

➢ **To find/find and replace special characters & formats:**
   ✦ **Using wild cards in the text search:**
      ❖ Use ***** as a wild card for any number of characters, either before or after text, for example, searching for ***CO** will find both **Cisco** and **Telco**.
      ❖ Use **?** as a wild card for a single character, for example, searching for **R?N** will find **Ron** and **Ran** but not **Rain**.
      ❖ To search for an asterisk, enter **~*** in the search box.

continued...

2

E
diting

Notes:

My Tips/ Shortcuts:

Finding/Finding & Replacing in a Single Sheet or in All Sheets (cont.)

In **Excel 2002 & Excel 2003**, use the **Find/Find and Replace** based on **Format** (see screenshot below).

Find and Replace	? X
Find **Replace**	
Find what: [▼] No Format Set Format... ▾	
Replace with: [▼] No Format Set Format... ▾	
Within: Sheet ▼ ☐ Match case	
Search: By Rows ▼ ☐ Match entire cell contents	
Look in: Formulas ▼ Options <<	
Replace All Replace Find All Find Next Close	

Related Tips:

Tip 40: Changing the Standard Font

Tip 42: Viewing and Capturing with a Toggle Button in Excel 2002/2003

Tip 43: Changing the Indentation in a Cell

Notes:

_____

_____

_____

_____

_____

_____

My Tips/
Shortcuts:

_____

_____

_____

_____

_____

Related
Tips:

Tip 40: Changing the Standard Font

Tip 42: Merging and Centering with a
Toggle Button in Excel 2002/2003

Tip 43: Changing the Indentation in a Cell

Displaying the Format Cells Dialog Box

Using keyboard shortcuts

✦ To display the *Format Cells* dialog box, press
<Ctrl+1>.

Using the mouse

✦ Select a cell, press **<Shift+F10>** or right-click a cell
and select **Format Cells** from the shortcut menu.

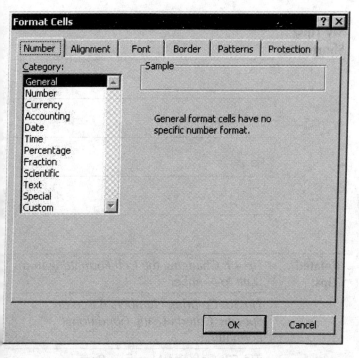

Notes:

_____

_____

_____

_____

_____

**My Tips/
Shortcuts:**

_____

_____

_____

_____

_____

Related Tips:	*Tip 49: Changing the Cell Formatting from Date to Number*
	Tip 50: Coloring Numbers Based on Specific Criteria Using Conditional Formatting
	Tip 53: Coloring Numbers Based on Specific Criteria

Copying Formatting

➤ **To copy the formatting, use the Format Painter icon:**

   ✦ Click the **Format Painter** icon to copy and apply formatting.

➤ **To repeatedly copy formatting:**

   ✦ Double-click the **Format Painter** icon to repeatedly apply formatting.

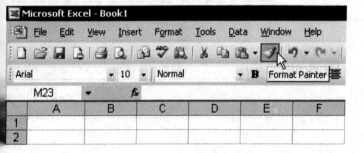

Notes:

**My Tips/
Shortcuts:**

**Related
Tips:**

Tip 43: Changing the Indentation in a Cell

*Tip 46: Adding a Shortcut for Wrapping
Text*

Tip 47: Preventing Text from Spilling Over

Changing the Standard Font

➤ **To change the standard font used in a new workbook:**

1. From the *Tools* menu, select **Options**, and then select the **General** tab.
2. From the **Standard font** dropdown list, select the desired font, and set the **Size**.
3. Click **OK**.

2

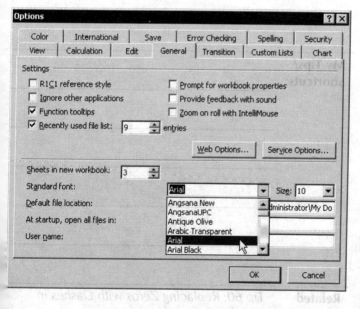

Formatting

Related Tips
Tip 60: Replacing Zeros with Dashes in Number Formatting

Tip 89: Coloring Gridlines

Tip 240: Hiding Errors in Cells before Printing

Notes:

_____

_____

_____

_____

_____

**My Tips/
Shortcuts:**

_____

_____

_____

_____

_____

_____

Related Tips:	*Tip 60: Replacing Zeros with Dashes in Number Formatting*
	Tip 89: Coloring Gridlines
	Tip 240: Hiding Errors in Cells Before Printing

Hiding the Display of Zero Values

➤ To hide zero value in specific cells:

The third section in the number custom formatting (after the second **;**) returns the formatting for a zero value. To hide the zero value, erase the **#** and **0** symbols in this section. The formatting will now display an empty cell (see *Tip #58*).

Example:

#,##0_;[Red](#,##0);;

➤ To hide zero values in a sheet:
1. From the *Tools* menu, select **Options**, and then select the **View** tab.
2. Deselect the **Zero values** checkbox and click **OK**.

➤ To hide zero values in all cells in the entire workbook:
1. From the sheet tab's shortcut menu, select **Select All Sheets**.
2. Follow the steps in the previous procedure.

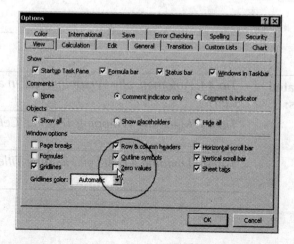

Notes:

**My Tips/
Shortcuts:**

| **Related
Tips:** | *Tip 44: Automatically Wrapping Text in a
Cell* |
| | *Tip 45: Manually Wrapping Text in a Cell* |
| | *Tip 48: Dividing a First Left Heading Title* |

Merging and Centering with a Toggle Button in Excel 2002/2003

In **Excel 2002** and **Excel 2003**, the **Merge and Center** icon works as a toggle button, which means it turns this functionality on and off by clicking the icon.

2

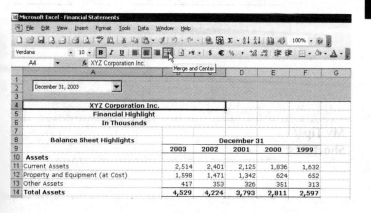

Notes:

**My Tips/
Shortcuts:**

Related Tips:	*Tip 44: Automatically Wrapping Text in a Cell*
	Tip 45: Manually Wrapping Text in a Cell
	Tip 48: Dividing a First Left Heading Title

Changing the Indentation in a Cell

➢ **To indent text in cells, for example, for a list of expenses under each department:**

1. Select the list of expenses below each division, for example, select cells **A2:A6** (a group of expenses for Department 1).

2. Click the **Increase Indent** icon on the **Formatting** toolbar several times, until you reach the desired indentation.

   OR

1. Select **A2:A6** and then press **<Ctrl+1>**.

2. Select the **Alignment** tab, and in the **Indent** box, change the number of characters to indent.

3. Click **OK**.

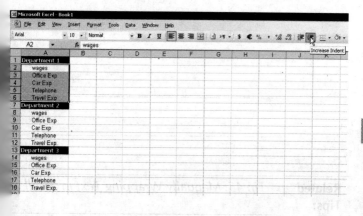

Notes:

_____

_____

_____

_____

_____

_____

_____

**My Tips/
Shortcuts:**

_____

_____

_____

_____

_____

_____

_____

Related Tips:	*Tip 45: Manually Wrapping Text in a Cell*
	Tip 46: Adding a Shortcut for Wrapping Text
	Tip 47: Preventing Text from Spilling Over

Automatically Wrapping Text in a Cell

> ### To automatically wrap text:
> 1. Type the following text into a cell: **"This is the best ExcelTip book"**.
> 2. Press **<Ctrl+1>**, and select the **Alignment** tab.
> 3. Select the **Wrap text** checkbox.
> 4. Click **OK**.

2

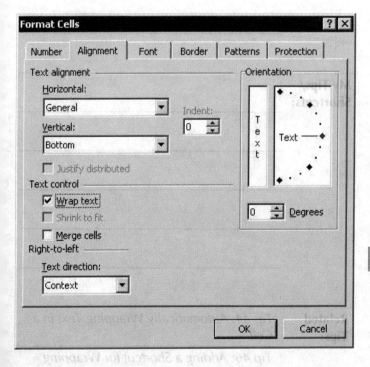

Notes:

**My Tips/
Shortcuts:**

Related Tips:	*Tip 44: Automatically Wrapping Text in a Cell*
	Tip 46: Adding a Shortcut for Wrapping Text
	Tip 47: Preventing Text from Spilling Over

Manually Wrapping Text in a Cell

Using keyboard shortcuts

➤ **To manually wrap text:**

1. Type the following text into a cell: **"This is the best ExcelTip book"**.
2. In the **Formula Bar**, place the cursor after the word **"best"**.
3. Press **<Alt+ Enter>**.

➤ **To cancel manual text wrapping:**

1. In the **Formula Bar**, place the cursor where you caused the text to wrap, that is, before the word **"Excel"**.
2. Press **<Backspace>**.

```
Microsoft Excel - Book1
 File   Edit   View   Insert   Format   Tools   Data   Window   Help
    A1        ▼ X ✔ ƒ  This is the best
        A          B         ExcelTip book
  1  ip book   best ExcelTip book
  2
  3
  4
  5
  6
  7
```

Notes:

**My Tips/
Shortcuts:**

Related Tips/ Shortcuts:	*Tip 44: Automatically Wrapping Text in a Cell*
	Tip 47: Preventing Text from Spilling Over

To display the **Style** box, press **<Alt+'>**.

Adding a Shortcut for Wrapping Text

 Using keyboard shortcuts

✦ **Step 1: Adding the Style Box to the Formatting Toolbar:**

1. Right-click one of the toolbars, and select **Customize**.

2. Select the **Commands** tab, and then select **Format**.

3. Drag the **Style** icon from the *Customize* dialog box to the **Formatting** toolbar, and drop it next to the **Font Size** box (or anywhere else you choose).

4. Click **Close**.

✦ **Step 2: Adding Wrapped Text to the Style Box:**

1. Enter text into a cell in the sheet, and press **<Ctrl+1>**.

2. Select the **Alignment** tab, select the **Wrap text** checkbox, and click **OK**.

3. In the **Style** box, enter the text **WrapText**.

4. To use the **Wrap text** shortcut, select a cell, and then select **Wrap text** from the **Style** box.

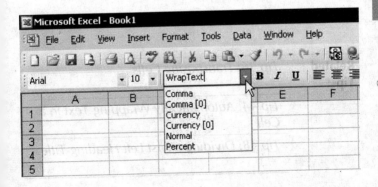

Notes:

_____

_____

_____

_____

_____

**My Tips/
Shortcuts:**

_____

_____

_____

_____

_____

Related Tips:	*Tip 36: Transposing Cells*
	Tip 44: Automatically Wrapping Text in a Cell
	Tip 48: Dividing a First Left Heading Title

Preventing Text from Spilling Over

In this example, enter a statement into cell **A59**, without the text spilling over into cells outside the area of the report (the report goes from column **A** to **D**).

> **To prevent text from extending beyond the report width:**

1. First, ensure that the typed text was only entered into cell **A59**.

2. Select cells **A59:E59**.

3. From the *Edit* menu, select **Fill** and then **Justify**.

4. Click **OK**. The following message appears: **Text will extend below selected range**. (Before clicking **OK**, ensure that the cells below row **60** are empty.)

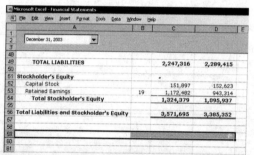

Notes:

_____

_____

_____

_____

_____

_____

_____

**My Tips/
Shortcuts:**

_____

_____

_____

_____

_____

_____

_____

Related Tips:	*Tip 44: Automatically Wrapping Text in a Cell*
	Tip 45: Manually Wrapping Text in a Cell
	Tip 47: Preventing Text from Spilling Over

Dividing a First Left Heading Title

➢ **To divide a title in a cell:**

1. In cell **A1**, enter the words: **Headings** and **Invoice Number**.

2. Select cell **A1**, and in the **Formula Bar**, place the cursor after the word **Headings**.

3. Press **<Alt+Enter>** twice (once to wrap the text and once for an additional empty row space).

4. Press **<Ctrl+Enter>** to accept the changes without moving from cell.

5. Press **<Ctrl+1>** to open the *Format Cells* dialog box.

6. Select the **Border** tab and select the left diagonal border.

7. Select the **Alignment** tab.

8. From both the **Horizontal** and **Vertical** dropdown lists, select **Justify**.

9. Click **OK**.

10. In the **Formula Bar**, place the cursor before the word **Headings** and press the **<Space Bar>** to add spaces and move the word to right.

	A	B	C	D	E	F
	Headings					
1	Invoice Number	Date	Customer Name	Market	Quantity	Income
2	1001	01/15/2002	Intel	Europe	252	2,523.00
3	1002	02/15/2002	eBay	Europe	4,585	45,852.00
4	1003	03/15/2002	ExcelTip	N.America	665	6,652.00
5	1004	04/15/2002	Toyota	Europe	185	1,854.00
6	1005	05/15/2002	Amazon	Africa	966	9,658.00
7	1006	06/15/2002	GM	N.America	1,255	12,554.00
8	1007	07/15/2002	Ford	Europe	1,463	14,632.00
9	1008	08/15/2002	GM	N.America	1,686	16,857.00
10	1009	09/15/2002	Microsoft	Europe	999	9,985.00

Notes:

_____

_____

_____

_____

_____

_____

**My Tips/
Shortcuts:**

_____

_____

_____

_____

_____

_____

Related Tips/ Shortcuts:	*Tip 143: Problem: Date Formatting Cannot Be Changed*
	Tip 149: Customizing Date Formatting

To apply the date format with the day, month and year, press **<Ctrl+Shift+#>**.

Changing the Cell Formatting from Date to Number

 Using keyboard shortcuts

➢ **To change the cell formatting from date to number:**

✦ Press **<Ctrl+Shift+~>**.

Example:

1. Enter today's date into a cell by pressing **<Ctrl+;>**. The result is **3/10/2004**.

2. Press **<Ctrl+Shift+~>** to change the format to **General** formatting.

	Microsoft Excel - Book1					
	File Edit View Insert Format Tools Data Window Help					
	A	B	C	D	E	F
1						
2	Before			3/10/2004		
3						
4	After pressing Ctrl+Shift+~			38056		
5						
6						
7						

Formatting

Related Tips: Tip 51: Coloring Numbers Based on Specific Criteria

Tip 55: Coloring Even Numbered Rows in a List

Tip 266: Applying Colors to Maximum/Minimum Values in List

Notes:

My Tips/ Shortcuts:

Related Tips:	Tip 53: Coloring Numbers Based on Specific Criteria
	Tip 55: Coloring Even Numbered Rows in a List
	Tip 260: Applying Colors to Maximum/Minimum Values in List

Coloring Numbers Based on Specific Criteria Using Conditional Formatting

➢ **To color numbers based on specific criteria using Conditional Formatting:**

1. Select a range of cells, and from the *Format* menu, select **Conditional Formatting**.

2. For **Condition 1**, select **Cell Value Is** and **less than** from the dropdown lists, and in the text box, type 0.

3. Click **Format**, and then select the **Font** tab.

4. From **Color**, select red, and then click **OK**.

5. Repeat steps 2 through 4 and add two more conditions for numbers less than 5000 and for numbers equal or greater than 5000.

   For each condition, click **Format**, select the **Font** tab, and then select **black** and **blue**, respectively.

6. Click **OK**.

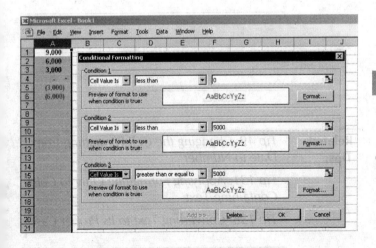

Notes:

_____

_____

_____

_____

_____

**My Tips/
Shortcuts:**

_____

_____

_____

_____

_____

_____

Related Tips:	*Tip 49: Changing the Cell Formatting from Date to Number*
	Tip 131: Applying Formatting Only to Cells Containing Text
	Tip 136: Converting Text to Its Proper Case

Changing a Numeric Heading to Text

When creating reports you might want to enter the year
numbers as headings above the figures:

➢ **To prevent the headings from being treated as
   numbers, change them to text:**

   ✦ Enter the ' (apostrophe) symbol before the number.
      for example, **'2003** will be treated as a text entry.

	A	B	C	D	E	F
1	2003					
2						
3						
4						

Notes:

**My Tips/
Shortcuts:**

| **Related
Tips/
Shortcuts:**	*Tip 96: Removing Icons Performing Two Different Tasks*
	Tip 264: Coloring and Filtering List According to Criteria
	To apply the outline border to the selected cells, press **<Ctrl+Shift+&>**.

"Tearing Off" Palettes from Toolbars

➢ **To "tear off" formatting palettes:**
1. From the **Formatting** toolbar, open the **Fill Color** icon palette.
2. Drag the palette to any place on the sheet to make it float.

2

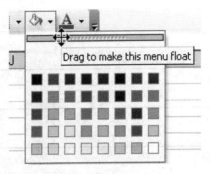

➢ **To "tear off" drawing palettes:**
1. From the **Drawing** toolbar, select **AutoShapes**, and then select **Stars and Banners**.
2. Drag the palette to any place on the sheet to make it float.

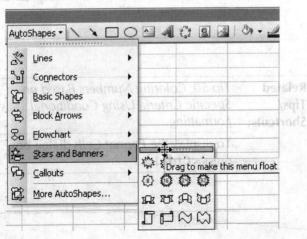

Notes:

**My Tips/
Shortcuts:**

Related Tips/ Shortcuts:	*Tip 50: Coloring Numbers Based on Specific Criteria Using Conditional Formatting*
	To display the *Format Cells* dialog box, press **<Ctrl+1>**.

Coloring Numbers Based on Specific Criteria

➢ **To color numbers, add criteria to the Custom Formatting:**

Color positive and/or negative numbers in any desired color. (Do not get too excited — the number of colors is limited to eight, and most are difficult to read!)

For example, **[BLUE] #,##0 ; [RED](#,##0)**

◆ The first formatting section (before the first **;**) refers to the formatting of positive numbers and is displayed in blue.

◆ The second formatting section (after the first **;**) refers to the formatting of negative numbers and is displayed in red.

◆ The number 0 uses the positive formatting information (if there are two sections in the syntax) and is therefore displayed in blue.

➢ **To add a condition to the formatting:**

◆ Each section is displayed in a different color:

[BLUE] [>5000]#,##0 ;[RED](#,##0); #,##0

❖ Positive numbers above 5,000 are blue.

❖ Negative numbers are red.

❖ Positive numbers up to 5,000 (and 0) are black.

Notes:

_____

_____

_____

_____

_____

_____

_____

**My Tips/
Shortcuts:**

_____

_____

_____

_____

_____

_____

_____

Related Tips:	*Tip 55: Coloring Even Numbered Rows in a List*
	Tip 258: Drawing Lines Between Sorted Groups
	Tip 259: Coloring Rows Based on Text Criteria

Coloring One Record in Each Group in a Range

➢ **To color one record in each group in a range, use Conditional Formatting:**

1. Select the range of cells (or select the entire column).

2. From the *Format* menu, select **Conditional Formatting**.

3. In the **Condition 1** box, select **Formula Is**.

4. Enter the following formula (make sure you are careful about the **Absolute** and **Relative** references):

   =COUNTIF($A$2:A2,A2)=1

5. Click **Format**, and select the **Patterns** tab.

6. Choose any color, and then click **OK** twice.

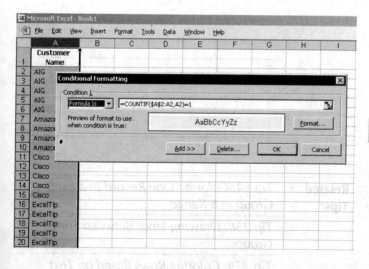

Notes:

_____

_____

_____

_____

_____

**My Tips/
Shortcuts:**

_____

_____

_____

_____

_____

_____

Related Tips:	*Tip 54: Coloring One Record in a Each Group in a Range*
	Tip 258: Drawing Lines Between Sorted Groups
	Tip 259: Coloring Rows Based on Text Criteria

Coloring Even Numbered Rows in a List

➤ **To color even numbered rows:**

1. Select a cell in the region and press **<Ctrl+Shift+*>** (in **Excel 2003**, press this or **<Ctrl+A>**) to select the **Current Region**.

2. From the *Format* menu, select **Conditional Formatting**.

3. For **Condition 1**, select **Formula Is**, and insert the following formula in the **Formula** box:

   =MOD(ROW(),2)<>0

4. Click **Format**, and select the **Patterns** tab.

5. Choose any color, and then click **OK** twice.

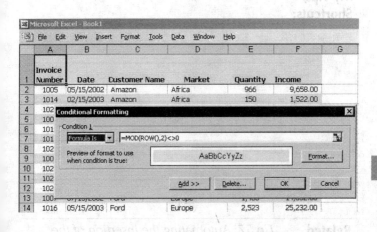

Notes:

_____

_____

_____

_____

_____

_____

_____

**My Tips/
Shortcuts:**

_____

_____

_____

_____

_____

_____

Related Tips:	*Tip 57: Automating the Insertion of the Euro Symbol*
	Tip 58: Symbols Used to Create Custom Formatting
	Tip 186: The Euro Currency Tools Add-In

Inserting Special Symbols into Custom Formats

➤ **To insert a symbol into a new number format in Excel 97 & Excel 2000:**

Example: Create and save a number format with the € (euro) symbol.

1. Press **<Alt+0128>** (use the numeric key pad).

   OR

   Select a cell and type the following formula:

   =CHAR(128)

2. Press **<F2>** and then **<F9>** to delete the formula and leave the value in the cell.

3. In the **Formula** bar, select the € symbol, and press **<Ctrl+C>** to copy it.

4. Select another cell, and press **<Ctrl+1>** to open the *Format Cells* dialog box.

5. Select the **Number** tab, and choose **Custom**.

6. In the **Type** box, press **<Ctrl+V>**.

7. Continue by typing the format code **#,##0**.

8. Click **OK**. The result is the following Custom Formatting **€ #,##0**, which can be applied to any other cell(s) or range(s).

	Microsoft Excel - Book1			
	File Edit View Insert Format Tools			
	B96 ▼ ƒ× =CHAR(A96)			
	A	B	C	D
93	125	}		
94	126	~		
95	127	▯		
96	128	€		
97	129	▯		
98	130	‚		
99	131	*ƒ*		
100	132	„		

continued...

131

Notes:

_____

_____

_____

_____

_____

_____

_____

My Tips/
Shortcuts:

_____

_____

_____

_____

_____

_____

_____

_____

_____

_____

continued...

Inserting Special Symbols into Custom Formats (cont.)

➢ **To add a symbol into a new number format in Excel 2002 & Excel 2003:**

1. From the *Insert* menu, select **Symbol**.
2. Select the **Euro** symbol and click **Insert**.
3. Continue with step 4 in the previous procedure.

2

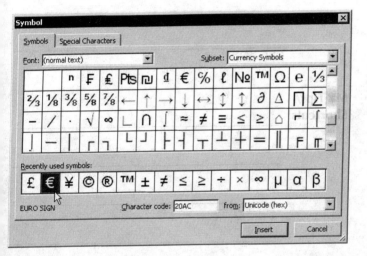

Notes:

_____

_____

_____

_____

_____

_____

_____

My Tips/
Shortcuts:

_____

_____

_____

_____

_____

_____

Related Tips:	*Tip 56: Inserting Special Symbols into Custom Formats*
	Tip 58: Symbols Used to Create Custom Formatting
	Tip 186: The Euro Currency Tools Add-In

Automating the Insertion of the Euro Symbol

> **To automatically insert the Euro symbol:**

1. Press **<Alt+0128>** (use the numeric key pad).

    OR

    Select a cell and type the following formula:

    =CHAR(128)

2. Press **<F2>** and then **<F9>** to delete the formula and leave the value in the cell.

3. Press **<Ctrl+C>** to copy the cell containing the **€** symbol.

4. From the *Tools* menu, select **AutoCorrect**.

5. In the **Replace** box, type **euro**, and in the **With** box, press **<Ctrl+V>**.

6. Click **Add**, and then click **OK**.

7. Check the result by typing the word **euro**. The text changes to the **€** symbol.

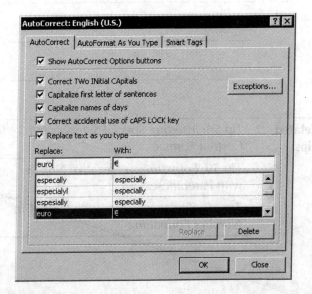

Notes:

**My Tips/
Shortcuts:**

Symbols Used to Create Custom Formatting

The following symbols are used in Custom Formatting:

✦ **0 (zero) symbol**: Displays a digit in a cell, including the digit 0. For example, the format **0.00** displays the number 0.987 as a number with two places after the decimal point, that is, 0.99 (without the 7). Places are omitted after the number is rounded. Any omitted insignificant digits cause the number to be rounded. In this case, 0.98 was rounded to 0.99.

✦ **# (pound) sign:** Displays significant digits and does not display insignificant zeros. For example, a format with two places after the decimal point, with or without the digit 0, for example, the format code for 50 cents:

❖ #.##: The cell displays .5.

❖ #.#0: The cell displays .50.

❖ 0.00: The cell displays 0.50.

✦ **, (comma):** Separates thousands. For example, with the format **#,##0**, the number 4543 is displayed as 4,543. The comma has a second use in the number format. If you place the comma at the end of the digits and the displayed number is be divided by 1,000 for each comma.

❖ #,##0,: Displays numbers in thousands.

❖ #,##0,,: Displays numbers in millions.

✦ **/ (forward slash) symbol**: The division sign for displaying a fraction.

✦ *** (asterisk) symbol:** Fills in empty characters, up to the beginning of the number. For example, the number 4,543 is displayed as $4,543 with the format **$ *#,##0**. The $ sign is displayed on the left side of the cell, and the number is displayed on the right side.

continued...

2

Formatting

Notes:

**My Tips/
Shortcuts:**

Symbols Used to Create Custom Formatting (cont.)

✦ **"TEXT"**: If text characters are enclosed in quotation marks and followed by a number format, the text is displayed and the digits are formatted. For example, with the format **"Balance" #,##0**, the number 4,543 is displayed as Balance 4,543. In the sheet cell, you only need to enter the digits, not the text.

✦ **\(backslash) <Any single character>**: Use the backslash followed by a single text character to display that character. For example, the following format will display a number in millions: **#,##0.0,,\M**. Using this format, 123,789,456 would be displayed as "123.8M".

Excel allows you to omit the backslash when displaying a capital letter K. This format will display a number in thousands: **#,##0,K**. Using this format, 123,789,456 would be displayed as 123,789K.

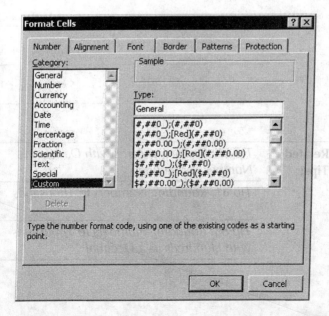

139

Notes:

**My Tips/
Shortcuts:**

**Related
Tips:**

*Tip 60: Replacing Zeros with Dashes in
Number Formatting*

Tip 61: Rounding Numbers to Thousands

*Tip 63: Rounding Numbers to Thousands
with Hundreds as a Decimal*

Formatting a Negative Number with Parentheses

➤ **To add parentheses to the display of negative numbers:**

1. Press **<Ctrl+1>** to open the *Format Cells* dialog box.

2. Select the **Number** tab, and from **Category**, select **Custom**.

3. In the **Type** box, enter the following syntax for customized formatting:

   #,##0 ;[Red](#,##0);- ;

Result:

✦ Original number: **-3,453,453**

✦ The displaying formatting number: **(3,453,453)**

Note: The number formatting syntax is:
Positive; Negative; 0; Text

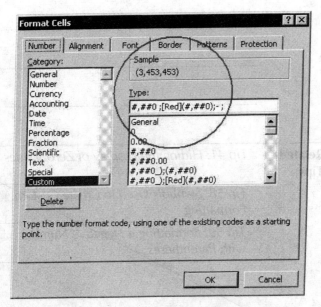

2

Formatting

141

Notes:

_____

_____

_____

_____

_____

My Tips/ Shortcuts:

_____

_____

_____

_____

_____

Related Tips:	*Tip 41: Hiding the Display of Zero Values*
	Tip 58: Symbols Used to Create Custom Formatting
	Tip 59: Formatting a Negative Number with Parentheses

Replacing Zeros with Dashes in Number Formatting

➢ **To replace zeros with dashes:**

1. Press **<Ctrl+1>** to open the *Format Cells* dialog box.

2. Select the **Number** tab, and from **Category**, select **Custom**.

3. In the **Type** box, enter the following Custom Formatting syntax:

   #,##0 ;[Red](#,##0);- ;

Note: The number formatting syntax is:
Positive; Negative; 0; Text

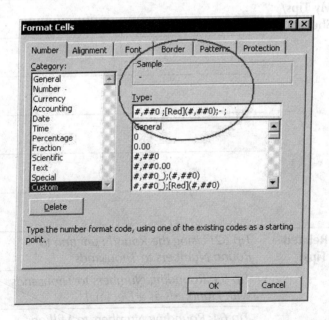

Notes:

**My Tips/
Shortcuts:**

| **Related
Tips:** | *Tip 62: Using the Round Function to
Round Numbers to Thousands* |
| --- | --- |
| | *Tip 63: Rounding Numbers to Thousands
with Hundreds as a Decimal* |
| | *Tip 64: Rounding Numbers to Millions* |

Rounding Numbers to Thousands

> ### To round numbers to thousands:

1. Press **<Ctrl+1>** to open the *Format Cells* dialog box.
2. Select the **Number** tab, and from **Category**, select **Custom**.
3. In the **Type** box, enter the following Custom Formatting syntax:

   #,##0, ;[Red](#,##0,);- ;

Result:

- ✦ Original number: **5,645,625**
- ✦ The displaying formatted number: **5,646**

Note: The number formatting syntax is:
Positive; Negative; 0; Text

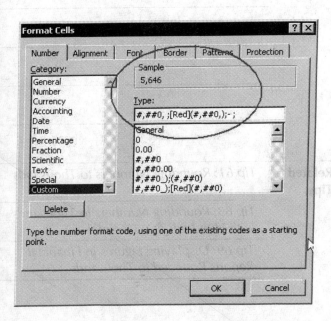

Notes:

**My Tips/
Shortcuts:**

Related Tips:	*Tip 61: Rounding Numbers to Thousands*
	Tip 63: Rounding Numbers to Thousands with Hundreds as a Decimal
	Tip 69: Displaying Figures in Financial Reports Rounded to Thousands

Using the Round Function to Round Numbers to Thousands

➤ **To round a number to thousands using the Round function, and display the number with three zeros:**

✦ For example, to round the number 5,233,501, use the **Round** function:

=Round(B1, -3)

The result is **5,234,000**.

➤ **To round a number to thousands using Custom Formatting:**

✦ For example, round the number 5,233,501 and display the number without the last three zeros, change the number formatting in the cell to: **#,###,**

The result is **5,234**.

	A	B	C	D
	Microsoft Excel - Book1			
	File Edit View Insert Format Tools Data Window Help			
	B3 fx =ROUND(B1,-3)			
1	Number	5,233,501		
2				
3	Round Function	5,234,000		=ROUND(B1,-3)
4				
5	Round Function, Number Formatting: #,###,	5,234		
6				
7				
8	The Number Format is: #,###,	5,234		5,233,501
9				

Notes:

_____

_____

_____

_____

_____

_____

**My Tips/
Shortcuts:**

_____

_____

_____

_____

_____

_____

Related Tips:	*Tip 61: Rounding Numbers to Thousands*
	Tip 62: Using the Round Function to Round Numbers to Thousands
	Tip 64: Rounding Numbers to Millions

Rounding Numbers to Thousands with Hundreds as a Decimal

➤ **To round a number to thousands with the hundreds shown as a decimal:**

1. Press **<Ctrl+1>** to open the *Format Cells* dialog box.

2. Select the **Number** tab, and from **Category**, select **Custom**.

3. In the **Type** box, enter the following Custom Formatting syntax:

   #,##0.0, ;[Red](#,##0.0,);- ;

Result:

✦ Original number: **5,645,625**

✦ The displaying formatting number: **5,645.6**

Note: The number formatting syntax is:
Positive; Negative; 0; Text

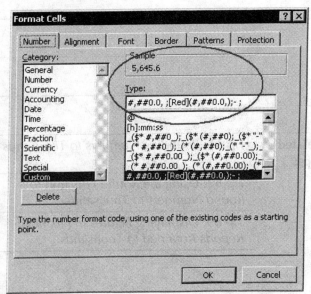

Notes:

_____

_____

_____

_____

_____

_____

**My Tips/
Shortcuts:**

_____

_____

_____

_____

_____

_____

Rounding Numbers to Millions

➤ **To round a numbers to millions:**

1. Press **<Ctrl+1>** to open the *Format Cells* dialog box.

2. Select the **Number** tab, and from **Category**, select **Custom**.

3. In the **Type** box, enter the following Custom Formatting syntax:

   #,##0,, ;[Red](#,##0,,);- ;

Result:

   ✦ Original number: **5,645,625**

   ✦ The displaying formatted number: **6**

Note: The number formatting syntax is:
Positive; Negative; 0; Text

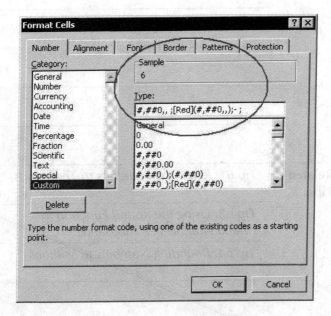

151

Notes:

**My Tips/
Shortcuts:**

**Related
Tips:**

Tip 61: Rounding Numbers to Thousands

*Tip 62: Using the Round Function to
Round Numbers to Thousands*

Tip 64: Rounding Numbers to Millions

Rounding Numbers to Millions with Thousands as a Decimal

➢ **To round a number to millions with the thousands shown as a decimal:**

1. Press **<Ctrl+1>** to open the *Format Cells* dialog box.

2. Select the **Number** tab, and from **Category**, select **Custom**.

3. In the **Type** box, enter the following Custom Formatting syntax:

   #,##0.0,, ;[Red](#,##0.0,,);- ;

Result:

✦ Original number: **5,645,625**

✦ The displaying formatted number: **5.6**

Note: The number formatting syntax is:
Positive; Negative; 0; Text

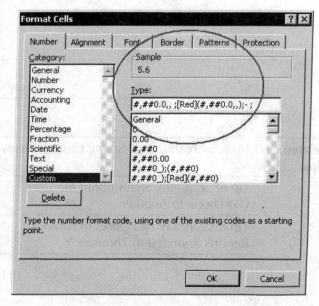

Notes:

_____

_____

_____

_____

_____

_____

My Tips/
Shortcuts:

_____

_____

_____

_____

_____

_____

Changing the Default Style

The default **Style** name is **Normal**.

➢ **To change the default Style:**
1. From the *Format* menu, select **Style**.
2. From the **Style name** dropdown list, select **Normal**.
3. Click **Modify**.
4. Select the **Number** tab.
5. In the **Category** box, select **Custom**.
6. In the **Type** box, enter the following format:

   #,##0;[Red]-#,##0;0;@ (or any other custom number formatting chosen)
7. Select the **Font** tab.
8. Select the font and the desired font size, and then click **OK**.

Note: This only changes the normal style for the current workbook.

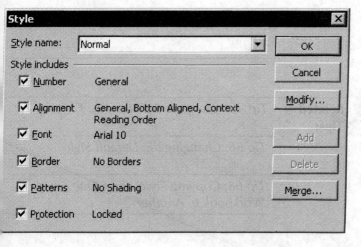

Notes:

_____

_____

_____

_____

_____

_____

**My Tips/
Shortcuts:**

_____

_____

_____

_____

_____

_____

**Related
Tips:**   _Tip 40: Changing the Standard Font_

Tip 66: Changing the Default Style

_Tip 68: Copying Styles from One
Workbook to Another_

Creating and Saving Custom Styles

➤ **To create a wide range of complex Styles, add Styles and save each one separately with a unique name:**

✦ **Step 1: Add the Style box to the Formatting toolbar:**

1. Place the mouse pointer on one of the toolbars, right-click, and from the shortcut menu, select **Customize**.

2. Select the **Commands** tab.

3. From **Format** categories, drag the **Style** box to the **Formatting** toolbar, and close the *Customize* dialog box.

✦ **Step 2: Save the Style:**

1. Select any cell and press **<Ctrl+1>**.

2. Select **Custom** on the **Number** tab and in the **Type** box, type the following number format:

    #,##0 ;[Red](#,##0);- ;

3. Select the font and the font size.

4. Press **<Alt+'>** (this keyboard shortcut opens the **Style** box).

5. In the **Style** box, enter the text **NegativeNumbersinBrackets, 0=-**.

6. Press **<Enter>**. This style can now be used for any cells in the current workbook.

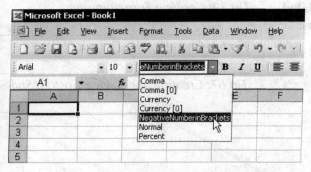

Styles

Notes:

**My Tips/
Shortcuts:**

Copying Styles from One Workbook to Another

Excel saves your defined **Styles** in the workbook where they were created and saved. To use the **Styles** in a different workbook, either use the **Merge** option, or copy the **Styles** from one workbook to another.

2

➢ **To merge Styles:**

1. Open a new workbook.
2. From the *Format* menu, select **Style**.
3. Click **Merge**.
4. In the *Merge Styles* dialog box, select the workbook where the **Styles** to merge were saved, and then click **OK**.
5. In the *Style* dialog box, click **OK**.

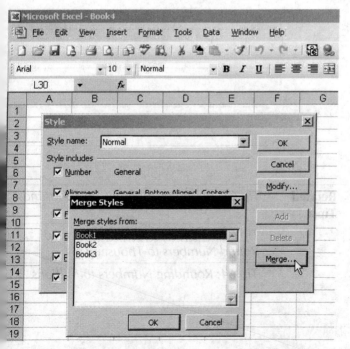

Notes:

**My Tips/
Shortcuts:**

**Related
Tips:**

Tip 61: Rounding Numbers to Thousands

*Tip 62: Using the Round Function to
Round Numbers to Thousands*

Tip 64: Rounding Numbers to Millions

Displaying Figures in Financial Reports Rounded to Thousands

By easily changing the **Style** in the **Style** box, you can quickly change the presentation of numbers in any report. For example, display and print reports with figures rounded to the thousands.

➤ **To apply a Style:**

1. Add the **Style** box to the **Formatting** toolbar (see *Tip #67*).

2. Create a new **Style** and name it **Round To Thousands** (see *Tip #67*).

3. Select the columns containing the numbers to round.

4. From the **Style** box, select **Round to Thousands**.

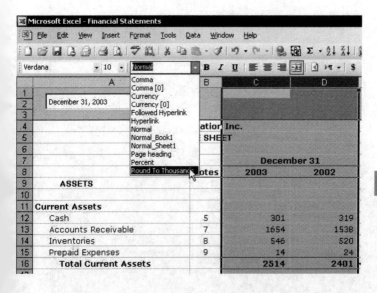

2

Styles

Displaying Figures in Financial Reports Rounded to Thousand

To display a figure or the amount in style in the Style box, you can quickly change the figure values into thousands, so that a report becomes easier to understand and right represents the figures.

To create a style:

1. Add the Style box to the Formatting toolbar (see Tip 183).

2. From Show Style... select the Round To Thousands dialog box.

3. Select the column containing the numbers to format.

4. From the Style box, select Round to Thousand.

Part 3 — Excel Environment

3

Information

Comments

Windows

Menus & Toolbars

Sheets

Workbooks

Notes:

_____

_____

_____

_____

_____

_____

**My Tips/
Shortcuts:**

_____

_____

_____

_____

_____

Related Tips:	*Tip 117: Displaying the Workbook's Path in the Address Box*
	Tip 118: Adding the Path of a Saved Workbook to the Title Bar
	Tip 243: Adding the Full Path of the Saved File to the Header/Footer

Cell Function Returns Sheet Name, Workbook Name and Path

The **Cell** function returns information about the formatting, location, or contents of the upper-left cell in a reference.

➢ **To get the sheet name:**

=MID(CELL("filename"),FIND("]",CELL("filename"))+1,255)

➢ **To get the workbook name:**

=MID(CELL("filename"),FIND("[",CELL("filename"))+1,(FIND("]",CELL("filename"))+1)-FIND("[",CELL("filename"))-2)

➢ **To get the path address & workbook name:**

=CELL("filename")

➢ **To get the path address:**

=MID(CELL("filename"),1,FIND("[",CELL("filename"))-1)

	A	B	C	D	E	F	G	H	I	J
	Microsoft Excel - Financial Statements									
	File Edit View Insert Format Tools Data Window Help									
	A3 ▼		fx	=MID(CELL("filename"),FIND("]",CELL("filename"))+1,255)						
1	**Sheet Name**									
2	=MID(CELL("filename"),FIND("]",CELL("filename"))+1,255)									
3	Sheet1				<--	Result				
4										
5	**Workbook Name**									
6	=MID(CELL("filename"),FIND("[",CELL("filename"))+1,(FIND("]",CELL("filename"))+1)-FIND("[",CELL("filename"))-2)									
7	Financial Statements.xls				<--	Result				
8										
9	**Path & File Name**									
10	=CELL("filename")									
11	C:\My Documents\[Financial Statements.xls]Sheet1				<--	Result				
12										
13	**Path**									
14	=MID(CELL("filename"),1,FIND("[",CELL("filename"))-1)									
15	C:\My Documents\				<--	Result				
16										

Notes:

My Tips/ Shortcuts:

Related Tips:	*Tip 72: Adding Data, Charts, or Other Information to a Cell Comment*
	Tip 73: Using a Picture to Watch Cell Values in Other Sheets
	Tip 75: Linking a Cell to a Text Box

Checking Cell Information at a Distance

The **Watch Window** (new in **Excel 2002** & **Excel 2003**) holds important information, such as **Book name**, **Sheet name**, **defined Name**, **Value**, and **Formula**. Specific cells can be added so that their information can be viewed at any time, even when located outside the viewing area.

➢ **To add cells to the Watch Window:**

1. Select a cell, press **<Shift+F10>** or right-click, and select **Add Watch** from the shortcut menu.

2. In *Watch Window* dialog box, click the **Add Watch** button, and then press **<F3>** to paste a **Name** defined for a cell, or select a cell in any sheet in the active workbook or in any open workbook.

➢ **To view information about a cell added to the Watch Window:**

1. Select a cell, press **<Shift+F10>** or right-click, and select **Add Watch** from the shortcut menu.

2. Double-click the cell address in the **Watch Window**.

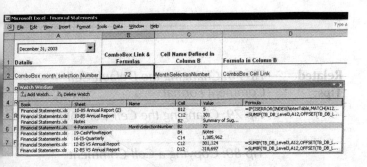

Notes:

**My Tips/
Shortcuts:**

Related Tips:	*Tip 78: Changing the Default Cell Comment Format*
	Tip 79: Changing the Cell Comment Shape
	Tip 80: Copying a Cell Comment

Adding Data, Charts, or Other Information to a Cell Comment

Want to see a photo, Chart, Financial Ratios report or sales information inside a cell **Comment**?

➢ **To add a picture to a cell Comment:**

1. Select a cell, press **<Shift+F2>** to add a new **Comment**; if a **Comment** is in the cell, and press **<Shift+F2>** to edit the **Comment**.

2. Select the edge of the **Comment** so that it is surrounded by dots, not slashes.

3. Right-click the **Comment** edge, and from **Format Comment**, select **Colors and Lines**.

4. In the **Fill** section, open the **Color** box.

5. Choose **Fill Effects**, click the **Picture** tab, and then click **Select Picture**.

6. Select a picture and click **OK** twice.

3

Information

169

Notes:

**My Tips/
Shortcuts:**

Using a Picture to Watch Cell Values in Other Sheets

Using keyboard shortcuts

> ## To paste a linked picture:
> 1. Select the relevant cells in the sheet, and press **<Ctrl+C>** to copy.
> 2. Select a different cell in any sheet.
> 3. Hold the **<Shift>** key, and from the *Edit* menu, select **Paste Picture Link**.

Using the mouse

> ## To use the Camera icon, add it to the regular toolbar:
> 1. Point with the mouse on any toolbar, right-click, and select **Customize** from the shortcut menu.
> 2. Select the **Commands** tab, and from the **Tools** category drag the **Camera** icon to the **Standard** toolbar and then close the *Customize* dialog box.
> 3. Select the relevant cells in the sheet and press the **Camera** icon.
> 4. Select any cell in the sheet (or in any other sheet) and paste the linking picture.

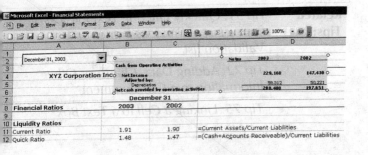

Notes:

_____

_____

_____

_____

_____

**My Tips/
Shortcuts:**

_____

_____

_____

_____

_____

_____

Using the Validation Input Message as a Cell Comment

➤ **To use the Validation Input Message as a cell Comment:**

1. Select a cell and from the *Data* menu, select **Validation**.
2. Select the **Input Message** tab.
3. Fill the two text boxes **Title** and **Input message**.
4. Click **OK**.

3

Information

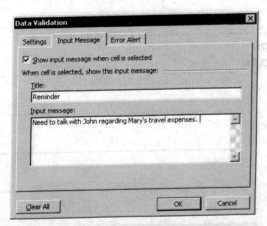

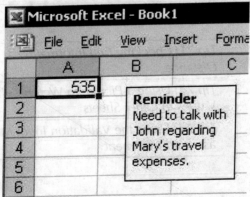

Notes:

_____

_____

_____

_____

_____

_____

**My Tips/
Shortcuts:**

_____

_____

_____

_____

_____

_____

Related Tips:	Tip 71: Checking Cell Information at a Distance
	Tip 73: Using a Picture to Watch Cell Values in Other Sheets
	Tip 74: Using the Validation Input Message as a Cell Comment

Linking a Cell to a Text Box

The advantage of linking a **Text Box** to a cell is the ability to format the text within the **Text Box** and change the **Text Box** color.

➤ **To link a cell to a Text Box object:**
1. From the **Drawing** toolbar, click **Text Box**.
2. Select the **Text Box**, and press **<F2>**.
3. In the **Formula Bar**, create a link to a cell by typing = and then selecting the cell.

The contents of the cell are displayed in the **Text Box**.

3

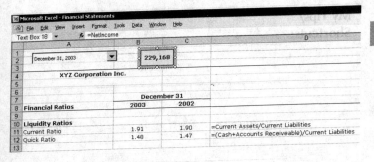

Related Tips: Tip 151: Filling a Range with a Series of Dates

                 Tip 216: Tracing Errors in Formula Results

Notes:

My Tips/
Shortcuts:

Related Tips:	*Tip 151: Filling a Range with a Series of Dates*
	Tip 218: Tracing Errors in Formula Results

Removing the Smart Tag Indicator

✦ What is a Smart Tag?

A **Smart Tag** is pop-up menu that allows access to more commands that are relevant to the current task.

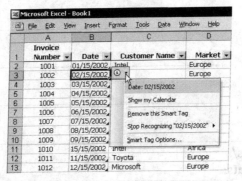

➢ To hide Smart Tags from view in the sheet:

1. From the **Smart Tag** shortcut menu, select **Smart Tag Options** to open the *AutoCorrect* dialog box.

   OR

   From the *Tools* menu, select **AutoCorrect Options**.

2. Select the **Smart Tags** tab, and from **Show smart tags as** dropdown list, select **None**.

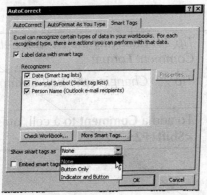

Notes:

**My Tips/
Shortcuts:**

| **Related
Tips/
Shortcuts:** | *Tip 78: Changing the Default Cell
Comment Format* |
| | *Tip 79: Changing the Cell Comment Shape* |

To add a **Comment** to a cell, press
<Shift+F2>.

Changing the Name of the Cell Comment's Author

By default, each cell **Comment** includes the author's name.

➤ **To change or cancel the name of the Comment's author:**

1. From the *Tools* menu, select **Options**, and then select the **General** tab.

2. In **User name** text box, change or clear the user name.

Options						? X
Color	International	Save	Error Checking	Spelling		Security
View	Calculation	Edit	General	Transition	Custom Lists	Chart

Settings

- ☐ R1C1 reference style
- ☐ Ignore other applications
- ☑ Function tooltips
- ☑ Recently used file list: 9 entries

- ☐ Prompt for workbook properties
- ☐ Provide feedback with sound
- ☐ Zoom on roll with IntelliMouse

Web Options...   Service Options...

Sheets in new workbook: 3

Standard font: Arial   Size: 10

Default file location: C:\My Documents

At startup, open all files in:

User name: Joseph Rubin

OK   Cancel

3

Comments

179

Notes:

_____

_____

_____

_____

_____

**My Tips/
Shortcuts:**

_____

_____

_____

_____

_____

Related Tips:	*Tip 72: Adding Data, Charts, or Other Information to a Cell Comment*
	Tip 79: Changing the Cell Comment Shape
	Tip 80: Copying a Cell Comment

Changing the Default Cell Comment Format

➤ **To change the default format of a cell Comments:**

1. Press **<⊞+M>** (the **<⊞>** key is located between the **<Ctrl>** and **<Alt>** keys) to minimize Excel and any other open programs.

2. Right-click the desktop and select **Properties** from the shortcut menu.

3. Select the **Appearance** tab.

4. Click **Advanced** (skip this step if using Windows 98).

5. In the **Item** box, select **ToolTip**, and change the color.

6. In the **Font** box, change the font as desired, and select the font size and color.

7. Click **OK** to accept the new selection.

8. Click **OK** again at the bottom of the dialog box.

Note: Changing the ToolTip impacts all ToolTips in Excel, including those that appear below the toolbar icons.

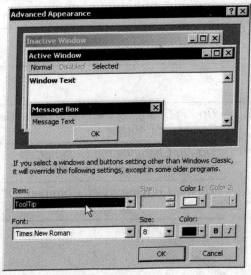

Notes:

**My Tips/
Shortcuts:**

| **Related
Tips:** | *Tip 77: Changing the Name of the Cell
Comment's Author* |
| | *Tip 78: Changing the Default Cell
Comment Format* |
| | *Tip 80: Copying a Cell Comment* |

Changing the Cell Comment Shape

➢ **To change the Comment shape:**

1. Follow the instructions in *Tip #72* and add a picture to the cell **Comment**.

2. Select the cell containing the **Comment** and press **<Shift+F2>** to edit the cell **Comment** or press **<Shift+F10>** (or right-click) and select **Show Comment** from the shortcut menu.

3. Select the edge of the **Comment** so that it is surrounded by dots, not slashes.

4. From the **Drawing** toolbar, click **Draw**, select **Change AutoShape**, and then select any shape.

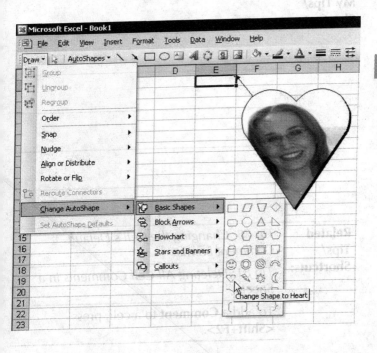

Notes:

_____

_____

_____

_____

_____

_____

My Tips/
Shortcuts:

_____

_____

_____

_____

_____

Related	*Tip 78: Changing the Cell's Default*
Tips/	*Comment Format*
Shortcuts:	*Tip 81: Deleting All Cell Comments in a*
	Sheet
	To add a **Comment** to a cell, press
	<Shift+F2>.

Copying a Cell Comment

➢ **To copy a cell Comment:**

1. Select a cell that contains a **Comment**, and press **<Ctrl+C>**.

2. Select a different cell, and press **<Shift+F10>** or right-click and select **Paste Special** from the shortcut menu.

3. Select the **Comments** option button, and click **OK**.

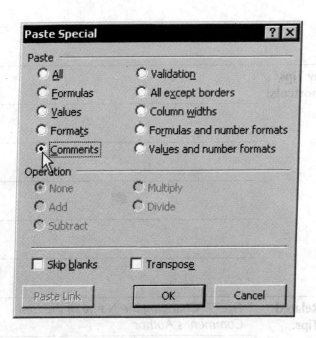

Notes:

**My Tips/
Shortcuts:**

**Related
Tips:**   *Tip 77: Changing the Name of the Cell
Comment's Author*

Tip 80: Copying a Cell Comment

Tip 82: Printing Cell Comments

Deleting All Cell Comments in a Sheet

➤ **To delete all Comments in a sheet:**

1. Press **<F5>** to open the *Go To* dialog box, and click **Special**.

2. In the *Go To Special* dialog box, select **Comments**.

3. Click **OK**. All cells containing **Comments** are selected.

   OR

   Skip steps 1 through 3 and press **<Ctrl+Shift+O>** (the letter **O**, not the number zero) to select all **Comments**.

4. Press **<Shift+F10>** or right-click, and select **Delete Comment** from the shortcut menu.

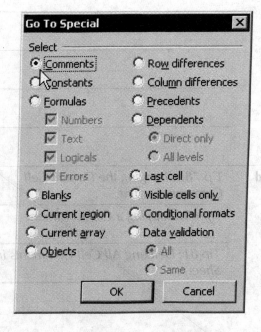

Notes:

My Tips/
Shortcuts:

Related
Tips:

Tip 78: Changing the Default Cell
Comment Format

Tip 80: Copying a Cell Comment

Tip 81: Deleting All Cell Comments in a
Sheet

Printing Cell Comments

➤ **To print the Comments within the print area:**

1. From the *File* menu, select **Page Setup**, and then click the **Sheet** tab.
2. Select one of the following options from the **Comments** dropdown list:

   ✦ **None:** No **Comments** are printed.
   ✦ **At end of sheet**: **Comments** are printed on a separate page after printing the sheet.
   ✦ **As displayed on sheet**: Only displayed **Comments** are printed.

➤ **To print a single Comment in cell:**

1. Select a cell containing a **Comment**.
2. From the *File* menu, select **Page Setup**, and then click the **Sheet** tab.
3. In the print area, insert the cell address.
4. From the **Comments** dropdown list, select **At end of sheet** and click **OK**.
5. Click the **Print** icon.

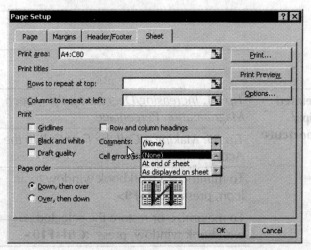

Notes:

**My Tips/
Shortcuts:**

**Related
Tips/
Shortcuts:**

Tip 84: Increasing/Decreasing the Screen Magnification Percentage

Tip 85: Making a Cell the First Cell in the Active Window

To minimize a workbook window to an icon, press **<Ctrl+F9>**.

To maximize or restore the selected workbook window, press **<Ctrl+F10>**.

Viewing All Data in a Sheet

➢ **To increase or reduce the selected data region to the size of the window:**

1. Select a range of cells containing data.
2. From the *View* menu, select **Zoom**.
3. In the *Zoom* dialog box, select **Fit Selection**.
4. Click **OK**.

continued...

Notes:

**My Tips/
Shortcuts:**

Viewing All Data in a Sheet (cont.)

➤ **To increase the number of cells appearing in the window, hide window elements, such as sheet tabs, toolbars, the formula bar, and the status bar:**

1. From the *Tools* menu, select **Options**, and then select the **View** tab.

2. Clear the checkboxes for **Row & Column headers**, **Horizontal scroll bar**, **Vertical scroll bar**, **Sheet tabs**, and **then** click **OK**.

3. Select **View** and deselect the **Formula Bar** and **Status Bar** checkboxes.

4. Select any one of the toolbars, right-click, and clear the checkboxes beside each of the displayed toolbars from the shortcut menu.

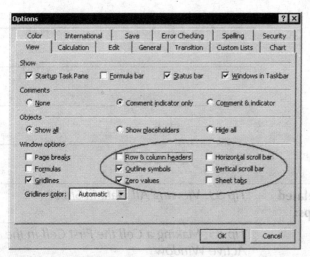

Result: Only the title row is displayed, and more rows are visible.

Notes:

My Tips/
Shortcuts:

Related
Tips:

Increasing/Decreasing the Screen Magnification Percentage

➤ **To quickly increase or decrease the screen magnification percentage:**

1. Select a cell.
2. Press **<Ctrl>**, and roll the mouse wheel forward (to increase the magnification) or backward (to decrease it).

3

	A	B	C	D	E	F	H	I	J
1	645	645	645	645	645	645	645	645	
2	645	645	645	645	645	645	645	645	
3	645	645	645	645	645	645	645	645	
4	645	645	645	645	645	645	645	645	
5	645	645	645	645	645	645	645	645	
6	645	645	645	645	645	645	645	645	
7	645	645	645	645	645	645	645	645	
8	645	645	645	645	645	645	645	645	
9	645	645	645	645	645	645	645	645	
10	645	645	645	645	645	645	645	645	
11	645	645	645	645	645	645	645	645	
12	645	645	645	645	645	645	645	645	
13	645	645	645	645	645	645	645	645	
14									

Windows

Notes:

**My Tips/
Shortcuts:**

Related Tips/ Shortcuts:	*Tip 83: Viewing All Data in Sheet*
	Tip 84: Increasing/Decreasing the Screen Magnification Percentage
	To display the active cell after using the Scrollbar, press **<Ctrl+Backspace>**.

Making a Cell the First Cell in the Active Window

> **To make the top-left cell of a report be the first cell in the active window:**

Before: Cell **C4** is the first cell in the **Financial Highlights** report:

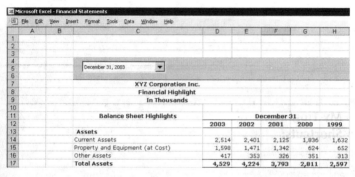

After: Cell **C4** is the first cell in the active window:

	C	D	E	F	G	H
4						
5	December 31, 2003 ▼					
6						
7	XYZ Corporation Inc.					
8	Financial Highlight					
9	In Thousands					
10						
11	**Balance Sheet Highlights**	December 31				
12		2003	2002	2001	2000	1999
13	**Assets**					
14	Current Assets	2,514	2,401	2,125	1,836	1,632
15	Property and Equipment (at Cost)	1,598	1,471	1,342	624	652
16	Other Assets	417	353	326	351	313
17	**Total Assets**	4,529	4,224	3,793	2,811	2,597
18						
19	**Liabilities and Stockholder's Equity**					
20	Current Liabilities	1,785	1,665	1,458	1,098	930
21	Long-Term Liabilities	1,325	1,255	1,250	865	915
22	Stockholder's Equity	1,419	1,304	1,085	848	752
23	**Total Liabilities and Stockholder's Equity**	4,529	4,224	3,793	2,811	2,597
24						

continued...

Notes:

_____

_____

_____

_____

_____

_____

**My Tips/
Shortcuts:**

_____

_____

_____

_____

_____

_____

_____

_____

_____

Making a Cell the First Cell in the Active Window (cont.)

1. Press **<Alt+F11>** to open the **VBE** (Visual Basic Editor).
2. Double-click any **Module** sheet under **VBAProject**.

   OR

   From the *Insert* menu, insert a new **Module**.
3. Type the following code in the **Module** sheet:

```
Sub ActiveCell_To_FirstCellCorner()

    Application.Goto ActiveCell, True

End Sub
```

4. Press **<Alt+F11>** to return to Excel.
5. Press **<Alt+F8>** and from the *Macro* dialog box, select the macro.
6. Click **Run** to operate the macro (see *Tip #19, page 3*).

Notes:

**My Tips/
Shortcuts:**

Related Tips:	*Tip 11: Selecting a Column(s) or Row(s) Using Keyboard Shortcuts*
	Tip 87: Protecting Data by Hiding a Row(s) and Column(s)
	Tip 257: Deleting Empty Rows

Hiding/Unhiding a Row(s) or Column(s)

Using keyboard shortcuts

➢ **To hide/unhide a row(s):**

✦ To hide a row(s), select a cell(s) and press
   <Ctrl+9>.

✦ To unhide a row(s), select the cells containing the
   range of the hidden row(s) and press
   <Ctrl+Shift+(>.

➢ **To hide/unhide a column(s):**

✦ To hide a column(s), select a cell(s) and press
   <Ctrl+0>.

✦ To unhide a column(s), select the cells containing
   the range of the hidden column(s) and press
   <Ctrl+Shift+)>.

➢ **To unhide rows & columns in a sheet:**

1. Press **<Ctrl+A>** to select all cells in the sheet (in
   Excel 2003, press **<Ctrl+A+A>** from a cell in the
   Current Region/List range) or click **Select All** at
   the top-left intersection of the rows and columns.

2. Press **<Ctrl+Shift+(>** and then **<Ctrl+Shift+)>**.

➢ **To unhide rows & columns in all sheets in the
   workbook at once:**

1. Group the sheets in the workbook by selecting
   Select All Sheets from the sheet tab's shortcut
   menu.

2. Press **<Ctrl+A>** to select all cells in the sheets (in
   Excel 2003, press **<Ctrl+A+A>** from a cell in the
   Current Region/List range) or click **Select All** at
   the top-left intersection of the rows and columns.

3. Press **<Ctrl+Shift+(>** and then **<Ctrl+Shift+)>**.

Notes:

_____

_____

_____

_____

_____

_____

My Tips/
Shortcuts:

_____

_____

_____

_____

_____

Related Tips:	*Tip 13: Moving Between Unprotected Cells in a Protected Sheet*
	Tip 107: Protecting the Sheet or the Cells in the Sheet
	Tip 109: Limiting the Movement in a Protected Sheet

Protecting Data by Hiding a Row(s) and Column(s)

Restrict the accessible area by hiding rows and columns.

➢ **To protect data in cells by hiding rows and columns:**

1. Select a column. For this example, select column **E** (see screenshot on the next page) and press **<Ctrl+Shift+Right Arrow>**.

2. Press **<Ctrl+0>**, or press **<Shift+F10>** and select **Hide** from the shortcut menu.

3. Select a row. For this example, select row **32** and press **<Ctrl+Shift+Down Arrow>**.

4. Press **<Ctrl+ 9>**, or press **<Shift+F10>** and select **Hide** from the shortcut menu.

Result: The unrestricted area is the visible area, range **A1:D31**.

continued...

3

Windows

Notes:

My Tips/ Shortcuts:

Protecting Data by Hiding Rows and Columns (cont.)

➢ **To unhide rows and columns:**

1. Select row **31**, and while placing the cursor on the row number, click and drag it slightly downward into the non-accessible area.

2. Release the mouse button and return the cursor to row **31**.

3. Press **<Ctrl+Shift+(>**, or press **<Shift+F10>** and select **Unhide** from the shortcut menu.

4. Select column **D**, and while placing the cursor on the column number, click and drag it slightly to the right into the non-accessible area.

5. Release the mouse button and return the cursor to column **D**.

6. Press **<Ctrl+Shift+)>**, or press **<Shift+F10>** and select **Unhide** from the shortcut menu.

	A	B	C	D
2	December 31, 2003			
4		XYZ Corporation Inc.		
5		BALANCE SHEET		
7			December 31	
8		Notes	2003	2002
9	ASSETS			
11	**Current Assets**			
12	Cash	5	301,124	318,697
13	Accounts Receivable	7	1,653,558	1,538,494
14	Inventories	8	546,173	520,133
15	Prepaid Expenses	9	13,552	23,659
16	**Total Current Assets**		2,514,407	2,400,982
18	**Property and Equipment (at Cost)**	10		
19	Land & Building		674,019	677,191
20	Machinery and Equipment		386,140	326,052
21	Furniture and Fixtures		59,410	47,906
22	Total Property and Equipment		1,119,569	1,051,150
23	Less: Accumulated Depreciation		(478,852)	(419,540)
24	**Net Book Value**		640,717	631,610
26	**Other Assets**			
27	Investment in Revenue Bond	11	364,321	300,260
28	Patents, Trademarks and Goodwill	12	52,250	52,500
29	**Total Other Assets**		416,571	352,760
31	**TOTAL ASSETS**		3,571,695	3,385,352

Notes:

**My Tips/
Shortcuts:**

| **Related
Tips:** | *Tip 13: Moving Between Unprotected Cells
in a Protected Sheet* |
| | *Tip 87: Protecting Data by Hiding a Row(s)
and Column(s)* |
| | *Tip 107: Protecting the Sheet or the Cells
in the Sheet* |

Allowing Multiple Users to Edit Specified Ranges

➤ **To allow users to only edit specific ranges when working in a shared workbook:**

✦ From the *Tools* menu, select **Protection**, and then **Allow Users to Edit Ranges**.

This advanced option allows multiple users (for example, when working on a network) to update data in a well-defined and private area. Each workbook user is allotted a range in the sheet with a unique password.

3

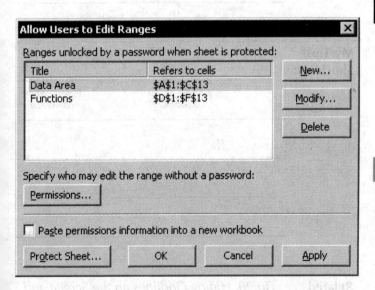

W
i
n
d
o
w
s

Notes:

**My Tips/
Shortcuts:**

**Related
Tips/
Shortcuts:**

Tip 90: Hiding Gridlines on the Screen and
when Printing

Tip 102: Coloring Sheet Tabs

To apply the outline border to the selected
cells, press <Ctrl+Shift+&>.

Coloring Gridlines

➢ **To color the gridlines:**

1. From the *Tools* menu, select **Options**, and then select the **View** tab.

2. In the **Window options** section, choose a color from **Gridlines color** dropdown list, and click **OK**.

Note: In **Excel 97** and **Excel 2000**, select the color from the **Color** dropdown list.

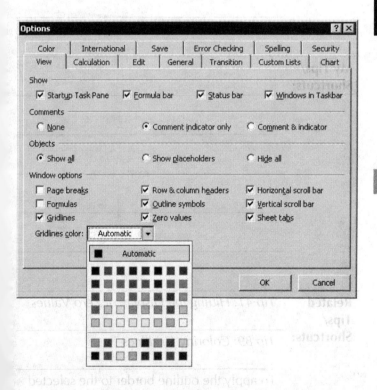

Notes:

_____

_____

_____

_____

_____

_____

**My Tips/
Shortcuts:**

_____

_____

_____

_____

_____

_____

Related Tips/ Shortcuts:	*Tip 41: Hiding the Display of Zero Values*
	Tip 89: Coloring Gridlines

To apply the outline border to the selected cells, press **<Ctrl+Shift+&>**.

Hiding Gridlines on the Screen and When Printing

➢ **To hide gridlines on the screen:**

1. From the *Tools* menu, select **Options**, and then select the **View** tab.

2. In **Window options** section, deselect the **Gridlines** box, and click **OK**.

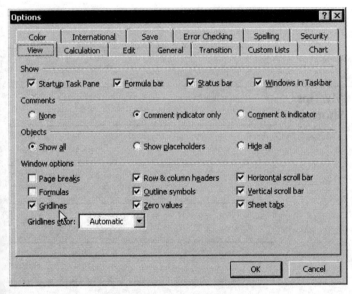

➢ **To hide gridlines when printing:**

1. From the *File* menu, select **Page Setup**, and then select the **Sheet** tab. By default, the checkbox for the **Gridlines** is deselected.

2. Click **OK**.

Notes:

My Tips/
Shortcuts:

Related Tips:	*Tip 12: Selecting Cells from Any Cell to the Last Cell in the Sheet's Used Range*
	Tip 250: Reducing the Workbook Size for Quick Sending via E-Mail

Reducing the Used Area in a Sheet

Why is it important to reduce the used area?

✦ The **vertical scroll bar** gets shorter as the used area of a sheet grows larger (as shown in the screenshots), making it inconvenient to use.

✦ Reducing the size of the used area also reduces the size of the workbook.

➤ **To reduce the used area:**

1. Find the last cell that contains data in the sheet.
2. Delete all rows after this cell, as well as the columns to the right of the cell that do not contain data (see *Tip #250*).
3. Press **<Ctrl+S>** to save the file. The address of the last cell in the used area is updated when the file is saved.

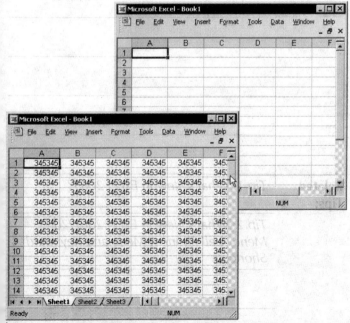

Notes:

_____

_____

_____

_____

_____

**My Tips/
Shortcuts:**

_____

_____

_____

_____

_____

**Related
Tips:**   *Tip 1: What's New in Excel 2003?*

*Tip 2: What's New in Excel 2002/2003:
Menu, Cell Shortcut Menu and Keyboard
Shortcuts*

_____

Using Task Panes

✦ What is the Task Pane?

The **Task Pane** is new from **Excel 2002**. It is a dialog box added to the right side of the sheet that expands existing features radically.

✦ Easy keyboard shortcut to open the Task Pane:

Open each of the **Task Panes** from the menu item to which the **Task Pane** belongs. For example, to open the **New Workbook Task Pane**, select **New** from the *File* menu.

3

❖ **Excel 2002** offers four **Task Panes**. Press **<Ctrl+C+C>** to open the **Clipboard Task Pane** (or select **Task Pane** from the *View* menu), and then select one of the **Task Panes** from the **Task Pane** dropdown list at the top-right corner of the **Task Pane**.

❖ **Excel 2003** offers 11 **Task Panes**. To make the **Task Pane** visible, press **<Ctrl+ F1>** and then choose one of the **Task Panes** from the **Task Pane** dropdown list at the top-right corner of the **Task Pane**.

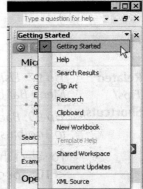

➢ **To hide the Task Pane:**

✦ Press **<Ctrl+F1>** (new in **Excel 2003**; it is a toggle).

Notes:

_____

_____

_____

_____

_____

_____

_____

**My Tips/
Shortcuts:**

_____

_____

_____

_____

_____

_____

_____

Related Tips/ Shortcuts:	Tip 97: Using the Empty Space in The Menu Bar by Adding Useful Icons
	Tip 99: Backing Up Customized Changes to Toolbars and Menus
	To select the Menu bar, press **<Alt>** or **<F10>**, or close an open menu and submenu at the same time.

Showing All Items When Choosing from a Menu

➢ **To display all items when choosing from a menu, select the Always show full menus checkbox:**

1. Place the mouse arrow on one of the toolbars, right-click, and select **Customize** from the shortcut menu.

2. In the *Customize* dialog box, select the **Options** tab.

3. Select the **Always show full menus** checkbox (in **Excel 2000**, deselect the **Menus show recently used commands first** checkbox) and then click **OK**.

3

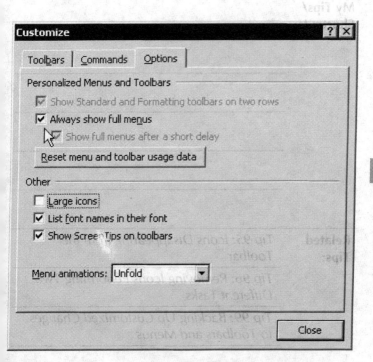

217

Notes:

_____

_____

_____

_____

_____

_____

**My Tips/
Shortcuts:**

_____

_____

_____

_____

_____

_____

Related Tips:	*Tip 95: Icons Disappearing from the Toolbar*
	Tip 96: Removing Icons Performing Two Different Tasks
	Tip 99: Backing Up Customized Changes to Toolbars and Menus

Customizing an Icon

Customizing an icon allows you to change the icon's image, assign a macro or hyperlink, and more.

➢ **To customize an icon:**

1. Place the mouse arrow over one of the toolbars, right-click, and select **Customize** from the shortcut menu.

2. Select any icon on an existing toolbar and right-click.

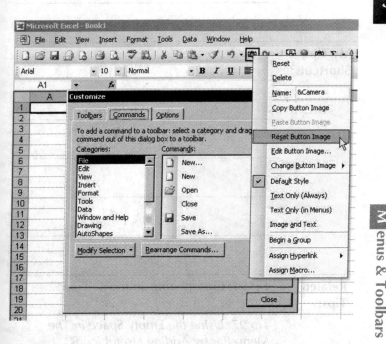

219

Notes:

_____

_____

_____

_____

_____

_____

My Tips/ Shortcuts:

_____

_____

_____

_____

_____

_____

_____

_____

Related Tips:	*Tip 94: Customizing an Icon*
	Tip 97: Using the Empty Space in The Menu Bar by Adding Useful Icons
	Tip 99: Backing Up Customized Changes to Toolbars and Menus

Icons Disappearing from the Toolbar

✦ **Troubleshooting:**

When adding new icons to the **Standard** and **Formatting** toolbars, some of the existing icons may disappear. This happens because there are too many icons to be displayed on one line.

Using keyboard shortcuts

➤ **To prevent icons from disappearing:**

✦ Remove unused icons from the toolbars by dragging them off the toolbar while pressing the **<Alt>** key.

OR

Change the icon positions on the toolbars. Move the most commonly used icons to the left side of the toolbar by pressing the **<Alt+ Shift>** keys while dragging the icons.

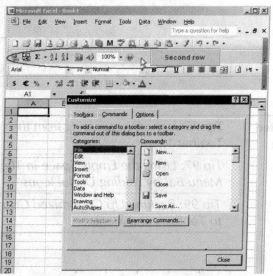

221

Notes:

_____

_____

_____

_____

_____

_____

**My Tips/
Shortcuts:**

_____

_____

_____

_____

_____

_____

**Related
Tips:**   *Tip 95: Icons Disappearing from the
            Toolbar*

            *Tip 97: Using the Empty Space in The
            Menu Bar by Adding Useful Icons*

            *Tip 99: Backing Up Customized Changes
            to Toolbars and Menus*

Removing Icons Performing Two Different Tasks

Some of the icons on the **Standard** and **Formatting** toolbars perform two different (but related) tasks. To toggle between the two tasks, press **<Shift>** while clicking the icon. The icons that perform different tasks are:

✦ **In the Standard toolbar:**
  ❖ Print <> Print Preview
  ❖ Sort Ascending <> Sort Descending
  ❖ Open <> Save

✦ **In the Formatting toolbar:**
  ❖ Increase Indent <> Decrease Indent
  ❖ Underline <> Double Underline
  ❖ Center <> Merge and Center
  ❖ Increase Decimal <> Decrease Decimal

Example: The **Open** icon changed to **Save** when pressing the **<Shift>** key.

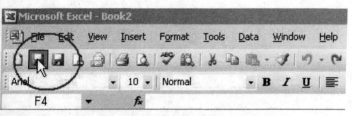

 Using keyboard shortcuts

➢ **To remove the double-task icons:**
  ✦ Drag the icon off the toolbar while holding the **<Alt>** key.

Notes:

My Tips/ Shortcuts:

Related Tips:

Tip 94: Customizing an Icon

Tip 95: Icons Disappearing from the Toolbar

Tip 98: Adding and Saving a New Customized Toolbar

Using the Empty Space in the Menu Bar by Adding Useful Icons

Almost 50% of the menu bar line is empty. Use this empty space to add useful icons such as **Page Setup**, **Custom Views**, **Macro**, and more.

➢ **To add icons to the menu bar:**

1. Place the mouse arrow on one of the toolbars, right-click, and select **Customize** from the shortcut menu.
2. Select the **Commands** tab.
3. From **Categories**, select **File** and drag the **Page Setup** icon to the menu bar.
4. Repeat step 3 for the **Custom Views** icon (from **View**) and for the **Macro** icon (from **Built-in Menus**).
5. Click **Close**.

Note: These new icons also have keyboard shortcuts, which are used by pressing **<Alt>** and the underlined letter. For example, to open the *Page Setup* dialog box, press **<Alt+u>**.

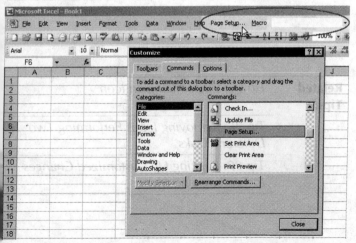

Notes:

**My Tips/
Shortcuts:**

Related Tips:	*Tip 94: Customizing an Icon*
	Tip 96: Removing Icons Performing Two Different Tasks
	Tip 99: Backing Up Customized Changes to Toolbars and Menus

Adding and Saving a New Customized Toolbar

➢ **To add and save a customized toolbar:**

1. Place the mouse arrow on one of the toolbars, right-click, and select **Customize** from the shortcut menu.

2. In the *Customize* dialog box, select the **Toolbars** tab.

3. Click **New**.

4. Type a name for the toolbar, and then click **OK**.

5. Select the **Commands** tab, and add icons from the **Commands** box to the new toolbar.

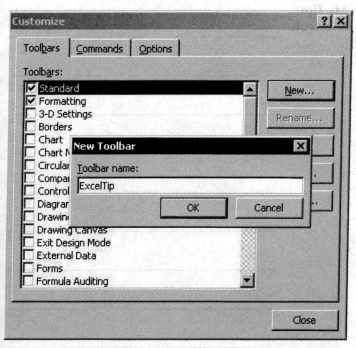

continued...

227

Notes:

**My Tips/
Shortcuts:**

Adding and Saving a New Customized Toolbar (cont.)

➢ **To attach the customized toolbar to a workbook:**

1. In the *Customize* dialog box, select the **Toolbars** tab.
2. Select **Attach**.
3. In the *Attach Toolbars* dialog box, select a toolbar from the **Custom** toolbars.
4. Click **Copy**, **OK**, and then **Close** in the *Customize* dialog box.
5. Press **<Ctrl+S>** to save the workbook.

3

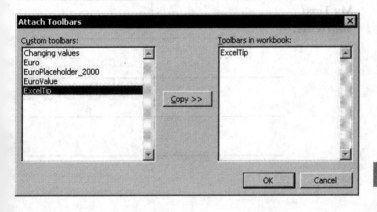

Menus & Toolbars

Tip 99

Notes:

_____

_____

_____

_____

_____

_____

**My Tips/
Shortcuts:**

_____

_____

_____

_____

_____

_____

_____

Related Tips:	*Tip 96: Removing Icons Performing Two Different Tasks*
	Tip 97: Using the Empty Space in The Menu Bar by Adding Useful Icons
	Tip 98: Adding and Saving a New Customized Toolbar

Backing Up Customized Changes to Toolbars and Menus

The customized changes made to menus and toolbars are saved in a file with the extension .XLB.

✦ In **Excel 97** and **Excel 2000**, the file name is the user's name followed by **.XLB**.

✦ In **Excel 2002** and **Excel 2003**, the file name is **Excel.XLB**.

➢ **To backup the file:**

1. Search for a file with the extension **.XLB**.

2. Copy the file and store it in a safe place.

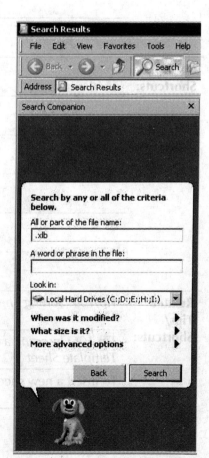

3

M
e
n
u
s

&

T
o
o
l
b
a
r
s

Notes:

**My Tips/
Shortcuts:**

Related Tips/ Shortcuts:	*Tip 104: Sorting Sheets in Ascending Order*
	Tip 106: Inserting a New Sheet from a Template Sheet
	To insert a new sheet, press **<Shift+F11>**.

Changing the Default Number of Sheets in a New Workbook

Excel can hold an unlimited numbers of sheets.

➤ **To change the default number of sheets in a new workbook:**

1. From the *Tools* menu, select **Options**, and then select the **General** tab.
2. In the **Sheets in new workbook** box, enter a new default number (up to 255 sheets).
3. Click **OK**.

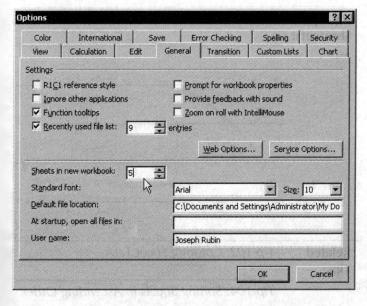

Notes:

_____

_____

_____

_____

_____

**My Tips/
Shortcuts:**

_____

_____

_____

_____

_____

_____

**Related
Tips:**

Changing the Font Size of the Sheet Name

➤ **To change the font size of the sheets tab:**

1. Minimize all open applications by pressing

   <⊞+M> (the ⊞ key is between the **<Ctrl>** and **<Alt>** keys), and right-click the desktop.

2. Select **Properties**, and then select the **Appearance** tab.

3. Click **Advanced** (skip this step if using Windows 98).

4. From the **Item** dropdown list, choose **Scrollbar**.

5. Change the **Size** and click **OK** twice.

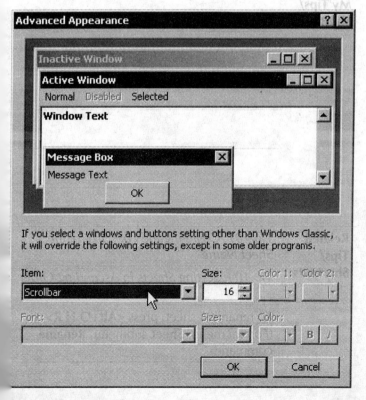

Notes:

**My Tips/
Shortcuts:**

Related Tips/ Shortcuts:	*Tip 101: Changing the Font Size of the Sheet Name*
	Tip 104: Sorting Sheets in Ascending Order
	To rename a sheet, press **<Alt+O H R>** (*Format* menu, **Sheet** submenu, **Rename** command)

Coloring Sheet Tabs

➢ **To color the Sheet tabs (new in Excel 2002 and Excel 2003):**

✦ Select a sheet tab, right-click, and select **Tab Color** from the shortcut menu.

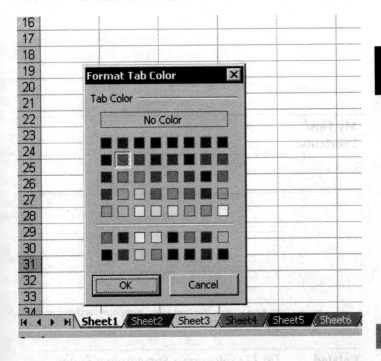

3

Notes:

**My Tips/
Shortcuts:**

**Related
Tips:**   *Tip 17: Selecting a Sheet from a Sorted
Sheets List*

Tip 105: Grouping/Ungrouping Sheets

*Tip 107: Protecting the Sheet or the Cells
in the Sheet*

Copying or Moving a Sheet

There is a difference between copying all the cells in a sheet and copying the sheet.

➤ To copy and paste all cells in a sheet:

1. Select the cells in the sheet by pressing **<Ctrl+A>** (in **Excel 2003**, select a cell in a blank area before pressing **<Ctrl+A>**, or from a selected cell in a **Current Region/List** range, press **<Ctrl+A+A>**).

   OR

   Click **Select All** at the top-left intersection of rows and columns.

2. Press **<Ctrl+C>**.
3. Press **<Ctrl+Page Down>** to select another sheet, then select cell **A1**.
4. Press **<Enter>**.

➤ To copy the entire sheet:

Copying the entire sheet means copying the cells, the page setup parameters, and the defined range **Names**.

✦ Option 1:

1. Move the mouse pointer to a sheet tab.
2. Press **<Ctrl>**, and hold the mouse to drag the sheet to a different location.
3. Release the mouse button and the **<Ctrl>** key.

continued...

3

Sheets

Notes:

My Tips/ Shortcuts:

Copying or Moving a Sheet (cont.)

✦ **Option 2:**

1. Right-click the appropriate sheet tab.

2. From the shortcut menu, select **Move** or **Copy**. The *Move or Copy* dialog box enables one to copy the sheet either to a different location in the current workbook or to a different workbook. Be sure to mark the **Create a copy** checkbox.

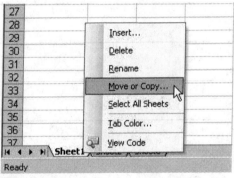

✦ **Option 3:**

1. From the *Window* menu, select **Arrange**.

2. Select **Tiled** to tile all open workbooks in the window.

3. Use Option 1 (dragging the sheet while pressing **<Ctrl>**) to copy or move a sheet.

Caution: Moving a sheet from a workbook with defined range **Names** or linked formulas will create links in the new workbook (see *Tip #220*).

241

Notes:

_____

_____

_____

_____

_____

_____

_____

**My Tips/
Shortcuts:**

_____

_____

_____

_____

_____

_____

Sorting Sheets in Ascending Order

➤ **To sort the sheets in ascending order:**

1. Press **<Alt+F11>**, and then select a **VBAProject** (for example, press **VBAProject (Financial Statements.xls)**).

2. From the *Insert* menu, select **Module**.

3. In the **Module**, type the code lines displayed in the **SheetInABC_Order** macro in the screenshot.

4. Operate the macro from the **Module** by pressing **<F5>**.

    OR

    Press **<Alt+F11>** and return to Excel, assign the macro to any Excel object as a button or icon, or press **<Alt+F8>** to select the macro, and then click **Run**.

Note: The **SheetInABC_Order** macro can be downloaded from www.exceltip.com/f1toc.

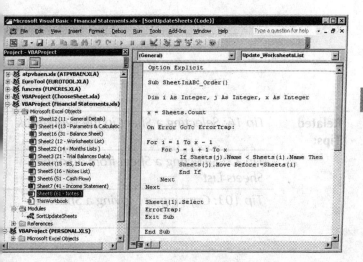

```
Sub SheetInABC_Order()

Dim i As Integer, j As Integer, x As Integer

x = Sheets.Count

On Error GoTo ErrorTrap:

For i = 1 To x - 1
    For j = i + 1 To x
        If Sheets(j).Name < Sheets(i).Name Then
        Sheets(j).Move Before:=Sheets(i)
        End If
    Next
Next

Sheets(1).Select
ErrorTrap:
Exit Sub

End Sub
```

Notes:

_____

_____

_____

_____

_____

_____

_____

**My Tips/
Shortcuts:**

_____

_____

_____

_____

_____

_____

_____

Related Tips:	Tip 16: Selecting a Sheet in the Workbook
	Tip 17: Selecting a Sheet from a Sorted Sheets List
	Tip 103: Copying or Moving a Sheet

Grouping/Ungrouping Sheets

Grouping sheets has the following advantages:

✦ Allows setting the print options for a number of sheets at once (see *Tip #231*).

✦ Allows changing an item from the **View** tab in the *Options* dialog box (*Tools* menu).

✦ Allows applying formats to many sheets.

✦ Allows unhiding of rows and/or columns simultaneously (see *Tip #86*).

✦ Allows typing/inserting text or formulas for the same cell address in all grouped sheets (see *Tip #28*).

➢ **To group all sheets in the workbook:**

✦ Select the first sheet in the workbook, hold the **<Shift>** key and click the last sheet tab in the workbook.

OR

From a sheet tab shortcut menu, select **Select All Sheets**.

➢ **To group continuous sheets:**

✦ Hold the **<Shift>** key and click a different sheet tab.

➢ **To group non-continuous sheets:**

✦ Hold the **<Ctrl>** key, click a different sheet tab and add it to the group.

➢ **To ungroup sheets:**

✦ Hold the **<Shift>** key and click the active sheet tab.

Notes:

**My Tips/
Shortcuts:**

| **Related
Tips/
Shortcuts:** | *Tip 17: Selecting a Sheet from a Sorted
Sheets List* |
| --- | --- |
| | *Tip 112: Opening/Closing a Workbook(s)* |

To select the next sheet, press **<Ctrl+Page
Down>**; to select the previous sheet, press
<Ctrl+Page Up>.

Inserting a New Sheet from a Template Sheet

For an explanation on how to create and save a new template workbook, see *Tip #124*.

In this example, the template workbook name is **Book.xlt** (except for **Excel 2000**, where the template workbook name will be **Sheet.xlt**).

➤ **To define a new customized sheet to be used as the default inserted sheet:**

1. Insert new sheets from a template named **Book.xlt** by right-clicking a sheet tab, and selecting **Insert** from the shortcut menu.

2. Double-click **Book.xlt**.

3. Delete all sheets except one.

4. Save the workbook as a template (see *Tip #124*) with the name **Sheet.xlt**, and then close it.

➤ **To insert one template sheet into a workbook:**

1. Right-click any sheet tab, and select **Insert** from the shortcut menu.

2. In the *Insert* dialog box, select the template **Sheet.xlt** and click **OK**. The inserted sheet is the customized sheet template.

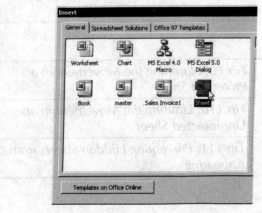

Notes:

_____

_____

_____

_____

_____

_____

My Tips/
Shortcuts:

_____

_____

_____

_____

_____

_____

_____

Related Tips:	Tip 109: Limiting the Movement in a Protected Sheet
	Tip 110: Limiting the Movement in an Unprotected Sheet
	Tip 111: Preventing Hidden Sheets from Appearing

Protecting the Sheet or the Cells in the Sheet

Protecting the sheet means that the content of cells cannot be changed and/or formulas can be hidden from view.

➢ **To protect a sheet:**
  ✦ From the *Tools* menu, select **Protection**, and then **Protect Sheet**.

➢ **To protect the cells in the sheet using the Protect Sheet option:**
  1. Press **<Ctrl+1>**, and select the **Protection** tab in the *Format Cells* dialog box.
  2. Select the **Locked** checkbox and click **OK**.
  3. Protect the sheet (see above). To protect formulas in cells, see *Tip #208*.

➢ **To hide text/formula in the Formula bar:**
  1. Press **<Ctrl+1>**, and select the **Protection** tab in the *Format Cells* dialog box.
  2. Select the **Hidden** checkbox and click **OK**.
  3. Protect the sheet (see above).

The new *Protect Sheet* dialog box in **Excel 2002** and **Excel 2003** provides various options for protecting and unprotecting different elements in the sheet.

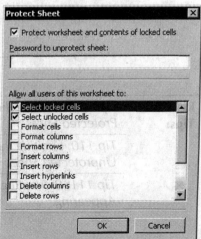

3

Sheets

249

Notes:

**My Tips/
Shortcuts:**

Related Tips:	*Tip 109: Limiting the Movement in a Protected Sheet*
	Tip 110: Limiting the Movement in an Unprotected Sheet
	Tip 111: Preventing Hidden Sheets from Appearing

Adding the Properties Icon to the Standard Toolbar

Why add the Properties icon to the Standard toolbar?

✦ By setting the **Scroll Area** range, you restrict the accessible area in the sheet (see *Tip #110*).

✦ By changing the **Enable Selection** option, you choose one of three different sheet movement options when the sheet is protected (see *Tip #109*).

✦ By selecting **XlSheetVeryHidden** from the **Visible dropdown list**, you prevent the sheet from appearing in the hidden sheets list when selecting **Sheet** and then **Unhide** from the *Format* menu (see *Tip #111*).

➢ **To add the Properties icon to the Standard toolbar:**

1. Place the mouse pointer over one of the toolbars, right-click, and select **Customize** from the shortcut menu.

2. Select the **Commands** tab.

3. From **Categories**, select **Control Toolbar** and from the **Commands** box, drag the **Properties** icon to the **Standard** toolbar.

4. Close the *Customize* dialog box.

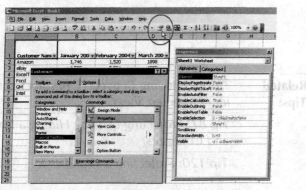

Notes:

_____

_____

_____

_____

_____

_____

_____

My Tips/ Shortcuts:

_____

_____

_____

_____

_____

_____

_____

_____

Related Tips:	*Tip 13: Moving Between Unprotected Cells in a Protected Sheet*
	Tip 87: Protecting Data by Hiding a Row(s) and Column(s)
	Tip 120: Protecting a Workbook

Limiting the Movement in a Protected Sheet

➢ **To limit the movement in a protected sheet** (for this example, protect cells containing formulas (see *Tip #208*)):

1. Click the **Properties** icon (see *Tip #108*).

   OR

   From the **Control Toolbox** toolbar, click the **Properties** icon.

2. There are three options in **EnableSelection**:

   ✦ **xlNoRestrictions:** In a protected sheet, selection is allowed for both locked and unlocked cells.

   ✦ **xlUnLockedCells:** In a protected sheet, selection is allowed for unlocked cells only (in the screenshot below a cell containing a formula cannot be selected).

   ✦ **xlNoSelection:** In a protected sheet, selection is not allowed for either locked or unlocked cells.

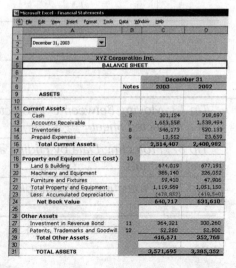

253

Notes:

_____

_____

_____

_____

_____

_____

_____

_____

My Tips/
Shortcuts:

_____

_____

_____

_____

_____

_____

_____

_____

Related Tips:	*Tip 13: Moving Between Unprotected Cells in a Protected Sheet*
	Tip 87: Protecting Data by Hiding a Row(s) and Column(s)
	Tip 120: Protecting a Workbook

Limiting the Movement in an Unprotected Sheet

In this example, the sheet is divided into two parts: an area where movement is allowed (the **Scroll Area**), and an area where movement is restricted (that is, a protected area), without protecting the sheet.

➢ **Set the Scroll Area range in the *Properties* dialog box:**

1. Click the **Properties** icon (see *Tip #108*).

   OR

   From the **Control Toolbox** toolbar, click the **Properties** icon.

2. In the **Scroll Area** text box, type the scroll area range, or type the defined **Name** for the range (this is flexible, if you plan to add more data to the range, it is better to use a defined **Name**).

3. To cancel the **Scroll Area** restricted range, clear the **Scroll Area** text box.

Note: You cannot add two **Scroll Areas** to the **Scroll Area** text box.

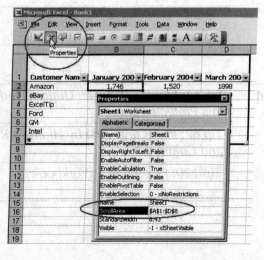

255

Notes:

**My Tips/
Shortcuts:**

Related Tips:	*Tip 13: Moving Between Unprotected Cells in a Protected Sheet*
	Tip 87: Protecting Data by Hiding a Row(s) and Column(s)
	Tip 120: Protecting a Workbook

Preventing Hidden Sheets from Appearing

When a sheet is hidden and the workbook is not protected, it will still appear in the list of hidden sheets in the **Unhide** box (from the *Format* menu, select **Sheet**, and then **Unhide**).

> **To prevent hidden sheets from appearing in the Unhide box:**

1. Click the **Properties** icon (see *Tip #108*).

    OR

    From the **Control Toolbox** toolbar, click the **Properties** icon.

2. From the **Visible** dropdown list, select **xlSheetVeryHidden**.

Properties - Sheet1	
Sheet1 Worksheet	
Alphabetic	Categorized
(Name)	Sheet1
DisplayPageBreaks	False
DisplayRightToLeft	False
EnableAutoFilter	False
EnableCalculation	True
EnableOutlining	False
EnablePivotTable	False
EnableSelection	0 - xlNoRestrictions
Name	Sheet1
ScrollArea	
StandardWidth	8.43
Visible	-1 - xlSheetVisible
	-1 - xlSheetVisible
	0 - xlSheetHidden
	2 - xlSheetVeryHidden

continued...

257

Notes:

**My Tips/
Shortcuts:**

Preventing Hidden Sheets from Appearing (cont.)

➤ **To cancel the xlSheetVeryHidden option for a hidden sheet:**

1. Press **<Alt+F11>** to open the **VBE**.

2. Under **VBAProject** in the left pane, double-click the sheet name you want to unhide.

3. Press **<F4>** or click the **Properties** icon to open the sheet's *Properties* dialog box.

4. In the **Visible** dropdown list, select **xlSheetVisible**.

5. Press **<Alt+F4>** to close the VBE.

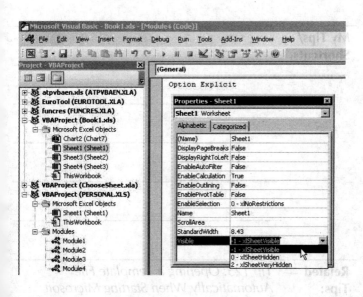

Notes:

**My Tips/
Shortcuts:**

Related Tips:	Tip 125: Opening a Template File Automatically When Starting Microsoft Excel
	Tip 126: Opening Workbooks from a List of Hyperlinks
	Tip 127: Opening a Copy of an Existing Workbook

Opening/Closing a Workbook(s)

Using keyboard shortcuts

Opening a Workbook

➢ **To open a new workbook:**
  ✦ Press **<Ctrl+N>**.

➢ **To open a recently saved workbook:**
  ✦ Press **<Alt+F>** and then the number of the file, as shown in the recently used file list (at the bottom of the *File* menu).

➢ **To open a linked workbook:**
  1. Select the cell with the linked formula, and press **<Ctrl+[>**.
     OR
  1. From the *Edit* menu, select **Links**.
  2. In the *Edit Links* dialog box, select the linked workbook and click **Open Source**.

➢ **To prevent a macro from running while opening a workbook:**
  ✦ Press the **<Shift>** key while opening.

Closing Workbooks

➢ **To close a workbook:**
  ✦ Press **<Ctrl+F4>**.

➢ **To close all open workbooks without closing Excel:**
  ✦ Press **<Shift>**, and from the *File* menu, select **Close All**.

Notes:

**My Tips/
Shortcuts:**

| **Related
Tips:**	*Tip 114: Changing the Default Auto-Save File Location*
	Tip 115: Auto-Recovering/Auto-Saving a Workbook
	Tip 117: Displaying the Workbook's Path in the Address Box

Changing the Number of Files Shown in the Recently Used File List

To see the maximum number of recently used files at the bottom of the *File* menu, change the **Recently used file list** option to 9.

➢ **To set the number of recently used files:**

1. From the *Tools* menu, select **Options**, and **then** select the **General** tab.
2. In the **Recently used file list** box, change the number to the maximum (**9**), and then click **OK**.

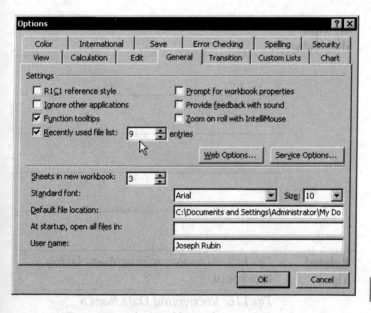

Notes:

_____

_____

_____

_____

_____

**My Tips/
Shortcuts:**

_____

_____

_____

_____

_____

Related Tips:	*Tip 115: Auto-Recovering/Auto-Saving a Workbook*
	Tip 116: Recovering Data from a Corrupted Workbook that cannot Be Opened
	Tip 120: Protecting a Workbook

Changing the Default Auto-Save File Location

➢ **To change the default auto-save file location:**

1. From the *Tools* menu, select **Options**, and then select the **General** tab.

2. In **Default file location** box, type the desired path and folder, then click **OK**.

Options ? ✕

| Color | International | Save | Error Checking | Spelling | Security |
| View | Calculation | Edit | General | Transition | Custom Lists | Chart |

Settings

- ☐ R1C1 reference style
- ☐ Ignore other applications
- ☑ Function tooltips
- ☑ Recently used file list: 9 entries

- ☐ Prompt for workbook properties
- ☐ Provide feedback with sound
- ☐ Zoom on roll with IntelliMouse

[Web Options...] [Service Options...]

Sheets in new workbook: 3

Standard font: Arial ▼ Size: 10 ▼

Default file location: C:\Joseph Rubin General Documents

At startup, open all files in:

User name: Joseph Rubin

[OK] [Cancel]

3

Workbooks

Notes:

**My Tips/
Shortcuts:**

Related Tips:	*Tip 114: Changing the Default Auto-Save File Location*
	Tip 118: Adding the Path of a Saved Workbook to the Title Bar
	Tip 120: Protecting a Workbook

Auto-Recovering/Auto-Saving a Workbook

In **Excel 97** and **Excel 2000**, the **Auto Save** option operates from the **Autosave Add-In**. In **Excel 2002** and **Excel 2003**, this option is automatic and the add-in no longer exists.

➢ **To enable the Autosave Add-In in Excel 97 and Excel 2000:**

1. Install the **Autosave Add-In** by selecting **Add-Ins** from the *Tools* menu, and then selecting the **Autosave Add-in** checkbox.

2. Click **OK**.

3. In the *Auto Save* dialog box, set the **Desired Every ... minutes**.

➢ **To change the default AutoRecovery option (if required):**

1. From the *Tools* menu, select **Options**, and then select the **Save** tab (this is a new tab in **Excel 2002** and **Excel 2003**).

2. Change the **Save AutoRecover info every: ... minutes**, set the **Auto Recover save location**, and then click **OK**.

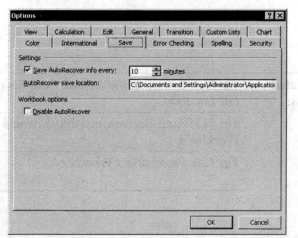

Notes:

**My Tips/
Shortcuts:**

Related Tips:	Tip 114: Changing the Default Auto-Save File Location
	Tip 115: Auto-Recovering/Auto-Saving a Workbook
	Tip 120: Protecting a Workbook

Recovering Data from a Corrupted Workbook That Cannot Be Opened

➤ **To recover data from a corrupted workbook:**

1. Add a new workbook, and save it using the name of the corrupted workbook, but in a different folder than the original (in the screenshot, the workbook name is **Financial Statements.xls**).

2. Change the new sheet names to those in the corrupted workbook (try to remember all of them), and then save the workbook.

3. Add a new workbook. In cell **A1** of the first sheet, insert a linked formula to cell **A1** in the newly created workbook (steps 1 and 2).

4. Copy the formula to all cells covering the data area (as you remember it to be) in the first sheet of the corrupted workbook.

5. Repeat steps 3 and 4 for all sheets, and then save and close the new workbook.

6. Change the linked source address. From the *Edit* menu, select **Edit Links**, and then click **Change Source**.

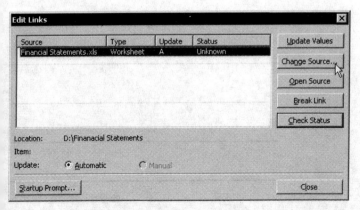

continued...

269

Notes:

**My Tips/
Shortcuts:**

Recovering Data from a Corrupted Workbook That Cannot Be Opened (cont.)

7. Locate the corrupted workbook, select it and then close the *Edit Links* dialog box.

8. Check the result. If the data appears in the new workbook, copy all cells in each sheet and paste them back as values (see *Tip #203*).

	A	B	C	D	E	F	G	H	I
	A1	▼		f_x ='D:\Finanacial Statements\[Financial Statements.xls]Balance Sheet'!A1					
1	0	0	0	0	0	0	0	0	0
2	0	0	0	0	0	0	0	0	0
3	0	0	0	0	0	0	0	0	0
4	XYZ Corpo	0	0	0	0	0	0	0	0
5	BALANCE	0	0	0	0	0	0	0	0
6	0	0	0	0	0	0	0	0	0
7	0	0	37986	0	0	Audit	0	0	0
8	0	Notes	2003	2002	0	2003	2002	0	0
9	AS!	0	0	0	0	0	0	0	0
10	0	0	0	0	0	0	0	0	0
11	Current As	0	0	0	0	0	0	0	0
12	Cash	5	301124.1	318697.1	0	0	0	0	0
13	Accounts I	7	1653558	1538494	0	0	0	0	0

F1 — Get the Most out of Excel!

Notes:

**My Tips/
Shortcuts:**

**Related
Tips:**

*Tip 118: Adding the Path of a Saved
Workbook to the Title Bar*

*Tip 121: Adding Passwords to Prevent
Unauthorized Opening of a Workbook*

*Tip 124: Saving a Customized Workbook
as a Template*

Displaying the Workbook's Path in the Address Box

➢ **To display the active workbook's path and name in the Address box:**

1. Place the mouse pointer over one of the toolbars, right-click, and select **Customize** from the shortcut menu.

2. Select the **Commands** tab, and then select **Web** in the **Categories** box.

3. From the **Commands** box, drag the **Address** box to the **Menu** bar and close the *Customize* dialog box.

3

	A	B	C	D	E	F
						Address
1						
2	December 31, 2003					
3						
4		XYZ Corporation Inc.				
5		BALANCE SHEET				
6						
7			December 31			
8		Notes	2003	2002		
9	ASSETS					
10						
11	Current Assets					
12	Cash	5	301,124	318,697		
13	Accounts Receivable	7	1,653,558	1,538,494		
14	Inventories	8	546,173	520,133		
15	Prepaid Expenses	9	13,552	23,659		
16	Total Current Assets		2,514,407	2,400,983		
17						

D:\Finanacial Statements - Financial Statements

File Edit Financial Statements View Insert Format Tools Data Window Help D:\Finanacial Statements\Financial Statements.xls

Related Tips:

Tip 115: Auto Recovering/Auto Saving a Workbook.

Tip 116: Displaying the Workbook's Path in the Address Box.

Tip 30: Adding the Full Path of the Saved File to the Header/Footer.

Workbooks

www.exceltip.com

Notes:

My Tips/
Shortcuts:

Related	*Tip 115: Auto-Recovering/Auto-Saving a*
Tips:	*Workbook*
	Tip 117: Displaying the Workbook's Path
	in the Address Box
	Tip 243: Adding the Full Path of the Saved
	File to the Header/Footer

Adding the Path of a Saved Workbook to the Title Bar

The blue line at the top of the window is the **Title bar**. Use the available empty space by adding information such as the **Path**, which shows where the active workbook is saved.

➢ **To add the path address to the Title bar:**
1. Press **<Alt+F11>** to open the **VBE**.
2. In the **VBAProject** pane, double-click **ThisWorkbook**.
3. At the top of the **Module**, open the left dropdown list (**General**) and select **Workbook**, then select the **Activate** event from the **Procedure** dropdown list on the right.

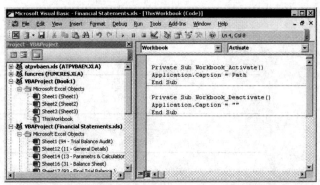

4. In the **Activate** macro, type the following code:

   Application.Caption=ThisWorkbook.Path
5. To cancel the displaying of the path when activating or opening a different workbook, add the **Deactivate** macro by selecting **Deactivate** from the **Procedure** dropdown list.

continued...

Notes:

**My Tips/
Shortcuts:**

Adding the Path of a Saved Workbook to the Title Bar (cont.)

6. In the **Deactivate** macro, type the code:

   Application.Caption=" "

7. Copy and insert the two macros to each **This Workbook** module of any workbook for which you wish to display the path.

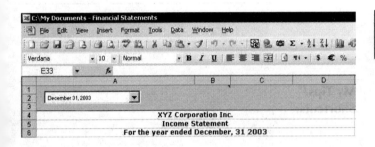

Notes:

**My Tips/
Shortcuts:**

**Related
Tips:**

Tip 120: Protecting a Workbook

Tip 121: Adding Passwords to Prevent
Unauthorized Opening of a Workbook

Tip 124: Saving a Customized Workbook
as a Template

Removing Personal Information from a Workbook

Why is it important to remove personal information from a workbook?

✦ When you do not want to expose your personal details when posting a question with an attached sample workbook to a Web forum.

✦ When sending a workbook by mail.

✦ When publishing a workbook on a Web site that allows downloading.

➢ **To remove personal information from a workbook:**

1. From the *Tools* menu, select **Options**, and then select the **Security** tab.

2. Check **Remove personal information from file properties on save** and then click **OK**.

3

Options   ? ✕

View	Calculation	Edit	General	Transition	Custom Lists	Chart
Color	International	Save	Error Checking	Spelling	Security

File encryption settings for this workbook

Password to <u>o</u>pen: [   ]   <u>A</u>dvanced...

File sharing settings for this workbook

Password to <u>m</u>odify: [   ]

☐ <u>R</u>ead-only recommended

<u>D</u>igital Signatures...

Privacy options

☑ <u>R</u>emove personal information from file properties on save

Macro security

Adjust the security level for files that might contain macro viruses and specify names of trusted macro developers.   Macro <u>S</u>ecurity...

[OK]   [Cancel]

Notes:

_____

_____

_____

_____

_____

_____

**My Tips/
Shortcuts:**

_____

_____

_____

_____

_____

_____

_____

Related Tips:	*Tip 107: Protecting the Sheet or the Cells in the Sheet*
	Tip 121: Adding Passwords to Prevent Unauthorized Opening of a Workbook
	Tip 123: Forgotten Your Password?

Protecting a Workbook

Why it is important to protect a workbook:

✦ To prevent the structure from being changed.

✦ To prevent sheets from being deleted.

✦ To prevent new sheets from being inserted.

✦ To prevent hidden sheets from being opened.

➢ **To protect a workbook:**

1. From the *Tools* menu, select **Protection** and then **Protect Workbook**.

2. Type a password in the **Password** box, and click **OK**.

3. Confirm the password, and click **OK** again.

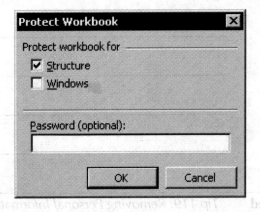

3

W orkbooks

Notes:

**My Tips/
Shortcuts:**

Related Tips:	*Tip 119: Removing Personal Information from a Workbook*
	Tip 122: Protecting Workbooks with a Digital Signature
	Tip 123: Forgotten Your Password?

Adding Passwords to Prevent Unauthorized Opening of a Workbook

➢ **To enter a password:**

1. From the *File* menu, select **Save as**.
2. From the **Tools** dropdown list, select **General Options** (in **Excel 97** select Options).
3. In the *Save Options* dialog box, enter passwords into **Password to open** and **Password to modify** boxes, and click **OK**.

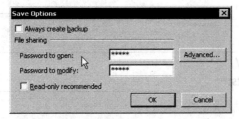

3

Excel 2002 and **Excel 2003** offer additional options:

1. From the *Tools* menu, select **Options**, and then select the **Security** tab.
2. Enter passwords in **Password to open** and **Password to modify** boxes and click **OK**.

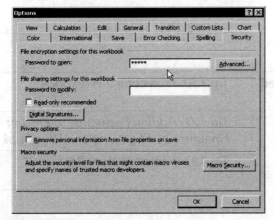

Notes:

**My Tips/
Shortcuts:**

**Related
Tips:**   Tip 120: Protecting a Workbook

              Tip 121: Adding Passwords to Prevent
              Unauthorized Opening of a Workbook

              Tip 123: Forgotten Your Password?

Protecting Workbooks with a Digital Signature

Excel 2002 and **Excel 2003** offer a new **Digital Signature** feature that ensures a higher level of security.

➢ **To set a Digital Signature:**
   1. From the *Tools* menu, select **Options**, and then select the **Security** tab.
   2. Click **Digital Signatures**. In the *Digital Signature* dialog box, add the signer's **Digital Signature**.

3

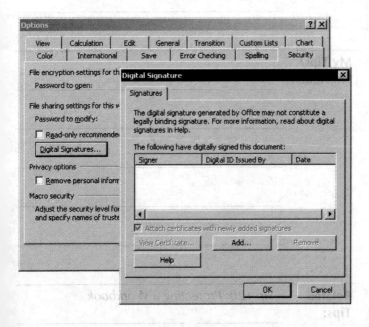

Notes:

**My Tips/
Shortcuts:**

Related Tips:	*Tip 120: Protecting a Workbook*
	Tip 121: Adding Passwords to Prevent Unauthorized Opening of a Workbook
	Tip 122: Protecting Workbooks with a Digital Signature

Forgotten Your Password?

If you forget your workbook password, go to your Internet browser, and type the words **excel password** into any search engine.

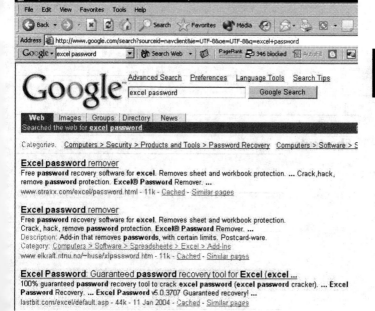

3

W
orkbooks

F1 — Get the Most out of Excel!

Notes:

**My Tips/
Shortcuts:**

| **Related
Tips:** | *Tip 125: Opening a Template File
Automatically When Starting Microsoft
Excel* |
| --- | --- |
| | *Tip 126: Opening Workbooks from a List
of Hyperlinks* |
| | *Tip 127: Opening a Copy of an Existing
Workbook* |

Saving a Customized Workbook as a Template

Why it is important to save a customized workbook as a template:

✦ Allows you to save custom **Styles**.

✦ Allows you to save **Print Setups** options as **Header/Footer** details.

✦ Allows you to save default option settings (from *Data*, select the *Options* dialog box).

✦ Enables many users to use the same design and structure.

3

➢ **To save a workbook as template:**

1. From the *File* menu, select **Save As**.

2. In the **File name** box, type a name for the new template file.

3. In the *Save As* dialog box, select **Template** from the **Save as type** box.

4. Select the **Templates** folder save the new template, and then click **Save**.

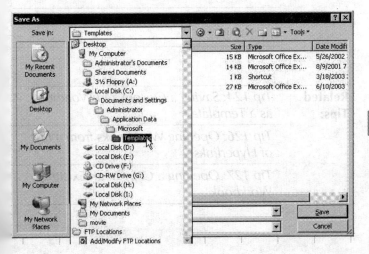

Workbooks

Notes:

**My Tips/
Shortcuts:**

Related Tips:	*Tip 124: Saving a Customized Workbook as a Template*
	Tip 126: Opening Workbooks from a List of Hyperlinks
	Tip 127: Opening a Copy of an Existing Workbook

Opening a Template File Automatically When Starting Microsoft Excel

➢ **To have Excel open a template upon starting:**
  ✦ **Option 1:**
    ❖ Save a template workbook file, named **Book.xlt** (in **Excel 2000**, the book name is **Sheet.xlt**), in the **XlStart** subfolder. When Excel starts, a customized workbook, **Book1.xls** (or **Sheet1.xls** in **Excel 2000**), is opened from within the template already saved, instead of the standard **Book1.xls**.
    ❖ The **XlStart** subfolder is located in the same folder as **Microsoft Office** on the hard drive.
    ❖ To open a new workbook from the template while working in Excel, press **<Ctrl+N>**, or in the **Standard** toolbar, click **New**.
  ✦ **Option 2:**
    1. Save the template workbook file as **MyWorkbook.xlt** (just a suggestion) in any folder.
    2. From the *Tools* menu, select **Options**, and then select the **General** tab.
    3. In the **At start up, open all files in** box (in **Excel 97** and **Excel 2000**, this is the **Alternate startup file location** box), enter the full path of the saved **MyWorkbook.xlt** file.
    4. Click **OK**.

Note: Do not use the two options simultaneously, unless you have created more than one template workbook. Otherwise, Excel will try to open the file with the same name twice.

3

W orkbooks

Notes:

_____

_____

_____

_____

_____

**My Tips/
Shortcuts:**

_____

_____

_____

_____

_____

Related Tips:	*Tip 112: Opening/Closing a Workbook(s)*
	Tip 127: Opening a Copy of an Existing Workbook
	Tip 128: Using a Workspace to Open a Number of Workbooks at Once

Opening Workbooks from a List of Hyperlinks

➢ **To add a workbook to a hyperlink list:**

1. Select a cell.

2. Press **<Ctrl+K>** or select the **Insert Hyperlink** icon from the **Standard** toolbar.

3. In the *Insert Hyperlink* dialog box, select the workbook, click **Bookmark**, and then click **OK**.

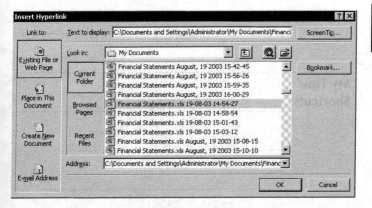

3

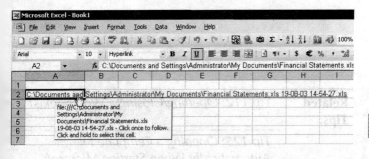

W o r k b o o k s

Notes:

_____

_____

_____

_____

_____

**My Tips/
Shortcuts:**

_____

_____

_____

_____

_____

_____

**Related
Tips:**

Tip 112: Opening/Closing a Workbook(s)

*Tip 125: Opening a Template File
Automatically When Starting Microsoft
Excel*

*Tip 126: Opening Workbooks from a List
of Hyperlinks*

Opening a Copy of an Existing Workbook

➤ **To open a copy of an existing workbook:**

1. Press **<Ctrl+F1>** (new in **Excel 2003**), or select **Task Pane** from the *View* menu.

2. In the **New Workbook Task Pane**, click **From existing workbook**.

3. In the *New from Existing Workbook* dialog box, find and select the workbook, and then click **Create new**.

3

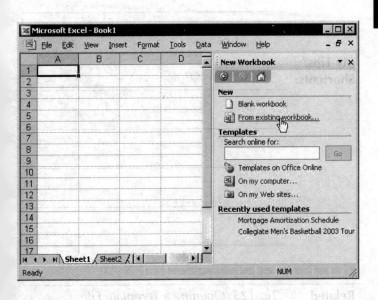

Notes:

**My Tips/
Shortcuts:**

Using a Workspace to Open a Number of Workbooks at Once

Saving open workbooks in a workspace enables them to be opened together at a later time. This is important when working with linked workbooks.

➢ **To save workbooks in a workspace:**
1. Open all the workbooks you want to store in the workspace, and close any other workbook not being stored in the workspace.
2. From the *File* menu, select **Save Workspace**.
3. In the *Save Workspace* dialog box, type the workspace name in the **File name** box and click **Save**.

➢ **To open all workbooks at once using the workspace:**
1. Press **<Ctrl+O>** to open the *Open* dialog box.

   OR

   From the *File* menu, select **Open**.
2. Select the workspace name to open the file.

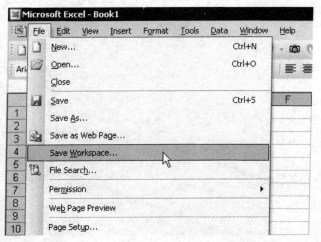

Part 4 — Text, Dates, Times

4

Text

Importing Text Files

Updating Internet Data

Dates

Times

Notes:

_____

_____

_____

_____

_____

_____

My Tips/
Shortcuts: _____

_____

_____

_____

_____

Related Tips:	*Tip 130: Combining Text and Formatted Values*
	Tip 132: Extracting Characters from Text Using Text Formulas
	Tip 134: Separating First and Last Names Using Formulas

Combining Text from Different Cells

Technique 1: Using the & (Ampersand)

The **&** symbol consolidates text information in the same way as the **+** symbol adds numbers. The space between quotation marks adds a blank character between the separated texts.

➢ **To combine text with the &:**

1. In cell **A1**, enter the text **F1**.
2. In cell **A2**, enter the text **Get the Most out of Excel!**
3. In cell **A3**, enter the text **The Ultimate Excel Tip Help Guide**.
4. In cell **A5**, type the formula:

    =A1&" "&A2&" "&A3

continued...

Notes:

**My Tips/
Shortcuts:**

Combining Text from Different Cells (cont.)

Technique 2: Using the Concatenate Formula

The **Concatenate** formula allows one to combine text from multiple cells into a single cell.

➤ **To combine text use the Concatenate formula:**

   ✦ The **Concatenate** formula is in the **Text** category in the *Insert Function* dialog box. To add a blank character between words, press **<Spacebar>** in the second and fourth argument box.

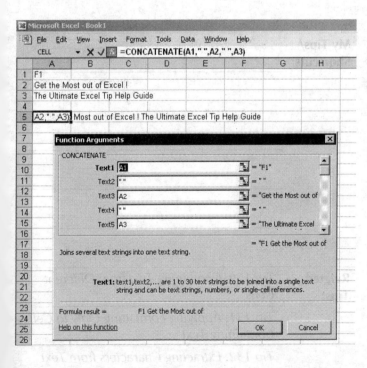

Notes:

_____

_____

_____

_____

_____

_____

My Tips/
Shortcuts:

_____

_____

_____

_____

_____

_____

_____

Related Tips:	*Tip 129: Combining Text from Different Cells*
	Tip 131: Applying Formatting Only to Cells Containing Text
	Tip 132: Extracting Characters from Text Using Text Formulas

Combining Text and Formatted Values

➢ **To combine text with a formatted value:**
  1. In cell **A1**, enter the text **IBM owe Limelight Media Inc**.
  2. In cell **A2**, enter the number **4222**.
  3. In cell **A3**, enter the text **for services supplied in March 2004**.
  4. In cell **A5**, enter the formula:

     =A1&" "& TEXT(A2,"$ #,##0") &" "&A3

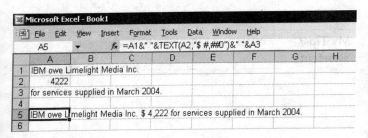

➢ **To format the number to present it in thousands:**
  ✦ Change the number format to **"$ #, K"**:

     =A1&" "& TEXT(A2,"$ #, K") &" "&A3

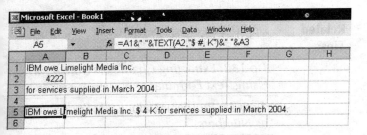

Notes:

_____

_____

_____

_____

_____

_____

_____

**My Tips/
Shortcuts:**

_____

_____

_____

_____

_____

Related Tips:	Tip 10: Selecting Special Cells
	Tip 132: Extracting Characters from Text Using Text Formulas
	Tip 141: Problem: Values Not Formatting as Numbers

Applying Formatting Only to Cells Containing Text

➤ **To apply formatting only to cells containing text, use the Conditional Formatting technique:**

1. Select a range of cells containing text.

2. From the *Format* menu, select **Conditional Formatting**.

3. In **Condition 1**, select **Formula Is** from the dropdown list.

4. In the **Formula Box**, enter the formula:

   =ISTEXT(A1)

5. Click **Format**.

6. Select the desired format from the *Format Cells* dialog box, and then click **OK**.

7. Click **OK** to close the *Conditional Formatting* dialog box.

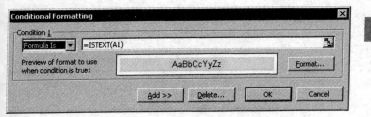

4

T
e
x
t

Notes:

**My Tips/
Shortcuts:**

Related Tips:	*Tip 131: Applying Formatting Only to Cells Containing Text*
	Tip 133: Extracting Characters from Text Without Using Formulas
	Tip 135: Separating First and Last Names Without Using Formulas

Extracting Characters from Text Using Text Formulas

➢ **To extract characters from text, use Text category formulas:**

✦ **Left:** Returns the first character(s) in a text string, based on the number of characters specified.

✦ **Mid:** Returns a specific number of character(s) from a text string, starting at the position specified based on the number of characters specified.

✦ **Right:** Returns the last character(s) in a text string, based on the number of characters specified.

✦ **Len:** Returns the number of characters in a text string.

	A	B	C	D	E	F	G	H
1	Text	F1 Get the Most out of Excel !						
2								
3	Extract 2 characters	F1			<-	=LEFT(B1,2)		
4								
5	Number of characters in the text	30			<-	=LEN(B1)		
6								
7	Extract all characters except first 2	Get the Most out of Excel !			<-	=RIGHT(B1,LEN(B1)-3)		
8								
9	Extract all characters except first 2	Get the Most out of Excel !			<-	Get the Most out of Excel !		
10								

B9 ▾ ƒx =MID(B1,4,LEN(B1)-3)

Notes:

**My Tips/
Shortcuts:**

Related Tips:	*Tip 132: Extracting Characters from Text Using Text Formulas*
	Tip 134: Separating First and Last Names Using Formulas
	Tip 135: Separating First and Last Names Without Using Formulas

Extracting Characters from Text Without Using Formulas

➤ **To extract characters from text:**

1. Select column **A**.

2. From the *Data* menu, select **Text to Columns**.

3. In **Step 1 of 3**, select **Fixed width**, and then click **Next**.

4. In **Step 2 of 3**, parse the data in the column by clicking the mouse between columns as needed for parsing, and then click **Next**.

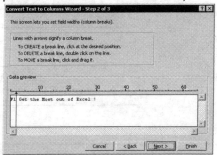

5. In **Step 3 of 3**, in the **Destination** box, enter cell **B1**, and then click **Finish**.

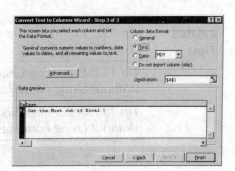

Notes:

_____

_____

_____

_____

_____

My Tips/ Shortcuts:

_____

_____

_____

_____

_____

Related Tips:	*Tip 132: Extracting Characters from Text Using Text Formulas*
	Tip 133: Extracting Characters from Text Without Using Formulas
	Tip 135: Separating First and Last Names Without Using Formulas

Separating First and Last Names Using Formulas

➢ **To separate the name John Smith, in cell A1, use two formulas:**

✦ The formula that extracts the first name is:

=LEFT(A1,FIND(" ",A1))

✦ The formula that extracts the last name is:

=MID(A1,FIND(" ",A1)+1,LEN(A1))

The **FIND** formula returns the starting position of one text string within another text string.

	A	B	C	D	E
	Microsoft Excel - Book1				
	File Edit View Insert Format Tools Data Window Help				
	B1 ▼	*fx* =LEFT(A1,FIND(" ",A1))			
1	**John Smith**	John	Smith		
2					
3	Formula in cell B1	=LEFT(A1,FIND(" ",A1))			
4					
5	Formula in cell C1		=MID(A1,FIND(" ",A1)+1,LEN(A1))		
6					
7					

4

Text

Notes:

**My Tips/
Shortcuts:**

Related Tips:	*Tip 132: Extracting Characters from Text Using Text Formulas*
	Tip 133: Extracting Characters from Text Without Using Formulas
	Tip 134: Separating First and Last Names Using Formulas

Separating First and Last Names Without Using Formulas

➤ **To separate first name and last names:**

1. Select Column **A** or the range of cells containing the list of names.

2. From the *Data* menu, select **Text to Columns**.

3. In **Step 1 of 3**, select **Delimited**.

4. In **Step 2 of 3**, select the **Space** checkbox.

5. In **Step 3 of 3**, in the **Destination** box, select cell **B1**, and then click **Finish**.

Notes:

_____

_____

_____

_____

_____

**My Tips/
Shortcuts:**

_____

_____

_____

_____

_____

_____

**Related
Tips:**   *Tip 137: Converting Text to Uppercase*

_____

*Tip 138: Converting Uppercase Letters to
Lowercase*

_____

Converting Text to Its Proper Case

Use the **PROPER** function to convert text to its proper case. The **Proper** function is in the **Text** category in the *Insert Function* dialog box.

Example:

✦ **Text in uppercase:** GEORGE W. BUSH

✦ **The function:** =PROPER(A1)

✦ **Result:** George W. Bush

	Microsoft Excel - Book1				
	File Edit View Insert Format Tools Data Window Help				
	C1 ▼ *fx* =PROPER(A1)				
	A	B	C	D	E
1	GEORGE W. BUSH		George W. Bush		
2					
3					
4					
5					

4

T
ext

Notes:

_____

_____

_____

_____

_____

_____

**My Tips/
Shortcuts:**

_____

_____

_____

_____

_____

_____

**Related
Tips:**

Tip 136: Converting Text to Its Proper Case

Tip 138: Converting Uppercase Letters to Lowercase

_____

Converting Text to Uppercase

Use the **UPPER** function to convert text to uppercase. The **UPPER** function is in the **Text** category in the *Insert Function* dialog box.

Example:

✦ **Text in lowercase:** george w. bush

✦ **The function:** =UPPER(A1)

✦ **Result:** GEORGE W. BUSH

	A	B	C	D	E
1	george w. bush		GEORGE W. BUSH		
2					
3					
4					
5					

C1 ▼ *fx* =UPPER(A1)

Notes:

My Tips/ Shortcuts:

Related Tips:

Tip 136: Converting Text to Its Proper Case

Tip 137: Converting Text to Uppercase

Converting Uppercase Letters to Lowercase

Use the **LOWER** function to convert all uppercase letters in a text string to lowercase. The **LOWER** function is in the **Text** category in the *Insert Function* dialog box.

Example:

◆ **Text in uppercase:** GEORGE W. BUSH

◆ **The function:** =LOWER(A1)

◆ **Result:** george w. bush

	A	B	C	D
	GEORGE W. BUSH		george w. bush	
2				
3				
4				
5				

Microsoft Excel - Book1

File Edit View Insert Format Tools Data Window Help

C1   ▼   *fx* =LOWER(A1)

4

T
ext

Notes:

_____

_____

_____

_____

_____

**My Tips/
Shortcuts:**

_____

_____

_____

_____

_____

Related Tips:	*Tip 140: Problem: Unnecessary Empty Characters in Cells*
	Tip 141: Problem: Values Not Formatting as Numbers
	Tip 142: Problem: The Minus Sign Appears to the Right of the Number

Problem: The Characters Are in Reverse Order

➢ **To reverse the character order, create and add a Custom Function to the *Insert Function* dialog box:**

1. Press **<Alt+F11>** to open the **VBE**.

2. In **VBAProject**, select any workbook name and insert a new **Module** by selecting **Module** from the *Insert* menu.

3. In the **Module** sheet, type the code lines as shown in the screenshot.

4. Press **<Alt+F11>** to return to Excel.

5. Select a cell and press **<Shift+F3>** to open the *Insert Function* dialog box.

6. From the **User Defined** category, insert the **ReverseText** function.

Note: The **ReverseText** macro can be downloaded from www.exceltip.com/f1toc.

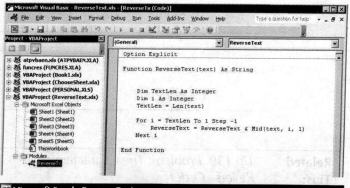

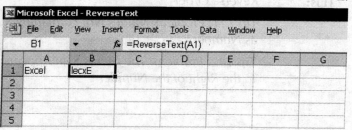

Notes:

_____

_____

_____

_____

_____

_____

My Tips/
Shortcuts:

_____

_____

_____

_____

_____

_____

Related Tips:	*Tip 139: Problem: The Characters are in Reverse Order*
	Tip 141: Problem: Values Not Formatting as Numbers
	Tip 142: Problem: The Minus Sign Appears to the Right of the Number

Problem: Unnecessary Empty Characters in Cells

To remove empty characters, use the **Trim** function. The **Trim** function is in the **Text** category in the *Insert Function* dialog box.

➢ To insert the Trim function:

1. Select a cell and type:

   =Trim

2. Press **<Ctrl+A>** to open the *Function Arguments* dialog box.

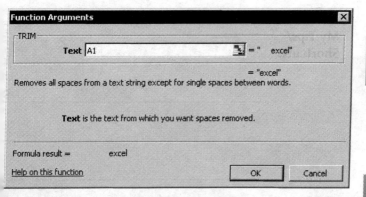

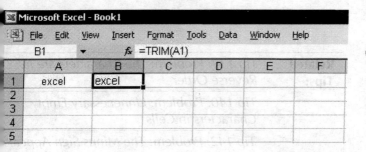

Notes:

**My Tips/
Shortcuts:**

| **Related
Tips:** | *Tip 139: Problem: The Characters are in
Reverse Order* |
| | *Tip 140: Problem: Unnecessary Empty
Characters in Cells* |
| | *Tip 142: Problem: The Minus Sign Appears
to the Right of the Number* |

Problem: Values Not Formatting as Numbers

✦ **Option 1: Change the column formatting from Text to General by multiplying the numbers by 1:**

1. Enter the number **1** into a cell and copy it.

2. Select the column formatted as text, press **<Shift+F10>** or right-click, and then select **Paste Special** from the shortcut menu.

3. Select the **Multiply** option button in the *Paste Special* dialog box, and then click **OK**.

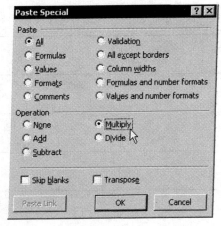

continued...

4

Importing Text Files

327

Notes:

**My Tips/
Shortcuts:**

Problem: Values Not Formatting as Numbers (cont.)

✦ **Option 2: Change the column formatting from Text to General using the Text to Columns technique:**

1. Select the column formatted as text.

2. From the *Data* menu, select **Text to Columns**.

3. In **Step 1 of 3**, select the **Fixed width** option button.

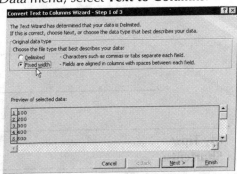

4. Skip **Step 2 of 3**.

5. In **Step 3 of 3**, select the **General** option button in the **Column data format** section, and then click **Finish**.

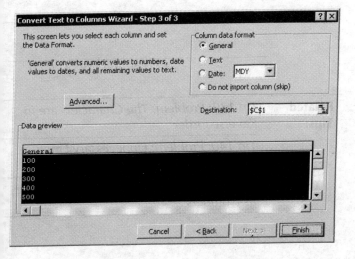

Notes:

_____
_____
_____
_____
_____
_____
_____
_____

**My Tips/
Shortcuts:**

_____
_____
_____
_____
_____
_____
_____

**Related
Tips:**

Tip 139: Problem: The Characters are in
Reverse Order

Tip 140: Problem: Unnecessary Empty
Characters in Cells

Tip 141: Problem: Values Not Formatting
as Numbers

Problem: The Minus Sign Appears to the Right of the Number

➢ **To move the minus sign from the right to the left:**

✦ Use the following function:

=VALUE(IF(RIGHT(A1,1)="-",RIGHT(A1,1)&LEFT(A1,LEN(A1)-1),A1))

	Microsoft Excel - Book1							
	File Edit View Insert Format Tools Data Window Help							
	B1 ▼		ƒx =VALUE(IF(RIGHT(A1,1)="-",RIGHT(A1,1)&LEFT(A1,LEN(A1)-1),A1))					
	A	B	C	D	E	F	G	H	I
1	32423-	-32423						
2								
3								
4								

In **Excel 2002** & **Excel 2003**, this problem is solved in the following manner:

1. In **Step 3 of 3** of the **Text Import Wizard**, or in **Step 3 of 3** of **Text to Columns** (select from *Data*), click **Advanced**.

2. In the *Advanced Text Import Settings* dialog box, select the **Trailing minus for negative numbers** checkbox.

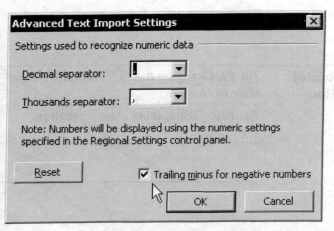

4

Notes:

_____

_____

_____

_____

_____

**My Tips/
Shortcuts:**

_____

_____

_____

_____

Related Tips:	*Tip 49: Changing the Cell Formatting from Date to Number*
	Tip 149: Customizing Date Formatting

Problem: Date Formatting Cannot Be Changed

➢ **To change the formatting from Text to Date, use Text to Columns technique:**

1. Select the column formatted as text.

2. From the *Data* menu, select **Text to Columns**.

3. In **Step 1 of 3**, select the **Fixed width** option button.

4. Skip **Step 2 of 3**.

5. In **Step 3 of 3**, check **Date** option button in **Column data format**, and click **Finish**.

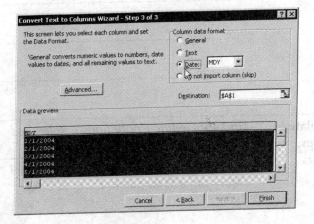

Notes:

**My Tips/
Shortcuts:**

**Related
Tips:**

*Tip 145: Getting Continuously Refreshed
Data from a Web site in Excel 2000*

*Tip 146: Getting Continuously Refreshed
Data from a Web Site in Excel 2002 &
2003*

Getting Continuously Refreshed Data from a Web Site in Excel 97

To get refreshed data from a Web site using **Excel 97**, save the site address (URL) for every new query in a text file with the extension **.iqy**.

➢ **To save an address in a text file as a query:**

1. Open the Web site that contains the information. For example, open the site www.bloomberg.com, which includes a table of various currency exchange rates. The address of the page containing the table of currency exchange rates is **http://www.bloomberg.com/ markets/index.html**.

2. Copy the address by selecting it in the address box and pressing **<Ctrl+C>**.

3. Open a new text file in Windows by selecting **Programs**, **Accessories**, and then **Notepad** from the *Start* menu.

4. Press **<Ctrl+V>** to paste the address into the text file, and then save the file with the extension **.iqy** (be sure to use lowercase). For example, save the file with the name **CrossCurrencyRates.iqy**.

5. Open **Excel 97**, and from the *Data* menu, select **Get External Data**, and then **Run Web Query**.

continued...

U pdating Internet Data

Notes:

**My Tips/
Shortcuts:**

Getting Continuously Refreshed Data from a Web Site in Excel 97 (cont.)

6. In the *Run Query* dialog box, search for and select the **CrossCurrencyRates.iqy** text file.

7. In the *Returning External Data to Microsoft Excel* dialog box, click **OK**.

8. Wait a few seconds. The data is transferred from the Web site to the Excel sheet.

➤ **To refresh the Internet data (the Web site does not have to be open):**

1. Select the cell in the sheet containing the data.

2. From the *Data* menu, select **Refresh Data**.

   OR

   Display the **External Data** toolbar and click the **Refresh Data** icon. To display the **External Data** toolbar, select one of the toolbars, right-click and select **External Data**, and click **OK**.

➤ **To automatically refresh the Internet data:**

1. On the **External Data** toolbar, click the **Data Range Properties** icon.

2. Select the **Refresh every** option, and set the number of minutes between each refresh action.

3. Select the **Refresh data on file open** checkbox to automatically refresh the data when the file is opened.

➤ **To run a saved query:**

1. From the *Data* menu, select **Get External Data**, and then **Run Web Query**.

2. Select the saved query, and click **Get Data**.

4

Updating Internet Data

337

Notes:

_____

_____

_____

_____

_____

_____

_____

_____

_____

**My Tips/
Shortcuts:**

_____

_____

_____

_____

_____

_____

_____

_____

Related Tips:	*Tip 144: Getting Continuously Refreshed Data from a Web site in Excel 97*
	Tip 146: Getting Continuously Refreshed Data from a Web Site in Excel 2002 & 2003

Getting Continuously Refreshed Data from a Web Site in Excel 2000

➢ **To import and refresh information from a Web site:**

1. Open **Excel 2000**, and from the *Data* menu, select **Get External Data**, and then **New Web Query**.

2. In the **Enter the address** box, paste the full address of the Web site. For example, open the site www.bloomberg.com, which includes a table of various currency exchange rates. The address of the page containing the table of currency exchange rates is **http://www.bloomberg.com/ markets/index.html**.

3. Copy the address by selecting it in the address box and pressing **<Ctrl+C>**.

4. Click **Save Query**, and type a name for the query.

5. Click **Save**, and then click **OK**.

6. In the *Returning External Data to Microsoft Excel* dialog box, click **OK**.

continued...

Updating Internet Data

4

Notes:

My Tips/ Shortcuts:

Getting Continuously Refreshed Data from a Web Site in Excel 2000 (cont.)

➤ **To refresh the Internet data (the Web site does not have to be open):**

1. Select the cell in the sheet containing the data.
2. From the *Data* menu, select **Refresh Data**.

   OR

   Display the **External Data** toolbar and click the **Refresh Data** icon. To display the **External Data** toolbar, select one of the toolbars, right-click and select **External Data**, and click **OK**.

➤ **To automatically refresh the Internet data:**

1. On the **External Data** toolbar, click the **Data Range Properties** icon.
2. Select the **Refresh every** option, and set the number of minutes between each refresh action.
3. Select the **Refresh data on file open** checkbox to automatically refresh the data when the file is opened.

➤ **To run a saved query:**

1. From the *Data* menu, select **Get External Data**, and then **Run Saved Query**.
2. Select the saved query, and click **Get Data**.

4

Notes:

**My Tips/
Shortcuts:**

**Related
Tips:**

*Tip 144: Getting Continuously Refreshed
Data from a Web site in Excel 97*

*Tip 145: Getting Continuously Refreshed
Data from a Web site in Excel 2000*

Getting Continuously Refreshed Data from a Web Site in Excel 2002 & 2003

Excel 2002 and **Excel 2003** enables selecting an exact data table on a Web site, and importing and refreshing only the needed data.

➢ **To import and refresh information from a Web site:**

1. Open **Excel 2002** or **Excel 2003**, and from the *Data* menu, select **Import External Data**, and then **New Web Query**.

2. In the **Address** box of the *New Web Query* dialog box, type or paste the address of the Internet site. For example, open the site www.bloomberg.com, which includes a table of various currency exchange rates. The address of the page containing the table of currency exchange rates is **http://www.bloomberg.com/markets/index.html**.

3. In the dialog box, notice the Web page. Click the small arrow in the upper left-hand corner of the table to select only the data table.

4. Click **Import**.

5. To save the query, click **Properties** in the *Import Data* dialog box.

continued...

343

Notes:

My Tips/ Shortcuts:

Getting Continuously Refreshed Data from a Web Site in Excel 2002 & 2003 (cont.)

6. In the *External Data Range Properties* dialog box, enter the query name in the **Name** box, select the **Save Query definition** checkbox, and then click **OK**.

7. In the *Import Data* dialog box, click **OK** to import.

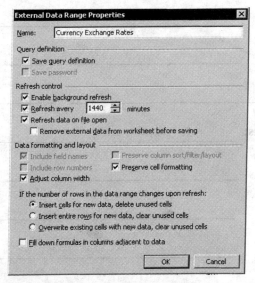

➤ **To refresh the Internet data (the Web site does not have to be open):**

1. Select the cell in the sheet containing the data.

2. From the *Data* menu, select **Refresh Data**.

   OR

   Display the **External Data** toolbar and click the **Refresh Data** icon. To display the **External Data** toolbar, select one of the toolbars, right-click and select **External Data**, and click **OK**.

continued...

4

Updating Internet Data

Notes:

**My Tips/
Shortcuts:**

Getting Continuously Refreshed Data from a Web Site in Excel 2002 & 2003 (cont.)

➢ **To automatically refresh the Internet data:**

1. On the **External Data** toolbar, click the **Data Range Properties** icon.

2. Select the **Refresh every** option, and set the number of minutes between each refresh action.

3. Select the **Refresh data on file open** checkbox to automatically refresh the data when the file is opened.

➢ **To run a saved query:**

1. From the *Data* menu, select **Import External Data**, and then **Import Data**.

2. Select the saved query , and click **Open**.

4

Notes:

_____

_____

_____

_____

_____

My Tips/
Shortcuts:

_____

_____

_____

_____

_____

Related
Tips/
Shortcuts:

	Tip 150: Quickly Typing Dates into Cells
	Tip 151: Filling a Range with a Series of Dates
	To enter the current time into a cell, press **<Ctrl+Shift+:>**.

Entering the Current Date into a Cell

 Using keyboard shortcuts

➢ **To enter the current date in a cell:**
  ✦ Select a cell and press **<Ctrl+;>**.

The formula that calculates the current date is:
=TODAY ()

	Microsoft Excel - Book1

| File | Edit | View | Insert | Format | Tools | Data | Window | Help |

| A1 | ▼ | fx | =TODAY() |

	A	B	C	D	E	F	G
1	4/9/2004						
2							
3							
4							
5							

Notes:

My Tips/ Shortcuts:

Related Tips/ Shortcuts:

Tip 149: Customizing Date Formatting

Tip 150: Quickly Typing Dates into Cells

To enter the current date into the cell, press **<Ctrl+;>**.

Changing the Default Date Separator from a Slash to a Dot When Entering a Date into a Cell

Excel recognizes a number as a date by its date format, which uses a slash (/) as a separator, for example, **1/25/2004** is recognized as a date by Excel.

➢ **To change the default setting for the date format:**

1. From the Windows *Start* menu, select **Settings**, **Control Panel**, and then **Regional and Language Options**.
2. In **Regional Options**, select **Customize**.
3. Select the **Date** tab, and in the **Date separator** dropdown list, change the slash (/) to a dot (.).
4. Click **Apply** and then click **OK**.

4

Customize Regional Options	? X

Numbers | Currency | Time | **Date**

Calendar
When a two-digit year is entered, interpret it as a year between:

1930 and 2029

Short date
Short date sample: 12/30/2003

Short date format: MM/dd/yyyy
Date separator: /

Long date
Long date sample: Tuesday, December 30, 2003

Long date format: MMMM dddd, yyyy

OK   Cancel   Apply

Dates

Notes:

**My Tips/
Shortcuts:**

Related Tips:	*Tip 147: Entering the Current Date into a Cell*
	Tip 148: Changing the Default Date Separator from a Slash to a Dot When Entering a Date into a Cell
	Tip 150: Quickly Typing Dates into Cells

Customizing Date Formatting

➢ **To customize the date formatting:**

1. Select cell **A1** in the sheet, and insert the current date by pressing **<Ctrl+;>**.

2. Press **<Ctrl+1>**, select the **Number** tab, and then select **Custom**.

3. Clear the **Type** box.

4. Enter the date format in the **Type** box, based on to the list of symbols below:

   ✦ **m (Month):** Display the month's number, without a leading 0 if the number is lower than 10.

   ✦ **mm (Month):** Display the month's number, including a leading 0 if the number is lower than 10.

   ✦ **mmm (Month):** Display the first three characters of the month's name.

   ✦ **mmmm (Month):** Display the month's full name.

   ✦ **mmmmm (Month):** Display the first character of the month's name.

   ✦ **d (Day):** Display the day's number, without a leading 0 if the number is lower than 10.

   ✦ **dd (Day):** Display the day's number, including a leading 0 if the number is lower than 10.

   ✦ **ddd (Day):** Display the day's name as three-character text.

   ✦ **dddd (Day):** Display the day's full name.

   ✦ **yy or y (Year):** Display the last two digits of the year.

   ✦ **yyy or yyyy (Year):** Display the full year.

4

D
a
t
e
s

Notes:

My Tips/
Shortcuts:

Quickly Typing Dates into Cells

Typing a large amount of data into cells can be tiring, especially if it includes a series of dates.

✦ Type the day (serial number only) into cell **A1** and add the following formula to insert the month and year into cell **B1**:

=DATE (YEAR(TODAY()), MONTH(TODAY()), A1)

✦ Type a full number in the cell and change it to a date by using the following formula:

=DATEVALUE(LEFT(A1,2)&"/"&MID(A1,3,2)&"/" &RIGHT(A1,2))

For example, type **122203**, the result is **12/22/03**.

	Microsoft Excel - Book1							
File	Edit	View	Insert	Format	Tools	Data	Window	Help
	B1	▼	*fx* =DATE(YEAR(TODAY()),MONTH(TODAY()),A1)					
	A	B	C	D	E	F	G	H	I
1	22	12/22/03	<--	=DATE(YEAR(TODAY()),MONTH(TODAY()),A1)				
2								
3	122203	12/22/03	<--	=DATEVALUE(LEFT(A3,2)&"/"&MID(A3,3,2)&"/"&RIGHT(A3,2))				
4								

4

Notes:

**My Tips/
Shortcuts:**

Related Tips:	*Tip 152: Calculating Differences Between Dates*
	Tip 153: Calculating the Week Number
	Tip 154: Calculating the Quarter Number

Filling a Range with a Series of Dates

➢ **To fill a range of cells with a series of dates:**

1. Select cell **A1**, and press **<Ctrl+;>**.

2. Select cells **A1** through **A10**.

3. From the *Edit* menu, select **Fill**, and then select **Series**.

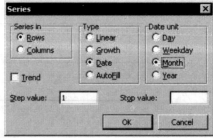

4. In the *Series* dialog box, check the **Date** and **Month** option buttons, and then click **OK**.

Note: To fill a series of quarters, change the **Step value** to **3**.

➢ **To fill a range of cells with a series of dates using a shortcut:**

1. Select cell **A1**, and press **<Ctrl+;>**.

2. Select the **Fill** handle in the bottom-right corner of the cell. The cursor changes to a plus sign.

3. Right-click, drag vertically, and then release the mouse.

4. From the shortcut menu, select the series as desired.

continued...

357

Notes:

**My Tips/
Shortcuts:**

Filling a Range with a Series of Dates (cont.)

A new feature from **Excel 2002** enables the use of a **Smart Tag** to automatically change a series of dates.

➢ **To use a Smart Tag:**

1. Select cell **A1**, and press **<Ctrl+;>**.
2. Click the **Fill handle** at the bottom-right corner of cell **A1**, and drag it to several cells in the column. Do not cancel the selection of the range of dates (Excel automatically creates a series according to days).
3. Click the arrow in the **Smart Tag**.
4. Select **Fill Months**.

4

	Microsoft Excel - Book 1.xls

	File	Edit	View	Insert	Format	Tools	Data	Window	Help

A1 ▼ *fx* 12/31/2003

	A	B	C	D	E	F
1	12/31/2003					
2	01/01/2004					
3	01/02/2004					
4	01/03/2004					
5		🔳▼				
6						
7		○ Copy Cells				
8		◉ Fill Series				
9		○ Fill Formatting Only				
10						
11		○ Fill Without Formatting				
12		○ Fill Days				
13		○ Fill Weekdays				
14						
15		○ Fill Months				
16		○ Fill Years				
17						

Dates

Notes:

_____

_____

_____

_____

_____

_____

_____

**My Tips/
Shortcuts:**

_____

_____

_____

_____

_____

_____

**Related
Tips:**

Tip 153: Calculating the Week Number

Tip 154: Calculating the Quarter Number

Tip 155: Calculating the Date at the End of a Month

Calculating Differences Between Dates

➤ **To calculate the difference between dates:**

✦ Use the **DATEDIF** function. The results of the calculation are displayed as days, full months, and full years.

Note: The **DATEDIF** function is not included in the *Insert Function* dialog box.

	A	B	C	D	E
	DATEDIF	**Start Date**	**End Date**	**Diffrence**	**Syntax Function**
2	Days	01/01/2003	12/31/2004	730	=DATEDIF(B2,C2,"d")
3	Months	01/01/2003	12/31/2004	23	=DATEDIF(B3,C3,"m")
4	Years	01/01/2003	12/31/2004	1	=DATEDIF(B4,C4,"y")
5					
6	Number of Months above Years	01/01/2003	12/31/2004	11	=DATEDIF(B6,C6,"ym")
7	Number of Days above Years	01/01/2003	12/31/2004	364	=DATEDIF(B7,C7,"yd")
8					

D2   *fx* =DATEDIF(B2,C2,"d")

4

Notes:

**My Tips/
Shortcuts:**

| **Related
Tips:** | *Tip 152: Calculating Differences Between
Dates* |
| --- | --- |
| | *Tip 154: Calculating the Quarter Number* |
| | *Tip 155: Calculating the Date at the End of
a Month* |

Calculating the Week Number

➤ **To calculate a week number:**

✦ Use the **WEEKNUM** function.

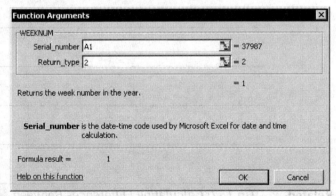

The second argument in the **WEEKNUM** function, **Return_type**, determines on which day the week begins, for example, **1** for Sunday, **2** for Monday, and so on.

Function Arguments		×
WEEKNUM		
Serial_number A1		= 37987
Return_type 2		= 2
		= 1
Returns the week number in the year.		
Serial_number is the date-time code used by Microsoft Excel for date and time calculation.		
Formula result = 1		
Help on this function	OK	Cancel

Note: This function is included in the **Analysis ToolPak** add-in. It is highly recommended that this **Add-In** be installed.

➤ **To install the Analysis ToolPak Add-In:**

1. From the *Tools* menu, select **Add-Ins**.
2. Select the **Analysis ToolPak** checkbox, and then click **OK**.

4

Dates

363

Notes:

**My Tips/
Shortcuts:**

**Related
Tips:**

*Tip 152: Calculating Differences Between
Dates*

Tip 153: Calculating the Week Number

*Tip 155: Calculating the Date at the End of
a Month*

Calculating the Quarter Number

➢ **To calculate the quarter number for a calendar year:**

◆ Enter the formula:

=INT((MONTH(A2)-1)/3)+1

➢ **To calculate the quarter number for a fiscal year ending in September:**

◆ Enter the formula:

=MOD(CEILING(22+MONTH(A2)-9-1,3)/3,4)+1

Note: The number **9** in the formula represents the number of the last month of the fiscal year (September).

Microsoft Excel - Book1

File Edit View Insert Format Tools Data Window Help

C2 ▾ *fx* =MOD(CEILING(22+MONTH(A2)-9-1,3)/3,4)+1

	A	B	C
1	Date	Quarter Number Calendar year basis	Quarter Number Fiscal year basis
2	January 31, 2004	1	2
3	February 29, 2004	1	2
4	March 31, 2004	1	2
5	April 30, 2004	2	3
6	May 31, 2004	2	3
7	June 30, 2004	2	3
8	July 31, 2004	3	4
9	August 31, 2004	3	4
10	September 30, 2004	3	4
11	October 31, 2004	4	1
12	November 30, 2004	4	1
13	December 31, 2004	4	1
14			

4

Dates

365

Notes:

My Tips/ Shortcuts:

Related Tips:

Tip 152: Calculating Differences Between Dates

Tip 153: Calculating the Week Number

Tip 154: Calculating the Quarter Number

Calculating the Date at the End of a Month

➢ **To calculate the date at the end of a month:**
  ✦ Use the **EOMONTH** function.

Microsoft Excel - Book1

File Edit View Insert Format Tools Data Window Help

B6   ▼   *fx* =EOMONTH(TODAY(),2)+5

	A	B	C	D	E	F
1	Today date	04/11/2004				
2	Date at end of previous month	03/31/2004	<--	=EOMONTH(TODAY(),-1)		
3	Date at the end of the current month	04/30/2004	<--	=EOMONTH(TODAY(),0)		
4	Date at the end of next month	05/31/2004	<--	=EOMONTH(TODAY(),1)		
5	Date at the end of two month	06/30/2004	<--	=EOMONTH(TODAY(),2)		
6	Date at the end of two month+5 days	07/05/2004	<--	=EOMONTH(TODAY(),2)+5		
7						
8						

4

Dates

367

Notes:

**My Tips/
Shortcuts:**

**Related
Tips:**

*Tip 139: Problem: The Characters are in
Reverse Order*

*Tip 152: Calculating Differences Between
Dates*

Tip 154: Calculating the Quarter Number

Adding a Custom Function That Returns the Quarter Number

➤ **To add a custom function to a Module in the Personal Macro Workbook** (To learn more about creating a **Personal Macro Workbook**, see *Tip #19*.)

1. Press **<Alt+F11>** to open the **VBE**.

2. Double-click a **Module** name in the **Personal Macro Workbook**, or insert a new **Module** into the **Personal Macro Workbook** by selecting **Module** from the *Insert* menu.

3. Enter the following code lines into the **Module**:

```
Function QuarterNum(Enter_Date)
    QuarterNum = DatePart("q", Enter_Date)
End Function
```

➤ **To test the Custom Function:**

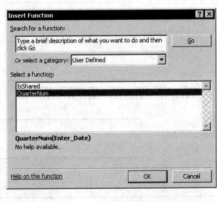

1. Select any empty cell and press **<Shift+F3>** to open the *Paste Function* dialog box.

2. In the **User Defined** category, select **QuarterNum**, and then click **OK**.

3. In the *Function Arguments* dialog box, enter the address of a cell containing a date, and click **OK**.

369

Notes:

**My Tips/
Shortcuts:**

Related Tips/ Shortcuts:	*Tip 150: Quickly Typing Dates into Cells*
	Tip 151: Filling a Range with a Series of Dates
	To enter the current date into the cell, press **<Ctrl+;>**.

Validating Date Entries

➤ **To validate date entries:**

1. Select a range of cells with the date to validate.
2. From the *Data* menu, select **Validation**, and then select the **Settings** tab.
3. In the **Allow** dropdown list, select **Date**.
4. In the **Data** dropdown list, select **between**.
5. In the **Start date** box enter **1/1/2004**.
6. In the **End date** box enter **12/31/2004**.
7. Click **OK**.

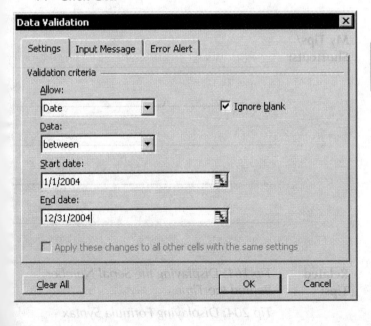

4

D a t e s

Notes:

**My Tips/
Shortcuts:**

**Related
Tips:**

*Tip 161: Displaying the Serial Number
Behind the Time*

Tip 204: Displaying Formula Syntax

Displaying the Serial Number Behind the Date

Excel handles dates and times numerically. The numbers for dates range from 1 to 2958465, with **1** indicating **January 1, 1900**, and **2958465** indicating **December 31, 9999**.

➢ **To see the serial number behind a date:**

✦ Press **<Ctrl+'>** (the ' key is to the left of the **1** key) to change the display of the cell's contents.

➢ **To convert a date to its serial number:**

✦ Press **<Ctrl+Shift+~>** to change the cell's contents.

Microsoft Excel - Book1		
File Edit View Insert Format Tools Data Window Help		
B4 ▼ ƒ× 3/10/2004		
A	B	C
1		
2	=TODAY()	
3		
4	38056	
5		
6		
7		

373

Notes:

**My Tips/
Shortcuts:**

**Related
Tips:**

*Tip 129: Combining Text from Different
Cells*

*Tip 130: Combining Text and Formatted
Values*

Combining Text and a Formatted Date

➢ **To combined text with a formatted date:**

1. In cell **A1**, enter the text **The book publication month is**.

2. In cell **A2**, enter the date **02/01/2004**.

3. In cell **A3**, enter the formula:

   =A1&" "& TEXT(A2,"mmmm yyyy")

	A	B	C	D	E	F	G
	Microsoft Excel - Book1						
	File Edit View Insert Format Tools Data Window Help						
	A3 ▼ *fx* =A1&" "& TEXT(A2,"mmmm yyyy")						
1	The book publication month is						
2	02/01/2004						
3	The book publication month is February 2004						
4							
5							

4

Notes:

**My Tips/
Shortcuts:**

**Related
Tips:**

*Tip 166: Converting Time to Decimal
Values*

*Tip 167: Converting a Number to a Time
Value*

Entering the Current Time into a Cell

Using keyboard shortcuts

➢ **To enter the current time into a cell:**
  ✦ Select a cell and press **<Ctrl+Shift+;>**.

➢ **To enter the current time into a cell by using a formula that returns the current date and time:**
  ✦ Enter the formula:

  =NOW ()

  ✦ To get a formula that calculates the current time, change the format of the cell containing the **NOW** formula to **h:mm** in the **Type** box.

4

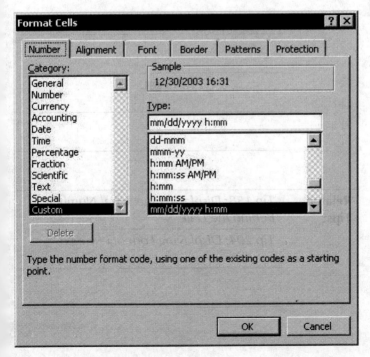

Notes:

**My Tips/
Shortcuts:**

**Related
Tips:**

Tip 158: Displaying the Serial Number
Behind the Date

Tip 204: Displaying Formula Syntax

Displaying the Serial Number Behind the Time

Using keyboard shortcuts

The time's serial number is between 0 and 1 (noon serial time = 0.50).

➢ **To display the serial number behind the time:**
1. Press **<Ctrl+Shift+;>** to insert the current time into cell **A1**.
2. Press **<Ctrl+'>** to display the serial number of the current time.

Microsoft Excel - Book1		
File Edit View Insert Format Tools Data Window Help		
A1 ▼ *fx* 6:19:00 PM		
A	**B**	**C**
1 0.763194444444444		
2		
3		
4		
5		

4

Related
Tips:

Tip 163: Calculating the Difference
Between Hours

Tip 164: Calculating Time Differences
Between Regions of the World

Tip 165: Rounding Hours Up

Times

Notes:

**My Tips/
Shortcuts:**

**Related
Tips:**

*Tip 163: Calculating the Difference
Between Hours*

*Tip 164: Calculating Time Differences
Between Regions of the World*

Tip 165: Rounding Hours Up

Totaling Time Values

Excel uses serial values to recognize time. The time's serial number is between 0 and 1 (noon serial time = 0.50).

The time format to display hours, minutes and seconds is **HH:MM:SS**. For example, a time of 14 hours and 56 minutes is displayed as 14:56:00.

Problem: The default time format does not allow a time value to exceed 24 hours. For example, by entering a time of **28:56:00**, the result is **04:56:00**.

Solution: Change the format of the cell by placing brackets around the hour, **[HH]:MM:SS**. The result is displayed as **28:56:00**.

In the screenshot below, cell **C5** uses the **SUM** function in a formatted cell to sum times correctly.

4

Microsoft Excel - Book1

File Edit View Insert Format Tools Data Window Help

C5 ▼ *fx* =SUM(C2:C4)

	A	B	C	D
1		**Summing Time**		
2		9:42	9:42	
3		14:22	14:22	
4		19:28	19:28	
5		19:32	43:32	
6	Formulas in Row 5	=SUM(B2:B4)	=SUM(C2:C4)	
7	Formatting in Row 5	h:mm	[hh]:mm	
8				

Times

Notes:

**My Tips/
Shortcuts:**

| **Related
Tips:**	*Tip 162: Totaling Time Values*
	*Tip 164: Calculating Time Differences
Between Regions of the World*
	Tip 165: Rounding Hours Up

Calculating the Difference Between Hours

➢ **To calculate an employee's working hours:**

✦ Enter the following formula into a cell:

=D4-C4+IF(C4>D4,1)

The number **1** in the **IF** formula equals 24 when working with time.

For example, in row **6**, the calculation is 6.00 - 20.31 + 24.00 = 9.29.

	Microsoft Excel - Book1				
	File Edit View Insert Format Tools Data Window Help				
	E4 ▾	fx =D4-C4+IF(C4>D4,1)			
A	B	C	D	E	F
1					
2	**Name**	**Start Time**	**End Time**	**Difference**	**Formula Syntax**
3					
4	Bill	05:44	10:40	04:56	=D4-C4+IF(C4>D4,1)
5	Joe	22:30	07:00	08:30	
6	Roy	20:31	06:00	09:29	
7					

4

T

Times

Notes:

**My Tips/
Shortcuts:**

Related Tips:	*Tip 162: Totaling Time Values*
	Tip 163: Calculating the Difference Between Hours
	Tip 165: Rounding Hours Up

Calculating Time Differences Between Regions of the World

➢ **To calculate time differences between regions of the world:**

  ✦ Enter the following formula:

  =$B$3+(C2/24)*-1

  and then apply the **HH:MM AM/PM** time formatting to the cells.

Microsoft Excel - Book 1.xls

File   Edit   View   Insert   Format   Tools   Data   Window   Help

C3   ▼   *fx* =$B$3+(C2/24)*-1

	A	B	C	D	E
		NY	**LA**	**London**	**Tokyo**
1					
2	Hours Difference		3	-5	-14
3	Local Time	9:00 AM	6:00 AM	2:00 PM	11:00 PM
4					

4

Notes:

_____

_____

_____

_____

_____

_____

**My Tips/
Shortcuts:**

_____

_____

_____

_____

_____

_____

_____

Related Tips:	*Tip 162: Totaling Time Values*
	Tip 163: Calculating the Difference Between Hours
	Tip 164: Calculating Time Differences Between Regions of the World

Rounding Hours Up

➢ **To round hours up:**

✦ Use the **CEILING** formula.

   The formula in cell **E6** in the screenshot is:

   =CEILING((+D6-C6)/0.04167,1)

Note: The number **0.04167** is a decimal value of 1/24.

	Name	Start Time	End Time	Round up	Formula Syntax
2	Name	Start Time	End Time	Round up	Formula Syntax
4	Bill	09:32	12:38	4	
5	Joe	05:43	14:32	9	
6	Roy	10:17	15:43	6	=CEILING((+D6-C6)/0.04167,1)

4

Times

Notes:

**My Tips/
Shortcuts:**

**Related
Tips:**

Tip 162: Totaling Time Values

*Tip 167: Converting a Number to a Time
Value*

Converting Time to Decimal Values

➢ **To convert time to decimal values:**

♦ Use the **HOUR** and **MINUTE** formulas to extract the hour and minute numbers from the time.

	Microsoft Excel - Book 1.xls			
	File Edit View Insert Format Tools Data Window Help			
	B2 ▼ _fx_ =HOUR(A2)+(MINUTE(A2)/60)			
	A	B	C	D
1	Time	Converting Time to Decimal	Syntax	
2	15:10:00	15.17	=HOUR(A2)+(MINUTE(A2)/60)	
3	23:38:00	23.63		
4				

4

Notes:

_____

_____

_____

_____

_____

_____

**My Tips/
Shortcuts:**

_____

_____

_____

_____

_____

**Related
Tips:**

Tip 162: Totaling Time Values

*Tip 166: Converting Time to Decimal
Values*

_____

Converting a Number to a Time Value

➢ **To quickly type time values into cells:**

◆ Enter the following formula:

**=IF(A3<1000,TIMEVALUE(LEFT(A3,1)&":"&RIGH
T(A3,2)),TIMEVALUE(LEFT(A3,2)&":"&RIGHT(A3,
2)))**

The formatting of the cells in column **B** is **HH:MM**.

	Microsoft Excel - Book1					
	File Edit View Insert Format Tools Data Window Help					
	B3 ▼	*fx* =IF(A3<1000,TIMEVALUE(LEFT(A3,1)&":"&RIGHT(A3,2)),TIMEVALUE(LEFT(A3,2)&":"&RIGHT(A3,2)))				
	A	B	C	D	E	F
1						
2	Number	Time Value				
3	1785	18:25				
4	959	9:59				
5	488	5:28				
6	1756	17:56				

4

Calculating

Summing

SUMIF Formula

Counting

Euro Currency Tools Add-In

Part 5 — Summing & Counting

5

Notes:

_____

_____

_____

_____

_____

_____

**My Tips/
Shortcuts:**

_____

_____

_____

_____

_____

Related Tips:	*Tip 26: Expanded Paste Icon Features in Excel 2002 & Excel 2003*
	Tip 169: Multiplying a Range by -1 in One Operation
	Tip 170: Performing a Quick Calculation in the Formula Bar

Adding, Subtracting, Multiplying and Dividing Without Using Formulas

➤ **To carry out simple mathematical calculations, use Paste Special → Operation:**

1. In this example, assume that columns **C** and **D** are sales figures to be added together.

2. Copy column **C**.

3. Select column **D**.

4. Press **<Shift+F10>** or right-click, and then select **Paste Special** from the shortcut menu.

5. In the **Operation** area, select the **Add** option button, and then click **OK**. The figures from column **C** are added to those in column **D**.

Paste Special	? ×
Paste	
⦿ All	○ Validation
○ Formulas	○ All except borders
○ Values	○ Column widths
○ Formats	○ Formulas and number formats
○ Comments	○ Values and number formats
Operation	
○ None	○ Multiply
⦿ Add	○ Divide
○ Subtract	
☐ Skip blanks	☐ Transpose
Paste Link	OK Cancel

5

Notes:

_____

_____

_____

_____

_____

_____

**My Tips/
Shortcuts:**

_____

_____

_____

_____

_____

_____

**Related
Tips:**

*Tip 26: Expanded Paste Icon Features in
Excel 2002 & Excel 2003*

*Tip 168: Adding, Subtracting, Multiplying
and Dividing Without Using Formulas*

*Tip 170: Performing a Quick Calculation in
the Formula Bar*

Multiplying a Range by -1 in One Operation

➢ **To multiply a range of numbers by -1:**

1. In any cell, type **-1**.
2. Select the cell and press **<Ctrl+C>** to copy.
3. Select the range to be multiplied by -1.
4. Press **<Shift+F10>** or right-click, and then select **Paste Special** from the shortcut menu.
5. Select the **Multiply** option button, and then click **OK**.

Note: ***-1** and parentheses are added in any cell with a formula.

Microsoft Excel - Book1

| | File | Edit | View | Insert | Format | Tools | Data | Window | Help |

| B1 | ▼ | *fx* | =(A1)*-1 |

	A	B	C	D	E	F	G
1	100	-100		-1			
2	200	-200					
3	300	-300					
4	400	-400					
5	500	-500					
6	600	-600					
7							

5

Notes:

_____

_____

_____

_____

_____

_____

My Tips/
Shortcuts:

_____

_____

_____

_____

_____

Related Tips:	*Tip 26: Expanded Paste Icon Features in Excel 2002 & Excel 2003*
	Tip 168: Adding, Subtracting, Multiplying and Dividing Without Using Formulas
	Tip 169: Multiplying a Range by -1 in One Operation

Performing a Quick Calculation in the Formula Bar

➢ **To perform a quick calculation in the Formula Bar:**

1. In the **Formula Bar**, type an equals (=) sign.

2. Type the numbers to multiply, for example, **9*5**.

3. Press **<F9>** to calculate and convert the formula to a value.

4. Press **<Ctrl+Enter>** to prevent moving down to the next cell. The value displayed in the cell is **45**.

Microsoft Excel - Book1						
File Edit View Insert Format Tools Data Window Help						
NOW ▼ ✕ ✓ *fx* =9*5						
A	B	C	D	E	F	G
1 =9*5						
2						
3						
4						

5

Related   Tip 168: Adding, Subtracting, Multiplying
Tips: and Dividing Without Using Formulas.

           Tip 169: Multiplying a Range by a Certain
           Operation.

           Tip 170: Performing a Quick Calculation in
           the Formula Bar.

Notes:

_____

_____

_____

_____

_____

**My Tips/
Shortcuts:**

_____

_____

_____

_____

_____

Related Tips:	Tip 168: Adding, Subtracting, Multiplying and Dividing Without Using Formulas
	Tip 169: Multiplying a Range by -1 in One Operation
	Tip 170: Performing a Quick Calculation in the Formula Bar

Seeing Calculation Results Immediately

➢ **To see calculations results immediately:**
  ✦ Right-click the **Status Bar** to open the fast
    calculation menu.

Note: Remember to select a range before using this
option.

Six functions are available:

✦ **Average**
✦ **Count**
✦ **Count Nums**
✦ **Max**
✦ **Min**
✦ **Sum**

5

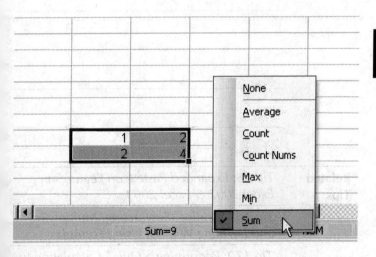

Notes:

**My Tips/
Shortcuts:**

| **Related
Tips:** | *Tip 26: Expanded Paste Icon Features in
Excel 2002 & Excel 2003* |
| --- | --- |
| | *Tip 168: Adding, Subtracting, Multiplying
and Dividing Without Using Formulas* |
| | *Tip 170: Performing a Quick Calculation in
the Formula Bar* |

Additional Functions in AutoSum

The **AutoSum** icon's functionality has been expanded in **Excel 2002** and **Excel 2003**. Click the arrow to the right of the **AutoSum** icon (a sigma) to select a function.

✦ **If the AutoSum icon does not appear in the Standard toolbar:**

1. Right-click one of the toolbars, and then select **Customize** from the shortcut menu.

2. Select the **Commands** tab, and from **Category**, click and drag the **AutoSum** icon onto the toolbar.

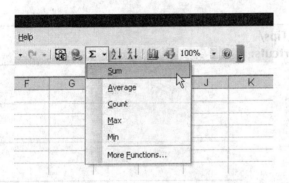

5

Notes:

**My Tips/
Shortcuts:**

**Related
Tips:**

Fast Summation

Using keyboard shortcuts

➤ **To sum the columns within the Current Region:**

1. Select a cell in the **Current Region/List** and press **<Ctrl+Shift+*>** (in **Excel 2003**, press this or **<Ctrl+A>**).

2. Press **<Alt+=>**.

   OR

   Click the **AutoSum** icon (sigma) on the **Standard** toolbar.

   The **SUM** formula is added automatically at the bottom of each column.

Before

	A	B	C	D
1	1	2	3	
2	2	4	6	
3	3	6	9	
4	4	8	12	
5	5	10	15	
6	6	12	18	
7	7	14	21	
8				
9				

After

	A	B	C	D
1	1	2	3	
2	2	4	6	
3	3	6	9	
4	4	8	12	
5	5	10	15	
6	6	12	18	
7	7	14	21	
8	28	56	84	
9				

continued...

Notes:

**My Tips/
Shortcuts:**

Fast Summation (cont.)

➢ **To add the SUM function to a vertical and horizontal range:**

1. Select the range of cells containing values, including an empty row and column surrounding the cells by selecting the first cell in data table, pressing **<Shift>**, and then selecting the empty cell in the first cross empty row and column (cell **D8** in the screenshot below).

2. Press **<Alt+=>**.

   OR

   Click the **AutoSum** icon.

   The **SUM** formula is added to the end of each row and the bottom of each column.

Before	**After**

Microsoft Excel - Book1					Microsoft Excel - Book1				
File Edit View Insert Format Tools					File Edit View Insert Format Tools Da				
	A	B	C	D		A	B	C	D
1	1	2	3		1	1	2	3	6
2	2	4	6		2	2	4	6	12
3	3	6	9		3	3	6	9	18
4	4	8	12		4	4	8	12	24
5	5	10	15		5	5	10	15	30
6	6	12	18		6	6	12	18	36
7	7	14	21		7	7	14	21	42
8					8	28	56	84	168
9					9				

continued...

5

Summing

Notes:

My Tips/
Shortcuts:

Fast Summation (cont.)

➢ **To quickly sum values in a range:**
1. Select the range of cells along with an empty cell in a vertical or horizontal direction.
2. Press **<Alt+=>**.

    OR

    Click the **AutoSum** icon.

    The **SUM** formula is added to the empty cell.

	A	B	C	D	E	F
1	1	2	3		<-	Before
2	2	4	6			
3						
4	1	2	3	5	<-	After
5	2	4	6			
6						

Microsoft Excel - Book1

File   Edit   View   Insert   Format   Tools   Data   Window   Help

5

Notes:

**My Tips/
Shortcuts:**

**Related
Tips:**

Tip 173: Fast Summation

*Tip 175: Extending the Range of the SUM
Formula*

*Tip 176: Summing Values at the
Intersection of Two Ranges*

Inserting Subtotals Quickly

Using keyboard shortcuts

➢ **To insert subtotals within a range of cells:**

1. Select row **4**, then press **<Ctrl++>** (the + sign) to insert a new row.

2. Select cell **A1**, then select the **Current Region** by pressing **<Ctrl+Shift+*>**(in **Excel 2003**, press this or **<Ctrl+A>**).

3. Press **<Alt+=>** or click the **AutoSum** icon.

4. Select any cell within the data area, then select the **Current Region** by pressing **<Ctrl+Shift+*>**, and repeat step 3.

5. Repeat the previous step after selecting any cell within the data area, (that is, select the **Current Region** and then repeat step 3).

	Microsoft Excel - Book1					
	File Edit View Insert Format Tools Data Window					
	C10	▼	*fx* =SUM(C9,C4)			
	A	B	C	D	E	F
1	1	2	3			
2	2	4	6			
3	3	6	9			
4	6	12	18	<--	=SUM(C1:C3)	
5	4	8	12			
6	5	10	15			
7	6	12	18			
8	7	14	21			
9	22	44	66	<--	=SUM(C5:C8)	
10	28	56	84	<--	=SUM(C9,C4)	
11						

Row **4** now contains **SUM** formulas for the data in rows **1:3**, row **9** contains **SUM** formulas for the data in rows **5:8**, and row **10** contains only the **SUM** formula for the two subtotal formulas (note that the formula in cell **C10** is **=SUM(C9,C4)**.

Notes:

_____

_____

_____

_____

_____

_____

_____

My Tips/ Shortcuts:

_____

_____

_____

_____

_____

_____

Related Tips:

Tip 173: Fast Summation

Tip 174: Inserting Subtotals Quickly

Tip 176: Summing Values at the Intersection of Two Ranges

Extending the Range of the SUM Formula

➢ **To extend the range of the SUM formula:**

1. In cell **C7** insert the **SUM** formula with the total for range **A1:A5**.

2. Select cell **C7**.

3. Press **<F2>** to enter edit mode.

   OR

   Click any place within the formula in the **Formula Bar**.

4. Drag the handle of the range to extend the range (the handle is located in the bottom-right corner of the range).

5. Press **<Enter>**.

	A	B	C	D	E	F
1	1	2	3			
2	2	4	6			
3	3	6	9			
4	4	8	12			
5	5	10	15			
6						
7			JM(A1:A5)			
8						

Microsoft Excel - Book1 — File Edit View Insert Format Tools Data Window Help — NOW =SUM(A1:A5)

5

Notes:

_____

_____

_____

_____

_____

_____

_____

_____

**My Tips/
Shortcuts:**

_____

_____

_____

_____

_____

_____

_____

Summing Values at the Intersection of Two Ranges

➢ **To sum figures at the intersection of two ranges:**

  ✦ Leave a space between the two argument ranges in the **SUM** formula.

    The **SUM** formula in cell **F3** totals the figures in range **B3:C5**.

    The **SUM** formula in cell **F5** totals the figures at the intersection of columns **B:C** and row **5:5**.

	A	B	C	D	E	F	G	H	I
1	1	2	3	4					
2	2	4	6	8					
3	3	6	9	12		60	<--	=SUM(B3:C5)	
4	4	8	12	16					
5	5	10	15	20		25	<--	=SUM(B:C 5:5)	
6	6	12	18	24					
7	7	14	21	28					
8	8	16	24	32					
9									

Microsoft Excel - Book1

File Edit View Insert Format Tools Data Window Help

G21

5

Notes:

_____

_____

_____

_____

_____

_____

**My Tips/
Shortcuts:**

_____

_____

_____

_____

_____

_____

Related Tips:	*Tip 28: Copying Cell Content Across Sheets*
	Tip 29: Copying/Moving a Cell(s) Between Sheets/Workbooks
	Tip 105: Grouping/Ungrouping Sheets

Summing Values from Cells in Different Sheets

In this example, we have a workbook with four successive sheets: **January**, **February**, **March** and **April**.

➢ **To total figures from the same cell address in different sheets:**

1. Select a cell and type **=SUM(**.
2. Select the tab for the first sheet, **January**.
3. Hold the **<Shift>** key, and then select the tab for the last sheet, **April**.
4. Select cell **B2**, and then press **<Enter>**.

The formula is now **=SUM(January:April!B2)**.

Microsoft Excel - Book1

File   Edit   View   Insert   Format   Tools   Data   Window   Help

B2   ▼   *fx* =SUM(January:April!B2)

	A	B	C	D	E	F	G	H
1								
2		4000						
3								
4								
5								
6								
7								
8								

\ January / February / March / April \ **Total** /

Ready   NUM

5

Notes:

_____

_____

_____

_____

_____

_____

_____

**My Tips/
Shortcuts:**

_____

_____

_____

_____

_____

_____

Related Tips:	*Tip 174: Inserting Subtotals Quickly*
	Tip 175: Extending the Range of the SUM Formula
	Tip 201: Array Formulas - the Technical Side

Summing Stock Lists

➤ **To total a stock list, use an Array Formula:**

1. Define **Names** to both the **Quantity** (**B2:B10**) and **Price** ranges (**C2:C10**). (To define a range **Name**, see *Tip #188*.)

2. Type the formula **=SUM(Quantity*Price)** into a cell.

3. To change the formula to an **Array Formula** (see *Tip #201*), press **<F2>** and simultaneously press **<Ctrl+Shift+Enter>**.

Summing

5

Microsoft Excel - Book1

File Edit View Insert Format Tools Data Window Help

D13 ▼ *fx* {=SUM(Quantity*Price)}

	A	B	C	D	E	F	G
1	Stock Number	Quantity	Price	Total			
2	AAA	345	$15.00	$5,175	<--	=B2*C2	
3	CCC	205	$12.00	$2,460			
4	BBB	257	$13.00	$3,341			
5	AAA	413	$18.00	$7,434			
6	AAA	413	$18.00	$7,434			
7	BBB	517	$20.00	$10,340			
8	CCC	621	$22.00	$13,662			
9	AAA	673	$23.00	$15,479			
10	CCC	725	$24.00	$17,400			
11				$82,725	<--	=SUM(D2:D10)	
12							
13	The Array Formula:			$82,725			
14							

Notes:

_____

_____

_____

_____

_____

**My Tips/
Shortcuts:**

_____

_____

_____

_____

_____

_____

Related Tips:	*Tip 61: Rounding Numbers to Thousands*
	Tip 178: Summing Stock Lists
	Tip 201: Array Formulas - the Technical Side

Summing Rounded Numbers

How Excel performs calculations:

Excel does not take number format into account when performing mathematical calculations. When performing a calculation, Excel operates on the entire number, using up to 15 significant digits, without considering the formatting.

Problem:

When the numbers displayed by the cells differ from the numbers Excel uses for calculations, there can be an apparent difference in the totals of those cells.

For example, in cells **B3** to **B7** in the screenshot, the numbers were rounded based on their number formats. Notice that the total in cell **B8** is not equal to the total of the displayed numbers, which is **16** (see explanations to the **Array Formula** in **C8** in the screenshot at the last page of this Tip).

	A	B	C	D
	Microsoft Excel - Book1			
	File Edit View Insert Format Tools Data Window Help			
	C8 ▼ *fx* {=SUM(ROUND(C3:C7,0))}			
1				
2				
3	1.11	1	1	
4	2.22	2	2	
5	3.33	3	3	
6	4.44	4	4	
7	5.55	6	6	
8	16.65	17	16	
9				
10	=SUM(A3:A7)	=SUM(B3:B7)	{=SUM(ROUND(C3:C7,0))}	
11				

continued...

421

Notes:

**My Tips/
Shortcuts:**

Summing Rounded Numbers (cont.)

Solution 1:

Deleting Number (Permanent — No Undo!)

1. From the *Tools* menu, select **Options**.
2. Select the **Calculation** tab, and then select the **Precision as displayed** option button.

All places after the decimal point are deleted in the cells. The numbers displayed in the cells are whole numbers, and the total is the sum of these whole numbers.

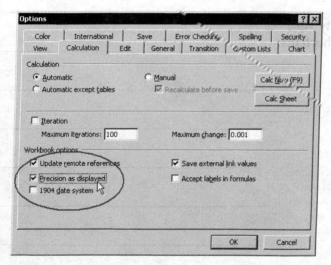

Disadvantage: There is no way to undo this operation, as the numbers have been permanently deleted.

continued...

Notes:

**My Tips/
Shortcuts:**

Summing Rounded Numbers (cont.)

Solution 2:

Use an Array Formula to Total Rounded Numbers

➢ **To total numbers rounded to the nearest integer:**

1. In cell **C8**, type **=ROUND** (see the screenshot in the first page of this Tip).

2. Press **<Ctrl+A>** for the *Function Arguments* dialog box, and in the first **Number** argument box of the **ROUND** formula, enter the range **C3:C7**.

3. In the **Num_digits** argument box, type **0** to round the number to the nearest whole digit and click **OK**.

4. After the equals (=) sign, type **SUM**.

5. Type **(** to open the parentheses, press **<End>**, and then type **)** to close the parentheses.

6. Press **<Ctrl+Shift+Enter>** to create an **Array Formula** (if the formula returns a **#VALUE** error, press **<F2>**, and then press **<Ctrl+Shift+Enter>**).

➢ **To total numbers rounded to thousands** (see the screenshot at the bottom):

✦ Follow the steps above and insert an **Array Formula** into cell **B8**, with **-3** in the **ROUND** formula's second argument box.

	A	B	C	• D	E	F	G
	Original Numbers	Rounding to Thousands					
2	1,252,501	1,253		Rounding to thousands by Formatting			
3	5,235,501	5,236		The formatting:		#,###,	
4	5,232,501	5,233					
5	11,720,503	11,722	<--	{=SUM(ROUND(B2:B4,-3))}			
6							

B5 — ƒx {=SUM(ROUND(B2:B4,-3))}

Notes:

_____

_____

_____

_____

_____

_____

_____

_____

**My Tips/
Shortcuts:**

_____

_____

_____

_____

_____

_____

_____

Related Tips:	*Tip 181: Totaling Two Ranges Using the SUMIF Formula*
	Tip 182: Summing Using Text Characters as Criteria
	Tip 229: The Power Combination

The SUMIF Formula – Using Comparison Operators (< >) as Criteria

Use the < or > comparison operators as criteria in the **SUMIF** formula.

Example:

1. In cell **E2**, type the criterion **>501**.
2. In cell **D2**, insert the **SUMIF** formula shown in the **Formula Bar**.

Result: The **SUMIF** formula returns only the total of cells **B12:B17** because the value of cells **A12** to **A17** are >501.

	Microsoft Excel - Book1					
File	Edit	View	Insert	Format	Tools	Data	Window	Help
	D2	▼		*fx* =SUMIF(A:A,E2,B:B)		

	A	B	C	D	E	F	G
1	Number	Amounts					
2	100	1		81	>501		
3	101	2					
4	200	3		81	<---	=SUM(B12:B17)	
5	201	4					
6	300	5					
7	301	6					
8	400	7					
9	401	8					
10	500	9					
11	501	10					
12	600	11					
13	601	12					
14	700	13					
15	701	14					
16	800	15					
17	801	16					
18							

SUMIF Formula

5

Notes:

_____

_____

_____

_____

_____

My Tips/
Shortcuts:

_____

_____

_____

_____

_____

Related Tips:	*Tip 180: The SUMS Formula - Using Comparison Operators (< >) as Criteria*
	Tip 198: Copying a Formula From Cell While Keeping the Absolute Reference or Relative Reference
	Tip 199: Copying Formulas from a Range of Cells Without Changing the Absolute or Relative References

Totaling Two Ranges Using the SUMIF Formula

➢ **To let the SUMIF formula add or subtract amounts from different ranges, insert two SUMIF formulas and combine them into a single formula:**

1. Insert the **SUMIF** formula to total the amounts based on the criterion **>701** into cell **E2**.

2. Insert the **SUMIF** formula to total the amounts based on the criterion **<300** into cell **E3**.

3. Select cell **E2** and copy the formula from the **Formula Bar** by selecting the formula and pressing **<Ctrl+C>**.

4. Select cell **E5** and press **<Ctrl+V>**.

5. Select cell **E3** and copy the formula from the **Formula Bar** without the equals (=) sign by selecting the formula and pressing **<Ctrl+C>**.

6. Select cell **E5** and enter a minus (-) sign after the formula in the cell, and then press **<Ctrl+V>**. The combined formula is now:

   =SUMIF(A:A,D2,B:B)-SUMIF(A:A,D3,B:B).

	A	B	C	D	E	F	G	H
				E5	=SUMIF(A:A,D2,B:B)-SUMIF(A:A,D3,B:B)			
1	Number	Amounts						
2	100	1		>701	31	<--	=SUMIF(A:A,D2,B:B)	
3	101	2		<300	10	<--	=SUMIF(A:A,D3,B:B)	
4	200	3						
5	201	4			21			
6	300	5						
7	301	6						
8	400	7						
9	401	8						
10	500	9						
11	501	10						
12	600	11						
13	601	12						
14	700	13						
15	701	14						
16	800	15						
17	801	16						

Notes:

**My Tips/
Shortcuts:**

Summing Using Text Characters as Criteria

The **SUMIF** formula can be used with a range of different criteria, including strings/characters.

The screenshot below displays the wide range of criteria available for **SUMIF** formulas.

Microsoft Excel - Book1

File　Edit　View　Insert　Format　Tools　Data　Window　Help

D2　　　ƒx　=SUMIF(A:A,C2&"*",B:B)

	A	B	C	D	E	F
1	Text	Amount	Criteria	Result	Formula Syntax	Criteria
2	AIG	(5,000)	Exc	(1,000)	=SUMIF(A:A,C2&"*",B:B)	3 Characters from Left
3	ExcelTip	(4,000)	A	(7,000)	=SUMIF(A:A,"A*",B:B)	1 Character from Left
4	AIG	(3,000)	???	(8,000)	=SUMIF(A:A,"A*",B:B)	3 Characters Only in Text
5	AIG	(2,000)	"Excel"	(1,000)	=SUMIF(A:A,C5,B:B)	Few Exact Characters from Left or in the Middle
6	Pacific Bell	(1,000)				
7	Motorola	0				
8	Amazon	1,000				
9	AIG	2,000				
10	ExcelTip	3,000				
11						

Notes:

**My Tips/
Shortcuts:**

**Related
Tips:**

*Tip 184: Counting the Number of Cells
Containing Text in a Range*

*Tip 185: Counting Based on Multiple
Criteria*

*Tip 270: Filter a List into Unique Records
Using the COUNTIF Formula*

COUNT Formulas

The **COUNT** formula comes in several forms:

✦ **Count:** Counts the number of cells containing numbers, as well as numbers within the list of arguments.

✦ **CountA:** Counts the number of cells that are not empty, as well as the values within the list of arguments.

✦ **CountBlank:** Counts empty cells in a specified range of cells.

✦ **CountIf:** Counts using criteria, as shown in the sample screenshot.

	A	B	C	D	E
	Microsoft Excel - Book1				
	File Edit View Insert Format Tools Data Window Help				
	B2	▼	ƒₓ =COUNTIF(A:A,C2)		
	Numbers & Text	**Result**	**Critera**	**Function Syntax**	**Detalis**
1					
2	1	4	< 5	=COUNTIF(A:A,C2)	Count cells contains numbers less than 5
3	2	4	*	=COUNTIF(A:A,C3)	Count cells contains text.
4	3	1	???	=COUNTIF(A:A,C4)	Count cells contains text 3 digits only.
5	4	2	A*	=COUNTIF(A:A,C5)	Count cells starts with the letter A.
6	5	1	*EXC*	=COUNTIF(A:A,C6)	Count cells contains the characters EXC.
7	6				
8	7				
9	8				
10	9				
11	10				
12					
13	AAA				
14	A				
15	Excel				
16					

Notes:

_____

_____

_____

_____

_____

_____

**My Tips/
Shortcuts:**

_____

_____

_____

_____

_____

_____

Related Tips:	*Tip 183: COUNT Formulas*
	Tip 185: Counting Based on Multiple Criteria
	Tip 295: Comparing Lists Using the COUNTIF Formula

Counting the Number of Cells Containing Text in a Range

✦ The **COUNTA** formula returns the number of cells that contain any type of data in a range.

✦ The **COUNT** formula returns the number of cells that contain only numeric data in a range.

Subtracting the two formulas will return the number of cells that contain text in the range defined by the **Name** table:

=COUNTA(Table)-COUNT(Table)

	A	B	C	D	E	F
	Table	▼	*fx* A			
	A	B	C	D	E	F
1	A	C	1	9	<--	=COUNTA(Table)
2	B	D	2	5	<--	=COUNT(Table)
3	4	5	3	4	<--	=COUNTA(Table)-COUNT(Table)
4						

Microsoft Excel - Book1

File   Edit   View   Insert   Format   Tools   Data   Window   Help

Counting

5

Notes:

**My Tips/
Shortcuts:**

Related Tips:	*Tip 183: COUNT Formulas*
	Tip 184: Counting the Number of Cells Containing Text in a Range
	Tip 270: Filter a List into Unique Records Using the COUNTIF Formula

Counting Based on Multiple Criteria

In this example, we will count the number of rows in which the text **ExcelTip** and **USA** appear in both columns **B** and **C** (the range **Name** for column **B** is **Customer_Name**, and for column **C** it is **Market**).

	A	B	C	D	E	F
	Invoice					
1	**Number**	**Customer Name**	**Market**	**Income**		
2	109	AIG	Asia	8,040.00		
3	118	AIG	Africa	25,129.90		
4	123	AIG	Europe	32,850.02		
5	138	Microsoft	USA	56,237.43		
6	110	Cisco	Asia	37,065.81		
7	136	Cisco	Africa	53,119.11		
8	139	Cisco	Africa	57,796.59		
9	101	ExcelTip	USA	2,136.75		
10	111	ExcelTip	Africa	15,452.00		
11	124	ExcelTip	Asia	34,409.18		
12	130	ExcelTip	Europe	43,764.14		
13	140	ExcelTip	USA	59,355.75		
14	102	Intel	USA	2,270.94		
15	114	Intel	Asia	23,084.00		
16						
17	2	{=SUM((Market="USA")*(Customer_Name="ExcelTip"))}				
18	9	{=SUM((Market="USA")+(Customer_Name="ExcelTip"))}				
19						

Cell reference A17, formula bar: {=SUM((Market="USA")*(Customer_Name="ExcelTip"))}

➢ **To count the number of rows that must satisfy criteria from two columns:**

✦ Insert the following **Array Formula** (see how to insert an **Array Formula** in page 2 of this Tip):

{=SUM((Market="USA")*(Customer_Name="Excel Tip"))}

The result of the calculation is **2**. The ***** symbol in the **Array Formula** returns a result equal to the **AND** operator.

continued...

Notes:

_____

_____

_____

_____

_____

_____

My Tips/
Shortcuts:

_____

_____

_____

_____

_____

_____

_____

Counting Based on Multiple Criteria (cont.)

➢ **To count the number of cells that satisfy at least one of two criteria from different ranges:**

✦ Replace the * symbol in the **Array Formula** with a + sign.

The return result calculation is **9**, that is, five cells in column **B** match the criteria **ExcelTip** and four cells in column **C** match the criteria **USA**.

Note: This can also be done by replacing the **Array Formula** with a **COUNTIF** formula:

**=COUNTIF (Market, "USA")+
COUNTIF(Customer_Name, "ExcelTip")**

Using keyboard shortcuts

The keyboard shortcut for inserting an **Array Formula** is as follows (see *Tip #201*):

✦ After entering the formula into the cell, select the cell, press **<F2>** to edit it, and then press **<Ctrl+Shift+Enter>**.

Notes:

_____

_____

_____

_____

_____

My Tips/
Shortcuts:

_____

_____

_____

_____

_____

Related **Tips:**	*Tip 2: What's New in Excel 2002/2003:* *Menu, Cell Shortcut Menu and Keyboard* *Shortcuts*
	Tip 56: Inserting Special Symbols into *Custom Formats*
	Tip 57: Automating the Insertion of the *Euro Symbol*

The Euro Currency Tools Add-In

✦ Step 1: Installing the Euro Currency Tools Add-In:

1. From the *Tools* menu, select **Add-In**.
2. Select the **Euro Currency Tool**s checkbox, and click **OK**.

✦ Step 2: Using the Euro Currency Tools:

1. Select cells containing values to be converted.
2. From the *Tools* menu, select **Euro Conversion**.
3. In the **Destination** range, select a cell.
4. From the **From** dropdown list, select the currency to which it is to be converted.
5. Click **OK**.

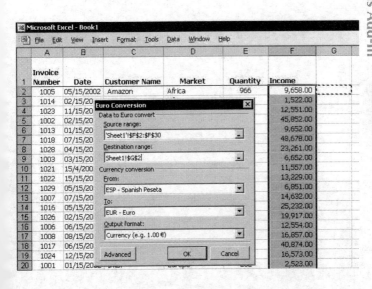

Part 6 — Formulas

6

Notes:

**My Tips/
Shortcuts:**

**Related
Tips:**

Tip 188: Defining a Range Name

Tip 189: Deleting a Range Name

*Tip 191: Using a Range Name in a
Formula*

Range Name Syntax

Name syntax rules:

✦ The **Name** string must begin with a text character, not a number, and consists of adjacent characters.

✦ Two words can be joined with an underscore (_), for example, to enter the **Name** "Excel Book", you should type **Excel_Book**.

✦ You cannot use a **Name** that could otherwise be confused as a cell reference, for example, A1 or IS2002, as these are already cell references.

Notes:

✦ There is no limit on the number of **Names** you can define.

✦ Be sure to define unique **Names** for a specific workbook. Defining **Names** that resemble **Names** in other sheets will only complicate your work.

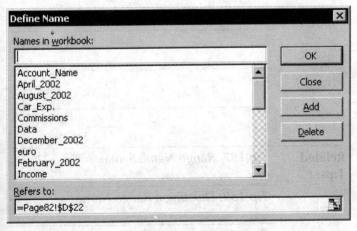

Notes:

**My Tips/
Shortcuts:**

**Related
Tips:**

Tip 187: Range Name Syntax

Tip 189: Deleting a Range Name

*Tip 190: Automatically Defining Names for
Ranges in Lists*

Defining a Range Name

➢ **To define a range Name, use one of the following two techniques:**

✦ **Type the text directly in the Name box**

1. Select cell **A1**.

2. In the **Name** box, type the text, and then press **<Enter>**.

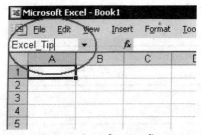

✦ **Define a Name using the *Define Name* dialog box**

1. Select cell **B1**.

2. Press **<Ctrl+F3>**.

   OR

   From the *Insert* menu, select **Name** and then **Define**.

3. Type the text in the **Names in workbook** box, and then click **OK**.

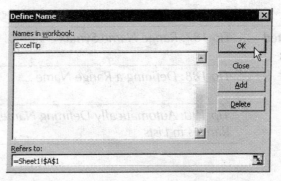

447

Notes:

**My Tips/
Shortcuts:**

**Related
Tips:**

Tip 187: Range Name Syntax

Tip 188: Defining a Range Name

*Tip 190: Automatically Defining Names for
Ranges in Lists*

Deleting a Range Name

Why it is highly recommended to delete unnecessary/unneeded range Names:

✦ Large number of range **Names** makes it more difficult to locate a specific **Name**.

✦ Range **Names** create references and unwanted links

➢ **To find unnecessary/unwanted range Names:**

1. Select a cell in a new sheet.

2. Press **<F3>** and click **Paste List**. A full list of range names and their references is pasted into the new sheet; delete each of the unwanted **Name**.

➢ **To delete a range Name:**

✦ Press **<Ctrl+F3>**, select the **Name**, and then click **Delete**.

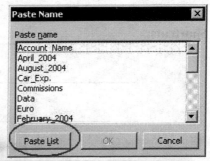

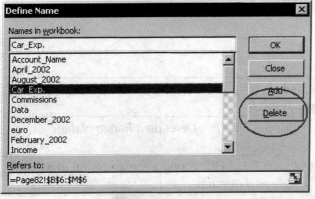

Notes:

_____

_____

_____

_____

_____

_____

**My Tips/
Shortcuts:**

_____

_____

_____

_____

_____

_____

Automatically Defining Names for Ranges in Lists

➢ **To automatically define Names according to the labels in the top row's cells and in the left column cell's:**

1. Select any cell in the data area and select the **Current Region** by pressing **<Ctrl+Shift+*>** (in **Excel 2003**, press this or **<Ctrl+A>**).

2. Press **<Ctrl+Shift+F3>**.

   OR

   From the *Insert* menu, select **Name** and then **Create**.

3. Select the **Top** row and **Left** column options, and then click **OK**.

   Each row and column range now defines its own range **Name**, for example: the range address for the defined **Name January_2004** is **$B$2:$B$11**, and the range address for the defined **Name Income** is **$B$2:$E$2**.

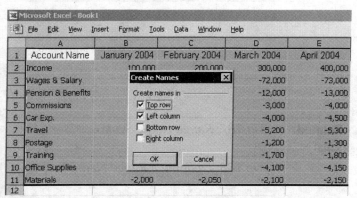

451

Notes:

**My Tips/
Shortcuts:**

Using a Range Name in a Formula

➤ **To use a range Name in a formula:**

1. Define the following range **Names** for ranges
   B2:B11, **C2:C11** and **D2:D11**, respectively (to
   define range **Name** see *Tip #188*): **January_2004**,
   February_2004, and **March_2004** (see the
   screenshot below).

2. Select a cell and type the formula **=SUM**.

3. Press **<Ctrl+A>**.

4. Select the first argument box and press **<F3>**.

5. Select the **Name January_2004**, and then click
   OK.

6. **Paste the Names February_2004** and **March_2004**
   in the next two argument boxes, and then click
   OK. The following formula has now been inserted
   into the cell:

=SUM(January_2004, February_2004, March_2004)

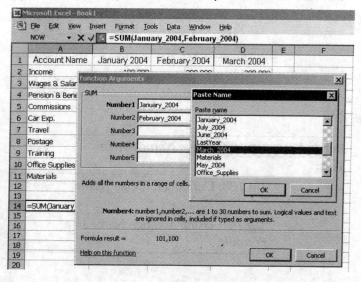

Notes:

_____

_____

_____

_____

_____

_____

_____

**My Tips/
Shortcuts:**

_____

_____

_____

_____

_____

_____

**Related
Tips:**

Tip 187: Range Name Syntax

Tip 188: Defining a Range Name

*Tip 191: Using a Range Name in a
Formula*

Saving a Frequently Used Formula/Numeric Value in the Define Name Dialog Box

Example 1:

Add a formula for calculating the number of the previous year: **= YEAR(TODAY())-1**

➤ **To define a Name that returns the result of a formula:**

1. Press **<Ctrl+F3>** for the *Define Name* dialog box.
2. In the **Names in workbook** box, type **LastYear**.
3. Type the formula **=YEAR(TODAY())-1** in the **Refers to** box, and then click **OK**.

➤ **To enter the formula into a cell:**

1. Type the **=** sign, and then press **<F3>** (for the *Paste Name* dialog box.
2. Select the **Name LastYear**, and then click **OK**.

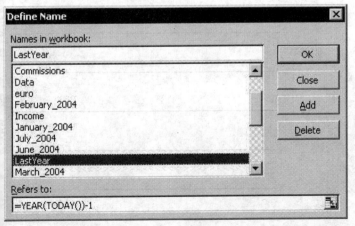

continued...

455

Notes:

**My Tips/
Shortcuts:**

Saving a Frequently Used Formula/Numeric Value in the Define Name Dialog Box (cont.)

Example 2:

Define a name that stores an exchange rate of **0.82** for **1 Euro** vs. **1 Dollar**.

➢ **To define a Name that stores a value:**

1. Press **<Ctrl+F3>** for the *Define Name* dialog box.
2. In the **Names in workbook** box, type **Euro**.
3. Type the formula **=0.82** in the **Refers to** box, and then click **OK**.
4. Enter a dollar amount in cell **A1**.
5. In cell **B1**, type the formula **=A1*Euro**.

➢ **To update a value saved as a Name:**

1. Press **<Ctrl+F3>** for the *Paste Name* dialog box.
2. Select the **Name Euro**.
3. Change the value of the exchange rate in the **Refers to** box, and then click **OK**.

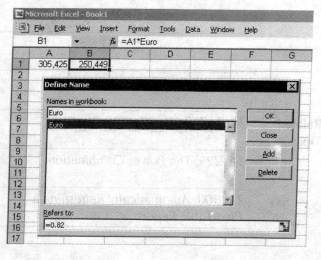

6

Notes:

_____

_____

_____

_____

_____

**My Tips/
Shortcuts:**

_____

_____

_____

_____

_____

_____

| **Related
Tips:** | *Tip 187: Range Name Syntax* |
| | *Tip 229: The Power Combination* |
| | *Tip 300: Automatically Refreshing a
PivotTable Report* |

Automatically Updating a Range Name Reference

Updating the size of a source data range is necessary in order to update the reference in any formula using range **Name**, especially when using a **PivotTable Report**.

➤ **To automatically update a range Name:**

✦ Insert the following formula into the **Refers to** box in the *Define Name* dialog box:

=OFFSET('Sheet1'!$A$1,0,0,COUNTA('Sheet1'!$A:$A),COUNTA(' Sheet1'!$1:$1))

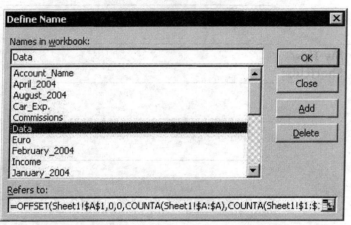

This **OFFSET** formula returns the measurement size of the data table (width and height). The syntax of the **OFFSET** formula is: **(Reference,Rows,Cols,**Height,Width).

✦ **Reference:** The reference from which you want to base the offset (in the example the reference is **A1**).

✦ **Rows,Cols:** The number of rows or columns that you want the upper-left cell to refer to (for example, **0** rows and **0** columns).

✦ **Height,Width:** The height or width, in number of rows (columns) that you want the returned reference to be, the numbers must be positive.

6

Notes:

**My Tips/
Shortcuts:**

Related Tips:	*Tip 195: Entering Formulas More Quickly by Shortening Sheet Names*
	Tip 196: Nesting Formulas
	Tip 198: Copying a Formula From Cell While Keeping the Absolute Reference or Relative Reference

Inserting/Editing Formulas

Using keyboard shortcuts

➢ **To open the *Insert Function* dialog box:**
  ✦ Select an empty cell and press **<Shift+F3>**.

➢ **To open a *Function Arguments* dialog box:**
  ✦ Select a cell containing a formula and press **<Shift+F3>**.

➢ **To insert a new Formula into a cell using the *Function Arguments* dialog box:**
  1. Select an empty cell, and then type the = sign.
  2. Type the formula name and press **<Ctrl+A>**.

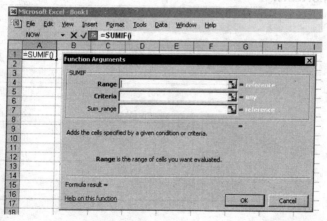

continued...

461

Notes:

**My Tips/
Shortcuts:**

Inserting/Editing Formulas (cont.)

➢ **To insert a formula by typing it while being guided by the formula syntax tooltip:**

1. Select an empty cell, and then type the **=** sign followed by the formula name and a **(** sign.

2. Press **<Ctrl+Shift+A>**.

Formulas

6

Notes:

_____

_____

_____

_____

_____

_____

**My Tips/
Shortcuts:**

_____

_____

_____

_____

_____

_____

**Related
Tips:**

Tip 196: Nesting Formulas

*Tip 197: Changing an Absolute Reference
to a Relative Reference or Vice Versa*

*Tip 198: Copying a Formula From Cell
While Keeping the Absolute Reference or
Relative Reference*

Entering Formulas More Quickly by Shortening Sheet Names

Formulas can be long and often take up several rows. Formulas can be made shorter by either using a range's defined **Names** for the references or shortening the sheet tab names.

➤ **To enter long Formulas into a cell more quickly:**

1. Rename the sheets to shorter names, such as **1**, **2** or **3**, to make the formulas shorter.

2. After entering the formulas, change the sheet names back to more meaningful names.

Formulas containing short sheet names:

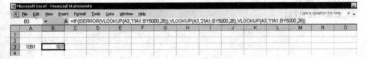

Formulas containing long sheet names:

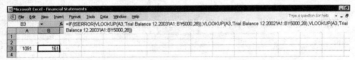

Notes:

_____

_____

_____

_____

_____

_____

**My Tips/
Shortcuts:**

_____

_____

_____

_____

_____

_____

Related Tips:	*Tip 197: Changing an Absolute Reference to a Relative Reference or Vice Versa*
	Tip 198: Copying a Formula From Cell While Keeping the Absolute Reference or Relative Reference
	Tip 199: Copying Formulas from a Range of Cells Without Changing the Absolute or Relative References

Nesting Formulas

Using keyboard shortcuts

A formula can be copied and pasted into the appropriate place in another formula in the **Formula Bar** by using the **<Ctrl+C>** and **<Ctrl+V>** keyboard shortcuts.

➢ **To combine Formulas into one long nested power Formula:**

1. Insert the following formula into a cell:

   =SUMIF(TB_DB_Level3,A12,G12)

2. Insert the following formula into an adjacent cell:

   =OFFSET(TB_DB_Level3,0,MonthSelectionNumb er+2)

3. In the **Formula Bar** of the second formula, select the formula without the **=** sign, and then press **<Ctrl+C>**.

4. Click **Cancel** or **Enter** (the two buttons between the **Name Box** and the formula in the **Formula Bar**) to exit edit mode.

5. Select the cell containing the first formula, and in the **Formula Bar**, select the reference **G12**, and then press **<Ctrl+V>**.

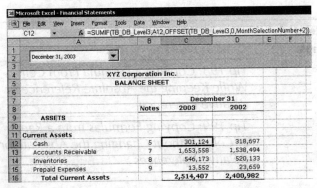

Notes:

_____

_____

_____

_____

_____

My Tips/ Shortcuts:

_____

_____

_____

_____

_____

Related Tips:	Tip 196: Nesting Formulas
	Tip 198: Copying a Formula From Cell While Keeping the Absolute Reference or Relative Reference
	Tip 199: Copying Formulas from a Range of Cells Without Changing the Absolute or Relative References

Changing an Absolute Reference to a Relative Reference or Vice Versa

✦ Relative Reference

When a formula is copied, a **Relative** reference is used. A **Relative** reference is the distance, in rows and columns, between the reference and the cell containing the formula.

For example: In cell **A1**, type the number **100**, and in cell **B1**, type the formula =A1. Cell **B1** is one column to the right of cell **A1**. When the formula is copied from cell **B1** to cell **B10**, the distance between the reference and the cell containing the formula remains one column, and the formula in cell **B10** is =A10.

✦ Absolute Reference

Select cell **B1** from the previous example. In the **Formula Bar**, select A1, and then press <F4>. The result is =$A$1.

Copy the contents of cell **B1** to cell **B10**. Notice that the formula does not change — the formula reference remains constant as =$A$1.

✦ The <F4> Key

The <F4> keyboard shortcut has four states:

❖ **State 1: Absolute** reference to the column and row, =$A$1

❖ **State 2: Relative** reference (column) and **Absolute** reference (row), =A$1

❖ **State 3: Absolute** reference (column) and **Relative** reference (row), =$A1

❖ **State 4: Relative** reference to the column and row, =A1

Formulas

6

Notes:

My Tips/ Shortcuts:

Related Tips/ Shortcuts:	*Tip 199: Copying Formulas from a Range of Cells Without Changing the Absolute or Relative References*
	Tip 200: Copying Formulas and Pasting Them in a Transposed Direction Without Changing the Relative References
	To display the *Function Arguments* dialog box, select a cell containing a Formula and press **<Shift+F3>**.

Copying a Formula from a Cell While Keeping the Absolute Reference or Relative Reference

Avoid the nightmare of pressing **<F4>** multiple times when coping and pasting formulas!

➢ **To copy/paste a Formula without changing the Absolute or Relative references:**

✦ **Option 1:** Select a cell under the cell containing a formula and press **<Ctrl+ '>**.

✦ **Option 2:** Copy and paste the formula from the **Formula Bar** to a cell, instead of from a **cell to another cell**.

For example, cell **C12** contains the formula:

1. Select the formula string in the **Formula Bar** and press **<Ctrl+C>** to copy it.

2. Leave the **Formula Bar** by clicking the **Enter** or **Cancel** icons to the left of the *fx* on the **Formula Bar**.

3. Select another cell and press **<Ctrl+V>**.

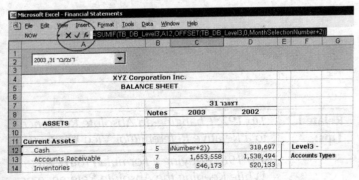

471

Notes:

_____

_____

_____

_____

_____

_____

_____

**My Tips/
Shortcuts:**

_____

_____

_____

_____

_____

_____

_____

_____

Related Tips:	*Tip 197: Changing an Absolute Reference to a Relative Reference or Vice Versa*
	Tip 198: Copying a Formula From Cell While Keeping the Absolute Reference or Relative Reference
	Tip 200: Copying Formulas and Pasting Them in a Transposed Direction Without Changing the Relative References

Copying Formulas from a Range of Cells Without Changing the Absolute or Relative References

➢ **To copy/paste Formulas from a range of cells without changing the Absolute or Relative references:**

1. Select the range of cells containing the formulas and press **<Ctrl+H>**.
2. In the **Find what** box, type the = sign.
3. In the **Replace with** box, type the # sign (to change the formulas to text).
4. Click **Replace All**, and then click **Close**.
5. Copy and paste the cells to a new location.
6. Repeat steps 1 through 3, reversing the # and = signs (to change the text to formulas).

Notes:

My Tips/
Shortcuts:

Related Tips/ Shortcuts:	*Tip 197: Changing an Absolute Reference to a Relative Reference or Vice Versa*
	Tip 199: Copying Formulas from a Range of Cells Without Changing the Absolute or Relative References
	To display the **Function Arguments** dialog box, select a cell containing a Formula and press **<Shift+F3>**.

Copying Formulas and Pasting Them in a Transposed Direction Without Changing the Relative References

➤ **To paste copied cells in a transposed direction:**

1. Select a range of cells in the sheet, and press **<Ctrl+C>**.
2. Select any cell in the sheet, right-click, and then select **Paste Special** from the shortcut menu.
3. In the *Paste Special* dialog box, select **Transpose**, and then click **OK**.

The **Transpose** option pastes the data in the opposite direction (that is, horizontally to vertically, or vice versa).

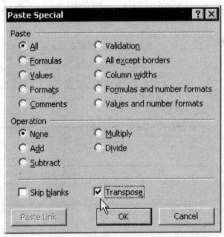

The *Paste Special* dialog box has a **Paste Link** option that enables to creating links to the source data while pasting copied cells in the new location.

Problem:

You cannot select the **Transpose** option together with the **Paste Link** option. In other words, you cannot create links while changing the direction using **Paste Special**.

continued...

Notes:

_____

_____

_____

_____

_____

_____

**My Tips/
Shortcuts:**

_____

_____

_____

_____

_____

_____

_____

_____

_____

_____

_____

Copying Formulas and Pasting Them in a Transposed Direction Without Changing the Relative References (cont.)

Solution:

Use the **TRANSPOSE** function together with the **Array Formula** technique to create links that change direction.

1. Select the range **A2:B6**, which has the range **Name Data** defined for it. The size of the range is **5Rx2C**, that is, four rows by two columns. (To quickly find the measurement, select the range and watch for the size in the **Name** box while pressing the mouse button.)

2. Select a range starting from cell **A8** whose size is **2Rx5C**, that is, the same size in the opposite direction.

3. Type the formula **=TRANSPOSE**, and then press **<Ctrl+A>**.

4. Press **<F3>**, paste the **Name Data**, and then press **<Ctrl+Shift+Enter>** (read more on **Array Formulas** in *Tip #201*).

	A	B	C	D	E
1					
2	Year	Sum			
3	2001	5,251			
4	2002	6,452			
5	2003	7,582			
6	Total	19,285			
7					
8	Year	2001	2002	2003	
9	Sum	5,251	6,452	7,582	
10					

A8 = {=TRANSPOSE(Data)}

Formulas

6

Notes:

**My Tips/
Shortcuts:**

Related Tips:	*Tip 178: Summing Stock Lists*
	Tip 179: Summing Rounded Numbers
	Tip 185: Counting Based on Multiple Criteria

Array Formulas – the Technical Side

To perform complex calculations, use an **Array Formula**.

Example: In this example there are two ranges to multiply (each item multiplies **Quantity** by **Price**) and totals the results.

1. For Range 1, the **Name** defined for range **B2:B10** is **Quantity** (see *Tip #188*).
2. For Range 2, the **Name** defined for range **C2:C10** is **Price**.
3. In cell **D16**, enter the following **Array Formula:**

   ={SUM(Quantity*Price)}

   The formula returns the result of the totals of the **Quantity** range, multiplied by the **Price** range.

To create an **Array Formula**, select the cell after manually entering the formula, press **<F2>**, and then press **<Ctrl+Shift+Enter>**.

The technical side of an array formula

An **Array** saves values or strings to temporary memory locations. The **Array** technique opens as many cells in memory as it needs to keep the multiplied numbers; the **Array Formula** returns the total (in this example) of these numbers from the temporary memory to the cell.

	Part Number	Quantity	Price	Total	
	A	B	C	D	E
1	Part Number	Quantity	Price	Total	
2	A657	345	15.00	5,175	
3	A658	205	12.00	2,460	
4	A659	257	13.00	3,341	
5	A660	413	18.00	7,434	
6	A661	413	18.00	7,434	
7	A662	517	20.00	10,340	
8	A663	621	22.00	13,662	
9	A664	673	23.00	15,479	
10	A665	725	24.00	17,400	
11					
12	Total			82,725	
13					
14				82,725	
15					

Microsoft Excel - Book1

File Edit View Insert Format Tools Data Window Help

D14 ▼ *fx* {=SUM(Quantity*Price)}

6

Formulas

Notes:

_____

_____

_____

_____

_____

My Tips/
Shortcuts:

_____

_____

_____

_____

Related **Tips:**	*Tip 139: Problem: The Characters are in* *Reverse Order*
	Tip 203: Pasting Values

Create a Custom Function

Custom Function Example

Create a function named **SalesTax** to calculate the amount of Sales Tax (or VAT tax) included in the total amount line in an invoice.

The function has two argument boxes.

✦ **The function:**

Type the code below into a regular **Module** sheet (read more on **VBE** & a **Module** sheet in *Tip #19*).

```
Function SalesTax (Total_Invoice,
Tax_percentage) As Single

SalesTax = Total_Invoice -
Total_invoice / (1+Tax_percentage)

End Function
```

Note: The **SalesTax** macro can be downloaded from www.exceltip.com/f1toc.

The formula structure is:

❖ **Function** name = **SalesTax**
❖ The **Function** arguments are placed in parentheses; the above example has two argument boxes.
❖ The last piece of the formula, **As Single**, defines the value type of the result returned by the **Function** (a number with two decimal places in this case).
❖ The **Function** receives the results of the calculation and returns the result to the cell.

continued...

6

Notes:

**My Tips/
Shortcuts:**

Create a Custom Function (cont.)

✦ **Activating the function:**

1. Type the total invoice into cell **B2** and the tax percentage into cell **B3**.

2. Select cell **D2**, and then press **\<Shift+F3\>** to open the *Paste Function* dialog box.

3. Select the **User Defined** category, and then select the **SalesTax Function**.

4. In the first argument box, select cell **B2**, and in the second argument box, select cell **B3**.

5. Click **OK**.

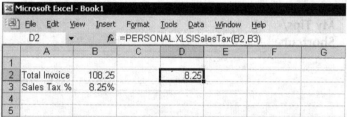

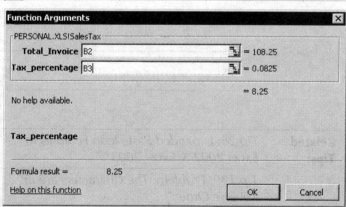

Notes:

**My Tips/
Shortcuts:**

**Related
Tips:**

*Tip 26: Expanded Paste Icon Features in
Excel 2002 & Excel 2003*

*Tip 139: Problem: The Characters are in
Reverse Order*

Pasting Values

 Using keyboard shortcuts

➤ **To paste the calculated value of a formula into a single cell (thus overwriting the formula):**
  ✦ Press **<F2>** to edit and then **<F9>** to calculate.

➤ **To paste the calculated value of a formula into a single cell under the cell containing the formula:**

  Press **<Ctrl+Shift+">**

➤ **To paste the calculated values from formulas in a range of cells, create and add a keyboard shortcut using the VBE:**
  ✦ Insert the code lines below into a regular **Module** in the **Personal Macro Workbook**, *read more from Tip #19 before adding the codes*:

```
Sub PasteValues()

' Keyboard Shortcut: Ctrl+Shift+V

    Selection.Formula = Selection.Value
End Sub
```

➤ **To paste values in a range of cells, use the *Paste Special* dialog box:**
  1. Copy a range of cells containing formulas, press **<Shift+F10>** or right-click, and then select **Paste Special** from the shortcut menu.
  2. Select **Values** and click **OK**.

continued...

6

ormulas

Notes:

**My Tips/
Shortcuts:**

Pasting Values (cont.)

➢ **To paste values using a shortcut menu:**

1. Select a range containing formulas.

2. With the mouse cursor over the selection border, drag the range while holding the right button.

3. Release the mouse button and select **Copy Here As Values Only** from the shortcut menu.

New in Excel 2002 and Excel 2003, see *Tip #26*

The **Paste** icon has been expanded, enabling some options from the *Paste Special* dialog box to be quickly accessed.

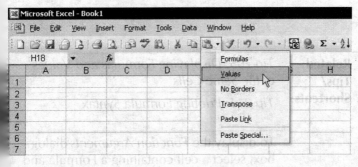

487

Notes:

**My Tips/
Shortcuts:**

| **Related
Tips/
Shortcuts:** | *Tip 205: Displaying Formulas and Values
of the Same Cells* |
| | *Tip 211: Printing Formula Syntax* |

To display the *Function Arguments* dialog
box, select a cell containing a Formula and
press **<Shift+F3>**

Displaying Formula Syntax

➤ **To display the syntax of all formulas in a sheet:**

✦ Press **<Ctrl+'>** (the **'** sign is located to the left of the number **1** on the keyboard).

OR

From the *Tools* menu, select **Options**, the **View** tab, **Formulas**, and then click **OK**.

✦ To return to the normal display, press **<Ctrl+'>** again (this keyboard shortcut is a toggle).

Normal Display

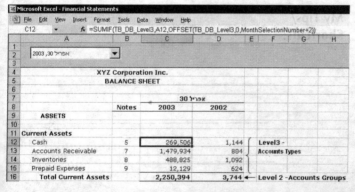

Displaying Formulas

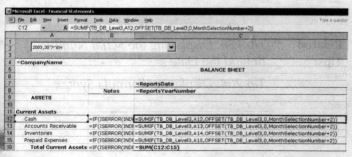

6

Notes:

**My Tips/
Shortcuts:**

**Related
Tips:**   Tip 158: Displaying the Serial Number
Behind the Date

Tip 204: Displaying Formula Syntax

Displaying Formulas and Values of the Same Cells

➤ **To display formulas and values of the same cells:**

1. From the *Window* menu, select **New Window**.

2. From the *Window* menu, select **Arrange**.

3. Select the **Horizontal** option button and click **OK**.

4. Select one of the two windows and press **<Ctrl+'>** (the key to the left of the number **1**).

To move between windows, press **<Ctrl+Tab>** or **<Ctrl+F6>**.

Formulas

Microsoft Excel

File   Edit   View   Insert   Format   Tools   Data   Window   Help

Book1:2

	A	B	C	D	E	F	G	H	I	J	K
1	Invoice Number	Date	Customer Name	Quantity	Unit Price	Income					
2	1001	01/15/2002	Intel	252	10	2,523					
3	1002	02/15/2002	eBay	4,585	10	45,852					
4	1003	03/15/2002	ExcelTip	665	10	6,652					
5	1004	04/15/2002	Toyota	185	10	1,854					
6	1005	05/15/2002	Amazon	966	10	9,658					

|◄ ◄ ► ►| \ **Sheet1** / Sheet2 / Sheet3 /

Book1:1

	B	C	D	E	F
1	Date	Customer Name	Quantity	Unit Price	Income
2	37271	Intel	252.3	10	=D2*E2
3	37302	eBay	4585.2	10	=D3*E3
4	37330	ExcelTip	665.2	10	=D4*E4
5	37361	Toyota	185.4	10	=D5*E5
6	37391	Amazon	965.8	10	=D6*E6
7	37422	GM	1255.4	10	=D7*E7
8	37452	Ford	1463.2	10	=D8*E8

6

Notes:

_____

_____

_____

_____

_____

_____

_____

**My Tips/
Shortcuts:**

_____

_____

_____

_____

_____

_____

**Related
Tips:**

Tip 10: Selecting Special Cells

*Tip 131: Applying Formatting Only to Cells
Containing Text*

_____

Selecting Cells That Contain Formulas

➤ **To select cells containing Formulas to color, delete, or protect, use the *Go To* dialog box:**

1. Press **<F5>**.

   OR

   From the *Edit* menu, select **Go To**.

2. In the *Go To* dialog box, click **Special**.

3. Select **Formulas**, and then click **OK**.

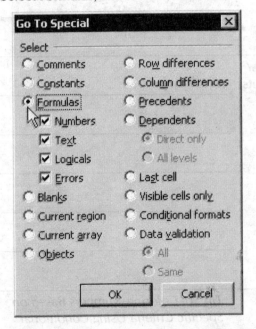

493

Notes:

_____

_____

_____

_____

_____

_____

My Tips/
Shortcuts:

_____

_____

_____

_____

_____

_____

Related
Tips:

Tip 50: Coloring Numbers Based on
Specific Criteria Using Conditional
Formatting

Tip 53: Coloring Numbers Based on
Specific Criteria

Formatting Cells Containing Formulas

➢ **To format cells containing Formulas using the *Conditional Formatting* dialog box, add a VBA Function:**

✦ **Step 1:** Add the following **VBA Function** to a regular **Module**, see *Tip #156*:

```
Function FormulaInCell(Cell) As Boolean

  FormulaInCell = Cell.HasFormula

End Function
```

✦ **Step 2:** Use the **Custom Function** to identify and format cells containing formulas:

1. Select the cells in the sheet by pressing **<Ctrl+A>**, in **Excel 2003** press **<Ctrl+A+A>** from a cell inside a region.

2. From the *Format* menu, select **Conditional Formatting**.

3. In **Condition 1**, select **Formula is** from the dropdown list.

4. In the formula box, type **=FormulaInCell(A1)**, and then click **Format**.

5. From the **Font** tab, select any desired color and click **OK** twice.

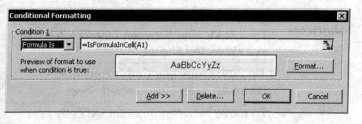

6

495

Notes:

_____

_____

_____

_____

_____

_____

My Tips/ Shortcuts:

_____

_____

_____

_____

_____

_____

Related Tips/ Shortcuts:	*Tip 10: Selecting Special Cells*
	Tip 13: Moving Between Unprotected Cells in a Protected Sheet
	Tip 209: Protecting Cells Containing Formulas in an Unprotected Sheet
	To move between unprotected cells in protected sheet, press **<Tab>**.

F
ormulas

Protecting Cells Containing Formulas in a Protected Sheet

➢ **To protect cells containing Formulas, two conditions must be met:**

✦ **The cell must be locked:**
   1. Select a cell in the sheet and press **<Ctrl+1>**.
   2. In the *Format Cells* dialog box, select the **Protection** tab.
   3. Select the **Locked** option.

✦ **The sheet must be protected:**
   1. From the Tools menu, select **Protection** and then **Protect Sheet**.
   2. Click **OK**.

Protecting cells containing Formulas, requires isolating the cells containing the Formulas from the rest of the cells in the sheet, locking them, and then protecting the sheet.

✦ **Step 1: Cancel the locked format of all the cells in the sheet:**
   1. Select all cells in the sheet by pressing **<Ctrl+A>**.
   2. Press **<Ctrl+1>**.
   3. Select the **Protection** tab, and deselect the **Locked** option.
   4. Click **OK**.

✦ **Step 2: Selecting cells containing Formulas:**
   1. Press **<F5>**.
   2. Click **Special**, and then select the **Formulas** option.
   3. Click **OK**.

continued...

6

Notes:

**My Tips/
Shortcuts:**

Protecting Cells Containing Formulas in a Protected Sheet (cont.)

✦ **Step 3: Locking cells containing Formulas:**

1. Press **<Ctrl+1>**.
2. Select the **Protection** tab, and then select the **Locked** option.
3. Click **OK**.

✦ **Step 4: Protecting the sheet:**

1. From the *Tools* menu, select **Protection**, and then **Protect Sheet**.
2. Click **OK** (a password is optional).

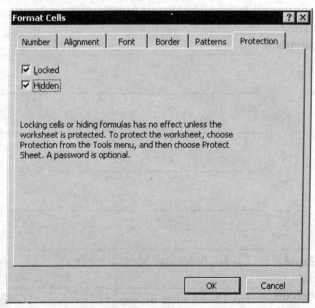

ormulas

6

499

Notes:

My Tips/
Shortcuts:

Related **Tips/** **Shortcuts:**	*Tip 10: Selecting Special Cells*
	Tip 13: Moving Between Unprotected Cells in a Protected Sheet
	To move between unprotected cells in a protected sheet, press **<Tab>**.

Protecting Cells Containing Formulas in an Unprotected Sheet

➢ **To protect cells containing Formulas in an unprotected sheet, use Validation:**

✦ **Step 1: Selecting cells containing formulas:**

1. Press **<F5>**.

2. Click **Special**, and then select the **Formulas** option.

3. Click **OK**.

✦ **Step 2: Validation:**

1. From the *Data* menu, select **Validation**.

2. Select the **Settings** tab, and select **Custom** from the **Allow** dropdown list.

3. In the **Formula** box, type **=""**, and then click **OK**.

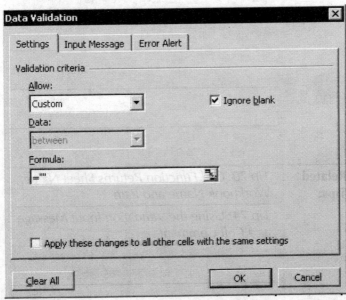

Notes:

**My Tips/
Shortcuts:**

**Related
Tips:**

*Tip 70: Cell Function Returns Sheet Name,
Workbook Name and Path*

*Tip 74: Using the Validation Input Message
as a Cell Comment*

Adding a Comment to a Formula

➢ **To add a Comment to a formula:**

1. At the end of the formula, add a **+** (plus) sign.

2. Type the letter **N**, and in parentheses, type your **Comment** in quotation marks. For example:

=CurrentAssets / CurrentLiabilities+ N("the formula calculates Current Ratio")

	A	B	C	D
2	December 31, 2003			
3				
4				
5	XYZ Corporation Inc.			
6				
7		December 31		
8	Financial Ratios	2003	2002	
9				
10	**Liquidity Ratios**			
11	Current Ratio	1.91	1.90	=Current Assets / Current Liabilities
12	Quick Ratio	1.49	1.47	=(Current Assets-Inventories) / Current Liabilities
13				
14	**Assets Management Ratios**			
15	Inventory Turnover	3.32	3.06	=Cost of Goods / Inventories
16	Asset Turnover	1.09	0.99	=Total Sales / Total Assets
17	Receivable turnover Days	156	167	=Accounts Receiveable*365 / Total Credit Sales

B11 ▾ ƒ =CurrentAssets/CurrentLiabilities+ N("the formula calculates Current Ratio")

Notes:

**My Tips/
Shortcuts:**

**Related
Tips:**

Tip 206: Selecting Cells That Contain
Formulas

Tip 208: Protecting Cells Containing
Formulas in a Protected Sheet

Printing Formula Syntax

Using keyboard shortcuts

➢ **To print the formula syntax for a range of cells:**

1. Display the formula syntax by pressing **<Ctrl+'>** (the key to the left of the number **1**).

2. Print the desired area.

Microsoft Excel - Financial Statements		Type a question
File Edit View Insert Format Tools Data Window Help		
C12 ▼ *fx* =SUMIF(TB_DB_Level3,A12,OFFSET(TB_DB_Level3,0,MonthSelectionNumber+2))		

	A	B	C
1			
2	2003, 30 אפריל	▼	
3			
4	=CompanyName		
5			BALANCE SHEET
6			
7			=ReportsDate
8		Notes	=ReportsYearNumber
9	ASSETS		
10			
11	Current Assets		
12	Cash	=IF(ISERROR(INDE	=SUMIF(TB_DB_Level3,A12,OFFSET(TB_DB_Level3,0,MonthSelectionNumber+2))
13	Accounts Receivable	=IF(ISERROR(INDE	=SUMIF(TB_DB_Level3,A13,OFFSET(TB_DB_Level3,0,MonthSelectionNumber+2))
14	Inventories	=IF(ISERROR(INDE	=SUMIF(TB_DB_Level3,A14,OFFSET(TB_DB_Level3,0,MonthSelectionNumber+2))
15	Prepaid Expenses	=IF(ISERROR(INDE	=SUMIF(TB_DB_Level3,A15,OFFSET(TB_DB_Level3,0,MonthSelectionNumber+2))
16	Total Current Assets	=IF(ISERROR(INDE	=SUM(C12:C15)

6

Related
Tips:

Tip 212: Checking Cell Information at a
Distance

Tip 213: Moving Between Precedent and
Dependent Cells

Tip 214: Circular References

Notes:

**My Tips/
Shortcuts:**

**Related
Tips:**

Tip 71: *Checking Cell Information at a
Distance*

Tip 213: *Moving Between Precedent and
Dependent Cells*

Tip 214: *Circular References*

Stepping into a Formula

The time spent evaluating complicated nested formulas can be enormous. This new, excellent technique will save time.

✦ From the *Tools* menu, select **Formula Auditing**, and then **Evaluate Formula**.

   OR

   From the **Formula Auditing** toolbar, click **Evaluate Formula**.

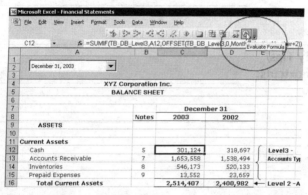

The *Evaluate Formula* dialog box allows moving between the arguments in a formula and checking the calculation result step-by-step. Click **Step In** to move between arguments.

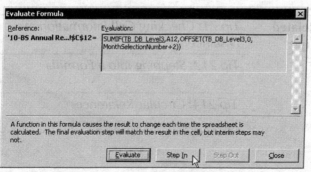

507

Notes:

_____

_____

_____

_____

_____

_____

_____

**My Tips/
Shortcuts:**

_____

_____

_____

_____

_____

_____

_____

Related Tips:	*Tip 71: Checking Cell Information at a Distance*
	Tip 212: Stepping into a Formula
	Tip 214: Circular References

Moving Between Precedent and Dependent Cells

Using keyboard shortcuts

➢ **To move to a precedent cell(s):**
  ✦ Select a cell containing a formula and press
     <Ctrl+[>.

  The **<Ctrl+[>** shortcut is one of the **most
  recommended** keyboard shortcuts, and is highly
  recommended. It can trace a precedent cell(s) in
  the active sheet, in another sheet in the workbook,
  or in a sheet in another open workbook, and it can
  open a closed workbook and select the precedent
  cell(s) after opening.

Using the mouse

✦ **Add three icons to the Standard toolbar**
  ❖ **Trace Precedents**
  ❖ **Trace Dependents**
  ❖ **Remove All Arrows**

continued...

6

Formulas

Notes:

**My Tips/
Shortcuts:**

Moving Between Precedent and Dependent Cells (cont.)

➢ **To add an icon to the toolbar:**

1. Right-click a toolbar, and then select **Customize** from the shortcut menu.

2. Select the **Commands** tab, and from **Categories**, select **Tools**.

3. Drag the three icons from the **Commands** area to the **Standard** toolbar and close the *Customize* dialog box.

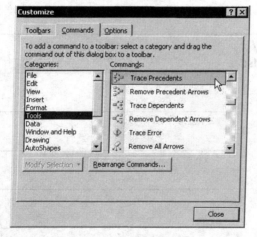

continued...

6

Notes:

**My Tips/
Shortcuts:**

Moving Between Precedent and Dependent Cells (cont.)

➤ **To use the Trace Precedents or Trace Dependents icons to move between linked cells in the same sheet:**

1. Type a number into cell **A1** and then type the formula **=A1** into cell **D1**.

2. Select cell **D1** and click **Trace Precedents**. Double-click the blue arrow between the cells to move between the precedent cell and the dependent cell.

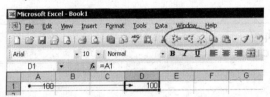

➤ **To use the Trace Precedents and Trace Dependents icons to move between linked cells outside the sheet:**

1. Insert a link formula **=[Book1.xls]Sheet1!$A$1** into cell **A1** in an open workbook.

2. Select cell **A1** in the new workbook and click **Trace Precedents**. Double-click the dotted-line arrow to open the *Go To* dialog box, select the address, and then click **OK**.

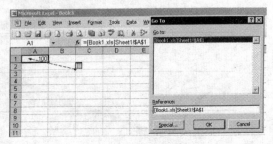

continued...

Notes:

My Tips/ Shortcuts:

Moving Between Precedent and Dependent Cells (cont.)

➢ **To move to a precedent cell:**

1. From the *Tools* menu, select **Options**.
2. Select the **Edit** tab, and deselect the **Edit directly in cell** checkbox.
3. Select a cell with a linked formula and double-click it to move to a precedent cell.

➢ **To return to the last four selected addresses:**

The *Go To* dialog box holds the last four references moved to via **Go To**.

✦ Press **<F5>** to open the *Go To* dialog box (the last step is shown in the **Reference** box). Check the address and click **OK**.

515

Notes:

_____

_____

_____

_____

_____

_____

_____

**My Tips/
Shortcuts:**

_____

_____

_____

_____

_____

_____

**Related
Tips:**

Tip 212: Stepping into a Formula

*Tip 213 Moving Between Precedent and
Dependent Cells*

_____

Circular References

How is a Circular Reference created?

A **Circular Reference** is created when a formula refers back to its own cell, either directly or indirectly.

The **Circular Reference** toolbar indicates the reference of the cell containing the circular reference. If you look at the formula or the **Status** bar (at the bottom of the sheet), you can pinpoint the source of the error and correct it.

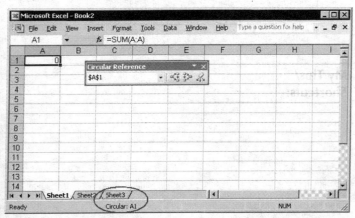

Formulas

6

Notes:

**My Tips/
Shortcuts:**

**Related
Tips:**

Tip 212: Stepping into a Formula

*Tip 213: Moving Between Precedent and
Dependent Cells*

Tip 214: Circular References

Iteration

➢ **To intentionally use a Circular Reference:**

In this example, a Value-added tax (VAT) gross-up
formula is in cell **B1** (the formula is **=B3-B2**).

1. In cell **A2**, enter the VAT percent (%) **0.20**.
2. In cell **B2**, insert the formula **=A2*B1** to calculate
   the VAT amount.
3. Click **OK** to dismiss the circular reference
   warning.
4. In cell **B3**, enter **100**. A **Circular Reference** is
   created in cell **B1**. The calculation of the amount
   without VAT is conditioned upon the calculation
   of VAT in cell **B2**.

Excel allows defining the number of iterations (that is, the
number of times the formula is calculated) performed to
resolve a circular reference.

➢ **To allow iteration and set the maximum iteration**
   numbers:

1. From the *Tools* menu, select **Options**.
2. In the **Calculation** tab, select the **Iteration**
   checkbox and click **OK**.

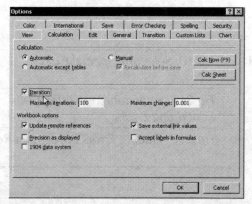

6

Notes:

**My Tips/
Shortcuts:**

Avoiding Error Displays when Formulas Return Result Calculations

➢ **To avoid errors being displayed, combine the IF formula with the ISERROR formula:**

1. In cell **A1**, type the number **100**.

2. In cell **B1**, type the formula **=A1/A2**. The calculation returns an error **#DIV/0!**, which occurs when trying to divide a number in a cell by 0 (**A2**).

3. To avoid displaying this error in a cell, in cell **C1**, enter the formula **=ISERROR(B1)**. The formula returns the result TRUE. That is, cell **B1** contains an error in the calculation of the formula (the **ISERROR** formula is located in the **Information** category in the *Paste Function* dialog box).

4. In cell **D1**, enter an **IF** formula **=IF(C1,0,B1)**.

5. Combine the formulas into one nested formula by copying the formula (without the = sign) from cell **C1**, and pasting it into cell **D1**.

6. From cell **B1**, copy the formula (without the = sign), and paste it twice.

    The result is one nested formula:
    =IF(ISERROR(A1/A2),0,A1/A2).

6

Notes:

_____

_____

_____

_____

_____

_____

**My Tips/
Shortcuts:**

_____

_____

_____

_____

_____

_____

_____

Related Tips:	*Tip 10: Selecting Special Cells*
	Tip 216: Avoiding Error Displays when Formulas Return Result Calculation
	Tip 218: Tracing Errors in Formula Results

Selecting/Formatting Cells Containing Errors

Selecting cells containing errors is important for fixing, coloring or deleting of those cells.

✦ **Option 1: Using the *Go To* dialog box:**

1. Press **<F5>**.

   OR

   From the *Edit* menu, select **Go To**.

2. In the *Go To* dialog box, click **Special**.

3. Select **Formulas**, and **Errors**, and then click **OK**.

✦ **Option 2: Using Conditional Formatting to format cells containing errors:**

1. Press **<Ctrl+A>** to select all cells in the active sheet, in **Excel 2003** press **<Ctrl+A+A>** from a cell in a region.

2. From the *Format* menu, select **Conditional Formatting**.

3. In **Condition 1**, select **Formula Is**.

4. In the formula box, type the formula **=ISERROR(A1)**.

5. Click **Format**, select the desired format, and then click **OK**.

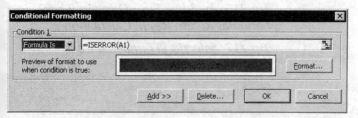

6

Notes:

**My Tips/
Shortcuts:**

**Related
Tips:**

Tip 212: Stepping into a Formula

*Tip 216: Avoiding Error Displays when
Formulas Return Result Calculation*

*Tip 217: Selection/Formatting Cells
Containing Errors*

Tracing Errors in Formula Results

➢ **To trace an error when using Excel 2002 & Excel 2003:**

1. Select cell **B1** (a cell containing an error), and click **Error Checking** (the first icon on the left of the **Auditing Formulas** toolbar).

   OR

   Use the **Smart Tag** to open the *Error Checking* dialog box.

2. Click **Options**.

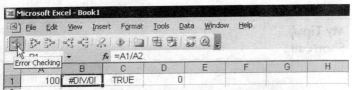

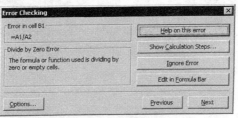

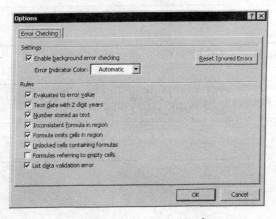

Notes:

_____

_____

_____

_____

_____

My Tips/
Shortcuts:

_____

_____

_____

_____

_____

Related
Tips:

Tip 223: Changing the Source Link

Tip 224: Finding and Deleting Unwanted and Orphaned Links

Quickly Creating Links Between Ranges

➢ **To use Paste Special to create links quickly:**

1. Copy a range of cells containing data, and select a cell in another sheet or workbook.

2. Press **<Shift+F10>** or right-click, and then select **Paste Special** from the shortcut menu.

3. Click **Paste Link**.

Paste Special ? ✕

Paste
- ⦿ **All**
- ○ Formulas
- ○ Values
- ○ Formats
- ○ Comments
- ○ Validation
- ○ All except borders
- ○ Column widths
- ○ Formulas and number formats
- ○ Values and number formats

Operation
- ⦿ None
- ○ Add
- ○ Subtract
- ○ Multiply
- ○ Divide

☐ Skip blanks   ☐ Transpose

| Paste Link | OK | Cancel |

Related   Tip 190 Defining a Range Name
Tips
         Tip 220 Quickly Creating Links Between
         Ranges

         Tip 222 Breaking Links Between
         Workbooks

527

Notes:

**My Tips/
Shortcuts:**

**Related
Tips:**

Tip 189: Deleting a Range Name

Tip 219: Quickly Creation Links Between Ranges

Tip 222: Breaking Links Between Workbooks

Unintentionally Creating Links Between Workbooks

Links are created unintentionally by moving sheets containing range defined **Names** from one workbook to another.

When moving or copying a sheet by selecting its tab (that is, by right-clicking, and then selecting **Move or Copy** from the shortcut menu), unwanted links can be created in the new workbook if the copied sheet contains **Named** ranges.

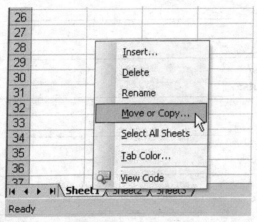

Broken links are created when the location of the precedent workbook is changed on the hard disk.

If you save a workbook that is linked to another workbook and then move or copy the linked workbook to another folder on the hard disk, the first workbook will (erroneously) refer to the original reference location.

6

Notes:

My Tips/
Shortcuts:

Related Tips:	*Tip 189: Deleting a Range Name*
	Tip 220: Unintentionally Creating Links Between Workbooks
	Tip 222: Breaking Links Between Workbooks

Canceling the Update Links Message While Opening a Linked Workbook

➤ **To cancel the Update Links message while opening a linked workbook:**

1. From the *Tools* menu, select **Options**, and then select the **Edit** tab.

2. Deselect the **Ask to update automatic links** checkbox, and then click **OK**.

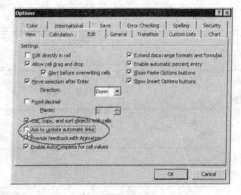

New in Excel 2002 and Excel 2003:

Choose one of three new options in the *Startup Prompt* dialog box:

✦ From the *Edit* menu, select **Links**, and then click **Startup Prompt**.

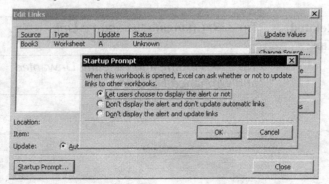

Notes:

My Tips/ Shortcuts:

Related Tips:

Tip 223: Changing the Source Link

Tip 224: Finding and Deleting Unwanted and Orphaned Links

Breaking Links Between Workbooks

➤ **To break unwanted or orphaned links between workbooks in Excel 2002 & Excel 2003:**

1. From the *Edit* menu, select **Links**.

2. In the *Edit Links* dialog box, select the **Source** workbook and click **Break Link**.

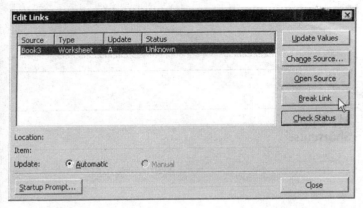

Notes:

_____

_____

_____

_____

_____

_____

**My Tips/
Shortcuts:**

_____

_____

_____

_____

_____

Related Tips:	Tip 220: Unintentionally Creating Links Between Workbooks
	Tip 222: Breaking Links Between Workbooks
	Tip 224: Finding and Deleting Unwanted and Orphaned Links

Changing the Source Link

Changing the source link allows changing the location of
the source workbook on the hard disk, or to exchange one
workbook for another.

➢ **To change the source link:**
1. From the *Edit* menu, select **Links**.
2. Select the source workbook you want to change,
   and then click **Change Source**.
3. Select the workbook that should be linked in the
   folder you have opened, and then click **OK**.

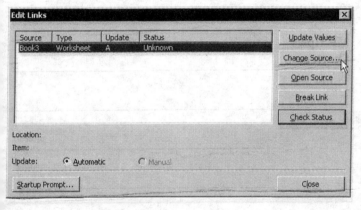

Notes:

_____

_____

_____

_____

_____

**My Tips/
Shortcuts:**

_____

_____

_____

_____

_____

_____

**Related
Tips:**

*Tip 220: Unintentionally Creating Links
Between Workbooks*

*Tip 222: Breaking Links Between
Workbooks*

Tip 223: Changing the Source Link

Finding and Deleting Unwanted and Orphaned Links

➢ **To find unwanted links created by range Names:**

1. Select a cell in the sheet.
2. Press **<F3>**, and click **Paste List**.
3. Check the list, and identify any defined **Names** you want to delete.
4. Press **<Ctrl+F3>**.
5. Select each **Name**, and click **Delete** (you cannot delete all of them at once).

➢ **To find unwanted links:**

1. Press **<Ctrl+F>**.
2. In the **Find** box, type a **[** (every externally linked formula has a square bracket).
3. Start the search, and delete any unwanted formulas (carefully!).

➢ **To check the *Edit Links* dialog box:**

1. From the *Edit* menu, select **Links**.
2. Select the source workbook whose links you want to delete, and then click **Change Source**.
3. In the folder, select the workbook you are currently working in (that is, link the workbook to itself), and click **OK**.

➢ **To save the workbook under a new name:**

If cells are having links to a non-existing workbook that is not shown in the *Edit Links* dialog box, there is a solution.

1. Save the workbook containing the links, using the name of the workbook to which it is linked. The links are automatically deleted (the new workbook is linked to itself).
2. Save the workbook again while renaming it.

Notes:

_____

_____

_____

_____

_____

_____

_____

My Tips/
Shortcuts:

_____

_____

_____

_____

_____

_____

Related
Tips:

Tip 226: Vlookup Formula - Eliminating
Errors

Tip 227: Index Formula Vs. Vlookup
Formula

Tip 228: Adding a Combo Box

Vlookup Formula – Organizing the Data Table

Rules for organizing the data table for proper use of the **Vlookup** formula:

✦ The **Vlookup** formula searches for the lookup criteria in the leftmost column of the data table. It is recommended that the whole sheet be used as the data table, so that **Vlookup** will automatically look at column **A** as the leftmost column.

✦ Defining a **Name** for the sheet (to use it as the **Table_array** (the second argument in the **Vlookup** formula) will eliminate the need of updating the range reference in any **Vlookup** formula.

➢ **To define a Name for the sheet:**

1. Select a cell, and click **Select All** (the button at the top-left corner of the intersection between rows and columns).

   OR

   Press **<Ctrl+A>**. (In **Excel 2003**, press **<Ctrl+A+A>** when selecting a cell in a region.)

2. Press **<Ctrl+F3>**, and in the **Names in workbook** box, type the **Name** for the data table.

3. Click **OK**.

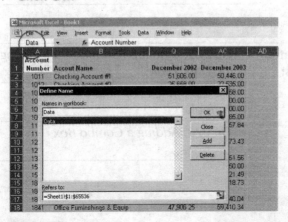

Notes:

**My Tips/
Shortcuts:**

Vlookup Formula – Eliminating Errors

➢ **To eliminate errors that occur when using the Vlookup Formula:**

✦ In the screenshot below are four **Vlookup** Formulas. In this example, we asume that the index number **1115** is not included in the index list in the leftmost column of the data table, the index number **1121** is included and the defined **Name** for the data table is **Data**:

❖ Cell **C2**: The fourth argument of the **Vlookup** Formula is empty, therefore, the formula returns a result according to a number equal to or less than the lookup number from the index list.

❖ Cell **C4**: In the fourth argument of the **Vlookup** Formula = **FALSE**, therefore, the formula returns errors when the lookup value is not included in the index list, which is the leftmost column of the data table.

❖ Cell **C6**: The **ISERROR** formula, nested in the **IF** formula, returns **TRUE** when **Vlookup** Formula returns an error, and therefore, the final result is **0**.

❖ Cell **C8**: The **ISERROR** formula nested in the **IF** formula returns **FALSE** and the **Vlookup** formula returns the appropriate result number.

Microsoft Excel - Book1

C6 = =IF(ISERROR(VLOOKUP(B6,Data,2,FALSE)),0,VLOOKUP(B6,Data,2,FALSE))

	A	B	C	D
1				
2	1	1115	Accounts Receivable	=VLOOKUP(B2,Data,2)
3				
4	2	1115	#N/A	=VLOOKUP(B3,Data,2,FALSE)
5				
6	3	1115	0	=IF(ISERROR(VLOOKUP(B6,Data,2,FALSE)),0,VLOOKUP(B6,Data,2,FALSE))
7				
8	4	1121	Allowance for doubtful accounts	=IF(ISERROR(VLOOKUP(B8,Data,2)),0,VLOOKUP(B8,Data,2,FALSE))
9				

L
ookup Formulas & Power Techniques

6

Notes:

**My Tips/
Shortcuts:**

Index Formula vs. Vlookup Formula

What are the advantages of using the Index Formula instead of Vlookup Formula?

✦ **How the Index formula calculates and returns results:**

The **Index** formula returns a value from the intersection between the row number and the column number in an **Array**. For example, in the screenshot below, the amount of **Petty Cash** for **December 2003** is **585**, which is the intersection cell of row **7** and column **29**.

The **Index** formula syntax is: **=Index(Data, 7, 29)**, where **Data** is the defined **Name** for the sheet (see *Tip #225*).

	Microsoft Excel - Book1			
	File Edit View Insert Format Tools Data Window Help			
	1	**2**	**17**	**29**
1	Account Number	Accout Name	December 2002	December 2003
2	1011	Checking Account #1	51,606.00	50,446.00
3	1012	Checking Account #2	25,658.00	22,535.00
4	1021	Payroll Checking Account	15,998.00	17,558.00
5	1051	Savings Account #1	150,000.00	160,000.00
6	1061	Money Market Account #1	75,000.00	50,000.00
7	1091	Petty Cash	435.00	585.00
8	1111	Accounts Receivable	1,538,493.60	1,653,557.84
9	1121	Allowance for doubtful accounts		
10	1201	Inventories for sale	520,133.25	546,173.43

✦ **How the Vlookup formula calculates and returns results:**

The **Vlookup** formula returns a value from the intersection between the found lookup value in the leftmost column and a column index number in the **Table Array**. For example, in the screenshot above, the **Account Number** (column A) for **Petty Cash** is **1091**, the column number for **December 2003** is **29**, and the amount for **Account Number 1091** and **December 2003** is **585**.

The **Vlookup** formula syntax is: **=Vlookup(1091, Data, 29)**.

continued...

Lookup Formulas & Power Techniques

6

Notes:

_____

_____

_____

_____

_____

_____

My Tips/
Shortcuts:

_____

_____

_____

_____

_____

_____

_____

_____

Index Formula vs. Vlookup Formula (cont.)

✦ **So, which one is better to use?**

The **main difference** between the two formulas is that when using **Index**, there is no need to organize the data table into a special format — you simply find the intersection between a row and a column. When using **Vlookup**, though, you always need to move the lookup column to the left side of the data table.

✦ **Use the Match formula to find the row, column and index column number when using both Vlookup & Index formulas**

The **Match** formula returns the cell number where the value is found in a horizontal or vertical range. For example, look at row **3** in the screenshot below. **December 2003** is in cell number **29** in row **1** (the **Name** defined for the list is **Row1**), see the screenshot on the previous page.

In row **7** in the screenshot below, two **Match** formulas are nested in an **Index** formula. The first calculates the row number where the text **Petty Cash** is found (row **7**) and the next one calculates the column number for **December 2003** (number **29**).

	A	B	C	D
1	Formula	Lookup Value	Result	Formula Syntax
2				
3	Match	December 2003	29	=MATCH(B3,Row1,0)
4				
5	Vlooup & Match	1091	585	=VLOOKUP(B5,Data,MATCH(B3,Row1,0),FALSE)
6				
7	Index & Match	Petty Cash	585	=INDEX(Data,MATCH(B7,Accout_Name,0),MATCH(B3,Row1,0))
8				

C7 ▼ _fx_ =INDEX(Data,MATCH(B7,Accout_Name,0),MATCH(B3,Row1,0))

6

Notes:

**My Tips/
Shortcuts:**

Related Tips:	Tip 225: Vlookup Formula - Organizing the Data Table
	Tip 227: Index Formula Vs. Vlookup Formula
	Tip 229: The Power Combination

Adding a Combo Box

✦ **Step 1: Defining two Names to be used in a Combo Box:**

1. Add a list of months to a new sheet, select cell **A2**, and then press **<Ctrl+Shift+Down Arrow>** to select the list.

2. Press **<Ctrl+F3>** and define the **Name MonthsList**.

3. Select cell **B2**, press **<Ctrl+F3>** and define the **Name MonthSelectionNumber**.

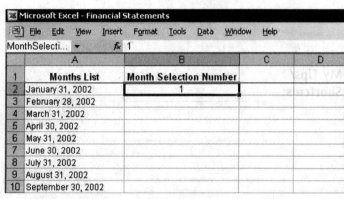

✦ **Step 2: Adding a Combo Box:**

1. In the sheet where the report is being created, place the mouse arrow over any toolbar, right-click, and then select **Forms** from the shortcut menu.

2. Click the **Combo Box** [Combo Box] icon. The cursor changes into a cross.

3. Select a cell in the sheet, and draw the shape of the **Combo Box**. When you are finished, a **Combo Box** appears.

continued...

Notes:

My Tips/ Shortcuts:

Adding a Combo Box (cont.)

4. Select the **Combo Box** you just created and make sure you are in edit mode (see the small circles in the screenshot below).

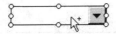

5. Right-click, and select **Format Control** from the shortcut menu.

6. Select the **Control** tab.

7. In the **Input Range** box, type the previously defined **Name, MonthsList**.

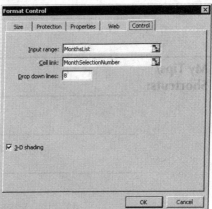

8. In the **Cell Link** box, type the defined **Name, MonthSelectionNumber**.

9. Select the **3-D shading** checkbox, and click **OK**.

	A	B	C	D
1				
2	December 31, 2003 ▼			
3				
4	XYZ Corporation Inc.			
5	BALANCE SHEET			
6				
7			December 31	
8		Notes	2003	2002
9	ASSETS			
10				
11	Current Assets			
12	Cash	5	301,124	318,697
13	Accounts Receivable	7	1,653,558	1,538,494
14	Inventories	8	546,173	520,133
15	Prepaid Expenses	9	13,552	23,659
16	Total Current Assets		2,514,407	2,400,982

Lookup Formulas & Power Techniques

Notes:

**My Tips/
Shortcuts:**

The Power Combination

Combining the **SUMIF** and **OFFSET** formulas, a **Validation** list and a **Combo Box** to return a summary from data to be selected by month — **truly a power combination!**

✦ **Step 1: Selecting items from Validation lists**

Selecting an item from a **Validation** list (column **A** in the screenshot) enables formulas entered into cells in columns **C** and **D** to identify the text and return the summary results from a column that contains the criteria (the chosen item) for the month selected in the **Combo Box**.

continued...

Notes:

**My Tips/
Shortcuts:**

The Power Combination (cont.)

➤ **To add a Validation list to a range of cells:**

1. Select the range of cells (in the screenshot on the previous page, the selected cells are **A12:A15**)

2. Select cells **A19:A23**.

3. From the *Data* menu, select **Validation**.

4. In the *Data Validation* dialog box, select the **Settings** tab, and the select **List** from the **Allow** box.

5. In the **Source** box, press **<F3>**, select the **Name** defined for the list (**Level3** in this example, see the screenshot on the last page for this tip), and click **OK**.

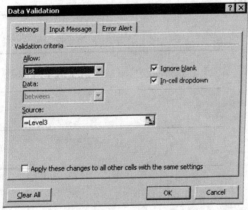

continued...

Notes:

_____

_____

_____

_____

_____

**My Tips/
Shortcuts:**

_____

_____

_____

_____

_____

_____

_____

_____

_____

The Power Combination (cont.)

✦ **Step 2: Entering formulas that return summary balances for chosen items**

The formula in cells **C12:C15** is:

=SUMIF(DataLevel3,A12,OFFSET(DataLevel3,0,MonthSelectionNumber+2))

The formula in cells **D12:D15** is:

=SUMIF(DataLevel3,A12,OFFSET(DataLevel3,0,MonthSelectionNumber+2-12))

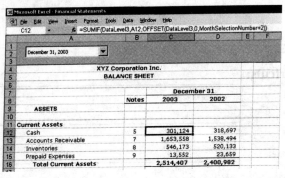

continued...

Lookup Formulas & Power Techniques

6

Notes:

**My Tips/
Shortcuts:**

The Power Combination (cont.)

Explanation:

The **SUMIF** formula in column **C** summarizes the balance amounts from the **December 2003** column; the **SUMIF** formula in column **D** summarizes the balance amounts from the **December 2002** column.

The **SUMIF** formula has three arguments:

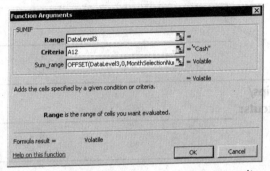

✦ **First argument:** The range to evaluate according to the criteria entered in the second argument of the **SUMIF** formula. In this example, the range is **DataLevel3**, which is the **Name** defined for column **C** in the **Balance Sheet** database. It contains **Level3** items of the **Balance Sheet**, such as **Cash**, **Accounts Receivable**, **Inventories**, and so on.

✦ **Second argument:** The criterion is the item chosen from the **Validation** list **Level3**.

continued...

Notes:

_____

_____

_____

_____

_____

_____

_____

**My Tips/
Shortcuts:**

_____

_____

_____

_____

_____

_____

_____

_____

_____

_____

The Power Combination (cont.)

✦ **Third argument:** The column from which the data will be summarized. This will be chosen according to the **OFFSET** formula for the month column, which is adjusted by the number selected from the **MonthsList** in the **Combo Box**. The **OFFSET** formula enables the selected month to be diverted from the base column (column **C** in the screenshot below).

✦ **How the OFFSET formula operates**

Column **29** is the column number for **December 2003** and the column number for **December 2002** is **17**, which is 12 columns before (see the screenshot below).

➢ **How to change the heading titles in a sheet from characters to numbers:**

1. From the *Tools* menu, select **Options**.

2. In the **General** tab, and check **R1C1 reference style**.

continued...

Notes:

_____

_____

_____

_____

_____

_____

_____

My Tips/
Shortcuts:

_____

_____

_____

_____

_____

_____

_____

The Power Combination (cont.)

When **December 2003** is selected from the **Combo Box** dropdown list (**Months List**), the month number in that list is **24** (this is calculated by determining the number of months between January 2002 to December 2003: 2 years * 12 months = 24). The linked cell to the **Combo Box** receives the value of **24**.

In the data sheet, column **3** is the base column that the **SUMIF** formula evaluates for the criteria in the second argument of the **SUMIF** formula. In this case, **December 2003** is distanced from column **C** by 24+ 2 = 26 (2= Column **D** & Column **E**).

In the third argument, the **Sum_range** should be 26 columns distant from the base column. The **OFFSET** formula returns the result of **26** and causes the **SUMIF** formula to summarize the figures from the **December 2003** column.

This Tip is taken from the Financial Statements.xls book.

Printing

Mailing

Part 7 — Printing & Mailing

Notes:

_____

_____

_____

_____

_____

_____

My Tips/ Shortcuts:

_____

_____

_____

_____

_____

_____

Related Tips/ Shortcuts:	*Tip 97: Using the Empty Space in The Menu Bar by Adding Useful Icons*
	Tip 98: Adding and Saving a New Customized Toolbar
	To display the *Print* dialog box, press **<Ctrl+P>**.

Adding the Page Setup Icon to the Excel Menu Bar

➢ **To add the Page Setup icon to the Excel Menu bar:**

1. Right-click one of the toolbars, and then select **Customize** from the shortcut menu.

2. In the *Commands* dialog box, select **File** from **Category**.

3. From **Commands**, drag the **Page Setup** icon onto the menu bar.

Using keyboard shortcuts

A new keyboard shortcut has been created:

After the **Page Setup** icon has been added to the Menu bar, press the **<Alt+u>** shortcut keyboard to open it.

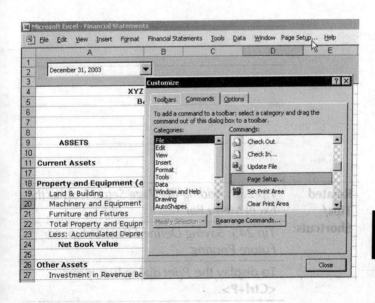

Notes:

My Tips/
Shortcuts:

Related Tips/ Shortcuts:	*Tip 230: Adding the Page Setup Icon to the Excel Menu Bar*
	Tip 245: Saving Defined Page Setups for Future Printing
	To display the *Print* dialog box, press **<Ctrl+P>**.

Copying the Page Setup to Other Sheets

➤ **To copy the page setup to other sheets in the workbook:**

1. Select the sheet whose print settings you want to copy.

2. To group the sheets in the workbook you want to copy the page setup, see *Tip #105, Grouping/Ungrouping Sheets*.

3. From the *File* menu, select **Page Setup**, and then click **OK**. The page settings from the sheet selected in step 1 are copied to all of the selected sheets.

4. To ungroup the sheets, hold the **<Shift>** key and click the active sheet tab or select the active sheet's tab, right-click and select **Ungroup Sheets** from the shortcut menu.

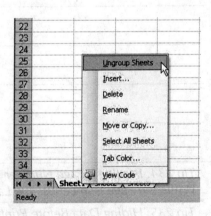

Notes:

My Tips/ Shortcuts:

Related Tips: *Tip 234: Printing a Page Number in Portrait While the Page Is in Landscape Layouts*

Tip 235: Hiding Data Before Printing

Tip 237: Printing Non-Continuous Areas

Removing All Page Breaks from the Sheet

➤ **To remove all page breaks from a sheet:**

1. Select all cells in the sheet by pressing **<Ctrl+A>**.
   In **Excel 2003**, press **<Ctrl+A+A>** from a cell in
   the **Current Region/List**.

   OR

   Click **Select All** at the corner of the sheet's
   headings.

2. From the *Insert* menu, select **Reset All Page
   Breaks**.

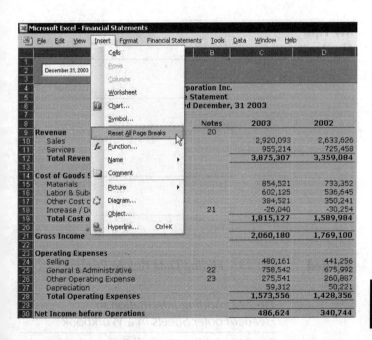

Notes:

_____

_____

_____

_____

_____

_____

**My Tips/
Shortcuts:**

_____

_____

_____

_____

_____

_____

**Related
Tips:**

Tip 235: Hiding Data Before Printing

Tip 242: Adding Information to Header/Footer Sheets in a Workbook

Tip 243: Adding the Full Path of the Saved File to the Header/Footer

Inserting a Watermark Behind the Text

➢ **To insert the text "Confidential" behind the data in a Financial Statements report:**

1. Select one of the toolbars, right-click, and select the **WordArt** toolbar from the shortcut.

2. On the **WordArt** toolbar, click the **Insert WordArt** icon.

3. From the **WordArt Gallery**, select any example, and then click **OK**.

4. In the *WordArt Edit Text* dialog box, type **Confidential**, select the font and size, and then click **OK**.

5. Right-click the WordArt, select **Format WordArt** from the shortcut menu, and then select the **Colors** and **Lines** tab.

6. In **Fill**, select **No Fill** from the **Color** dropdown list.

7. In **Line**, select a color that is not too light from the **Color** dropdown list, and then click **OK**.

8. Right-click, select **Order** from the shortcut menu, and then **Send to Back**.

9. Adjust the object's size and location to suit the sheet.

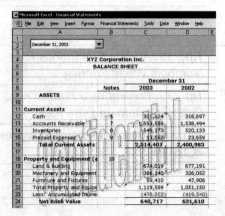

Notes:

**My Tips/
Shortcuts:**

**Related
Tips/
Shortcuts:**

Tip 238: Adding Continuous Page
Numbers While Printing

Tip 239: Preventing a Printed Area from
Extending onto an Extra Page

To display the *Print* dialog box press
<Ctrl+P>.

Printing a Page Number in Portrait While the Page Is in Landscape Layout

Problem:

Assume that one of the pages in a report is set up in landscape layout, while all the other pages are in portrait layout.

When all the pages are combined into a single report, the page number that should be at the bottom of the landscape page will not be printed at the bottom, but at the right side (the footer of a page printed in landscape layout).

Solution:

Print the page number from a cell in the sheet, not from the **Header/Footer** in **Page Setup**.

Example: The **Income Statement** (see the screenshot at the end of this tip) has many columns, and is printed in landscape layout while all other pages are printed in portrait mode.

➢ **To print the page number from a cell in the sheet:**

1. Select column **A** (see the screenshot at the end of this tip).

2. Right-click, and select **Insert** from the shortcut menu.

3. In cell **A3**, type the number of the page in the report (in this example, **5**).

4. Select the range **A3:A26**, and press **<Ctrl+1>** to format the cells, and then select the **Alignment** tab.

continued...

Notes:

**My Tips/
Shortcuts:**

Printing a Page Number in Portrait While the Page Is in Landscape Layout (cont.)

5. In **Text Alignment**, select **Left** from the **Horizontal** dropdown list (in **Excel 97**, select **Right**), and **Center** from the **Vertical** dropdown list.

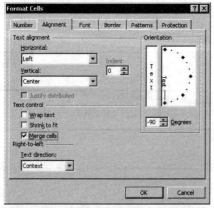

6. In **Text Control**, check **Merge cells**.
7. In **Orientation**, change the text orientation to -90 degrees (if the sheet direction is right to left, text orientation should be +90 degrees), and then click **OK**.

➢ **To update the print area:**

1. From the *File* menu, select **Page Setup**.
2. Select the **Sheet** tab.
3. In **Print Area**, change **B3** to **A3**. The new print area is now **A3:J26** (that is, the print area includes the new column).
4. Select the **Margins** tab, and reduce the right margin to **0** (so that the page number will appear at the bottom of the printed page).
5. Select the **Header/Footer** tab, and then select **Custom** footer.

continued...

Notes:

**My Tips/
Shortcuts:**

Printing a Page Number in Portrait While the Page Is in Landscape Layout (cont.)

6. Delete **Page** (if it appears in one of the sections), and then click **OK**. The page number, **5**, is displayed horizontally and centered in Column **A**.

	December 2003		YTD				Previous Year		
	XYZ Inc.								
	Income Statement for December 2003								
			Month	%	YTD	%	Month	%	$	%
	Income									
	Sales		252,121	94.26%	995,251	99.05%	214,958	94.26%	880,996	99.05%
	Interest		10,220	3.82%	9,552	0.95%	8,709	3.82%	8,455	0.95%
	Total Income		267,466	100.00%	1,004,803	100.00%	227,935	100.00%	889,452	100.00%
	Cost of goods sold		125,652	46.98%	622,531	61.96%	107,081	46.98%	551,064	61.96%
	Gross income		141,814	53.02%	382,272	38.04%	120,854	53.02%	338,387	38.04%
	General & Administrative		38,521	14.40%	199,856	19.89%	32,828	14.40%	176,913	19.89%
	Selling		25,854	9.67%	98,541	9.81%	22,033	9.67%	87,228	9.81%
	Total		64,375	24.07%	298,397	29.70%	54,860	24.07%	264,141	29.70%
	Net Earnings		77,439	28.95%	83,875	8.35%	65,994	28.95%	74,246	8.35%
	Interest Exp.		5,621	2.10%	5,332	0.53%	4,790	2.10%	4,720	0.53%
	Net before income taxes		71,818	26.85%	78,543	7.82%	61,203	26.85%	69,526	7.82%
	Income taxes		25,854	9.67%	35,652	3.55%	22,033	9.67%	31,559	3.55%
	Net Earnings		45,964	17.18%	42,891	4.27%	39,170	17.18%	37,967	4.27%

Notes:

**My Tips/
Shortcuts:**

**Related
Tips:**

Tip 236: Preventing the Printing of Objects

*Tip 240: Hiding Errors in Cells Before
Printing*

*Tip 241: Adding a Picture to a
Header/Footer*

Hiding Data Before Printing

➢ **To hide data before printing, use one of the following techniques:**

✦ **Hiding a column(s) and/or row(s):**

To hide a column(s), select it and press **<Ctrl+0>**; to hide a row(s, select it and press **<Ctrl+9>**. (To select a row(s) or column(s), see *Tip #11*.)

✦ **To hide data within the cells:**

Change the font color to white.

✦ **To hide numbers:**

Use Custom Formatting, for example, to eliminate the display of negative figures, use "**#,##0 ; ;** " for the format (see *Tip #58* for the symbols used in Custom Formatting).

✦ **To hide areas:**

Adding a white text box with clear borders from the **Drawing** toolbar.

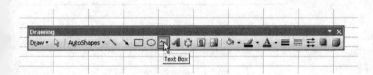

Notes:

<hr>

**My Tips/
Shortcuts:**

<hr>

Preventing the Printing of Objects

➢ **To prevent objects from being printed:**

   ✦ **Technique 1:**
   1. From the *File* menu, select **Page Setup**.
   2. Select the **Sheet** tab.
   3. In **Print**, select the **Draft quality** checkbox, and then click **OK**.

   ✦ **Technique 2:**
   1. Right-click the object, and select **Format Control**.
   2. Select the **Properties** tab.
   3. Deselect the **Print object** checkbox, and then click **OK**.

   ✦ **Technique 3:**

Objects make printing slower, so you may want to temporarily hide them before printing.

1. Press **<Ctrl+6+6>** to hide objects in the sheets.
2. After printing, press **<Ctrl+6>** to unhide the objects in the sheet.

Notes:

_____

_____

_____

_____

_____

_____

_____

My Tips/
Shortcuts:

_____

_____

_____

_____

_____

_____

_____

Related Tips:	*Tip 231: Copying the Page Setup to Other Sheets*
	Tip 232: Removing All Page Breaks from the Sheet
	Tip 239: Preventing a Printed Area from Extending onto an Extra Page

Printing Non-Continuous Areas

> **To set non-continuous areas and add them all to the Print area:**

1. Select a range of cells.

2. Press **<Ctrl>** and select another area. Repeat this as many times as you need.

3. Click the **Print Area** icon (if the icon is displayed in the **Standard** toolbar).

   OR

   From the *File* menu, select **Print Area**, and then **Set Print Area**.

   Each area within the print area will be printed on a separate page.

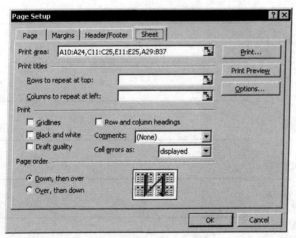

continued...

Notes:

**My Tips/
Shortcuts:**

Printing Non-Continuous Areas (cont.)

➤ **To combine non-continuous ranges into a single range in Excel 2000, Excel 2002 and Excel 2003:**

1. Copy each range (in **Excel 2000**, the **Clipboard** can hold up to 12 different copied areas).

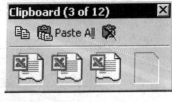

2. In **Excel 2000**, press **<Ctrl+C+C>** to display the **Clipboard**; in **Excel 2002** & **Excel 2003**, press **<Ctrl+C+C>** to open the **Clipboard Task Pane**.

3. Select the **Paste All** icon and paste all copied ranges into one single range.

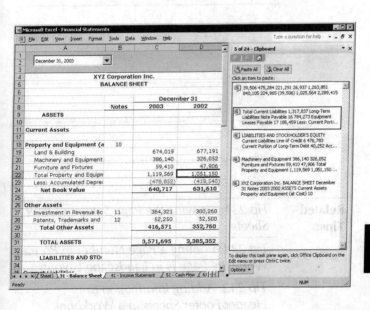

585

Notes:

**My Tips/
Shortcuts:**

Related Tips:	*Tip 231: Copying the Page Setup to Other Sheets*
	Tip 234: Printing a Page Number in Portrait While the Page Is in Landscape Layouts
	Tip 242: Adding Information to Header/Footer Sheets in a Workbook

Adding Continuous Page Numbers While Printing

Excel offers a number of options for printing continuous page numbers.

◆ When printing from one sheet, enter a number in the **First page number** box in the **Page** tab of that sheet's *Page Setup* dialog box.

◆ When printing a report from a few sheets, manually enter a page number in the **Custom Footer** in the **Header/Footer** tab of each sheet's *Page Setup* dialog box.

◆ Enter the page number into a cell when printing a page in landscape layout while the page number is in portrait layout (see *Tip #234*).

◆ Use the automatic option for continuous numbers when using **Report Manager** (see *Tip #248*).

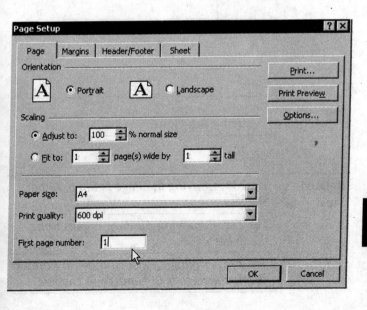

587

Notes:

**My Tips/
Shortcuts:**

Preventing a Printed Area from Extending onto an Extra Page

A common problem that occurs while printing is when a small area wraps onto an extra page. For example, if you select a print area that includes columns **A** to **F**, columns **A** to **E** may be on one page, while column **F** is printed on an extra page.

➢ **To force the last column(s) to be within the printed area:**
1. From the *File* menu, select **Page Setup**.
2. Select the **Page** tab.
3. In **Scaling**, select the **Fit to** option button, and set the area to be **1** page wide by **blank** page tall (that is, leave the **tall** input box blank).

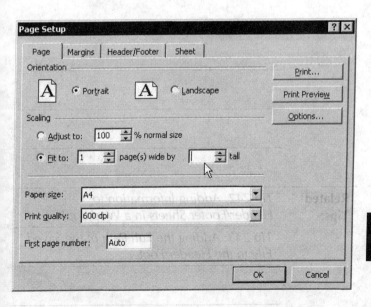

Notes:

**My Tips/
Shortcuts:**

Related Tips:	*Tip 242: Adding Information to Header/Footer Sheets in a Workbook*
	Tip 243: Adding the Full Path of the Saved File to the Header/Footer

Hiding Errors in Cells Before Printing

➢ **To hide errors in cells before printing in Excel 97 and Excel 2000:**
1. Select the **Print Area** in the Sheet, and from the *Format* menu, select **Conditional Formatting**.
2. In **Condition1**, select **Formula Is**.
3. In the **Formula** box, type **=ISERROR(A1)** (assuming the print area starts at cell **A1**).
4. Click **Format** and select the **Font** tab.
5. In **Color**, select white and click **OK**.
6. In the *Conditional Formatting* dialog box, click **OK**.

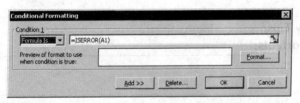

➢ **To hide errors in cells before printing in Excel 2002 and Excel 2003:**
1. From the *File* menu, select **Page Setup**.
2. Select the **Sheet** tab.
3. From **Cell errors as**, select **<blank>**, and then click **OK**.

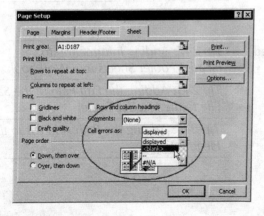

591

Notes:

My Tips/ Shortcuts:

Adding a Picture to a Header/Footer

> **To add a picture (such as a company logo) to the header/footer in Excel 97 and Excel 2000:**

1. Select cell **A1**.
2. From the *Insert* menu, select **Picture**, and then select **From File**.
3. Select the picture you want, and click **Insert**.
4. Adjust the picture to the height and width of the row.
5. From the *File* menu, select **Page Setup**.
6. Select the **Sheet** tab.
7. Select **Rows to repeat at top**.
8. Select row **1**, and then click **OK**.
9. To copy **Page Setup** parameters to other sheets in the workbook read *Tip #231*.

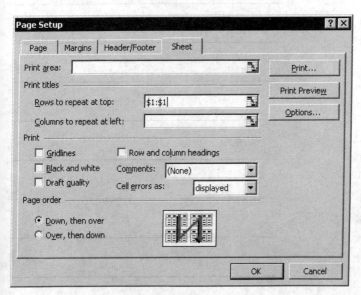

continued...

Notes:

_____

_____

_____

_____

_____

_____

**My Tips/
Shortcuts:**

_____

_____

_____

_____

_____

_____

_____

_____

_____

_____

Adding a Picture to a Header/Footer (cont.)

➤ **To add a picture (such as a company logo) to the header/footer in Excel 2002 and Excel 2003:**

1. From the *File* menu, select **Page Setup**.
2. Select the **Header/Footer** tab.
3. Select **Custom Footer**.
4. Select **Left section**.
5. Click the **Picture** icon (the second icon from the right).
6. In the *Insert Picture* dialog box, search for and select the logo or picture you want to add.
7. To format the picture, click the **Format Picture** icon (the first icon from the right).
8. Click **OK**.

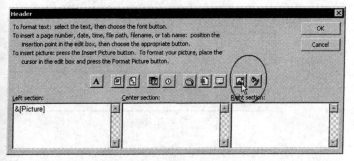

Notes:

**My Tips/
Shortcuts:**

| **Related
Tips:** | *Tip 241: Adding a Picture to a
Header/Footer* |
| --- | --- |
| | *Tip 243: Adding the Full Path of the Saved
File to the Header/Footer* |

Adding Information to Header/Footer Sheets in a Workbook

➢ **To add information such as workbook name, sheet name, printing date and time (and in Excel 2002 and Excel 2003, the path address):**

1. From the *View* menu, select **Header/Footer**.
2. Select the **Header/Footer** tab.
3. Select **Custom Footer**.
4. Select **Left section**.
5. Click the **Tab**, **File**, **Path**, **Time**, and **Date** icons (the **Path** icon is new in **Excel 2002** and **Excel 2003**, see *Tips #243 & 244*), and then click **OK**.
6. To copy the **Page Setup** to selection sheets in the workbook, see *Tip #231, Copying the Page Setup to Other Sheets.*

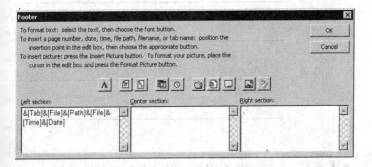

Notes:

_____

_____

_____

_____

_____

_____

_____

_____

**My Tips/
Shortcuts:**

_____

_____

_____

_____

_____

_____

_____

Related Tips:	*Tip 70: Cell Function Returns Sheet Name, Workbook Name and Path*
	Tip 117: Displaying the Workbook's Path in the Address Box
	Tip 118: Adding the Path of a Saved Workbook to the Title Bar

Adding the Full Path of the Saved File to the Header/Footer

> ### To add the path to a header or footer with Excel 2002 and Excel 2003:

1. From the *File* menu, select **Page Setup**.
2. Select the **Header/Footer** tab.
3. Select **Custom Footer**.
4. Select **Left section**.
5. Click the **Path** icon, and then click **OK**.

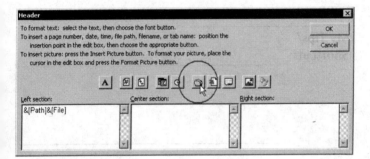

Notes:

My Tips/ Shortcuts:

Related Tips:

Tip 97: Using the Empty Space in The Menu Bar by Adding Useful Icons

Tip 117: Displaying the Workbook's Path in the Address Box

Tip 118: Adding the Path of a Saved Workbook to the Title Bar

Adding the Path Address to the Header/Footer

To add the **Path** to a header or footer while printing when
using **Excel 97** & **Excel 2000**, add an **Event** (macro code
lines) that will automatically cause information, including
the **Path**, to appear on each sheet you print from the
workbook.

➤ **To add the path to a header or footer:**

1. Open the **VBE** (Visual Basic Editor) by pressing
   <Alt+F11>.

2. In the **Project Explorer**, double-click the
   ThisWorkbook Module.

3. From the **Object** dropdown list, select **Workbook**,
   and from the **Procedure** dropdown list, select
   BeforePrint (these two dropdown lists are at the
   top of the **Module** sheet).

4. In the **Event** procedure, between the automatically
   generated opening and closing statements, type
   the following code:

   ```
   ActiveSheet.PageSetup.LeftFooter="&A
   &F&T&D" & ActiveWorkbook.Path
   ```

   The letters **A**, **F**, **T**, **D** are the sheet name,
   workbook name, time, and date, respectively.

   When using **Excel 2002** and **Excel 2003**, the line
   of code will be shorter (Z is for the path address):

   ```
   LeftFooter="&A&F&T&D"&Z"
   ```

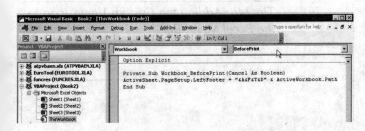

7

Notes:

**My Tips/
Shortcuts:**

Related Tips:	*Tip 231: Copying the Page Setup to Other Sheets*
	Tip 246: Adding the Custom Views Icon to the Excel Menu Bar

Saving Defined Page Setups for Future Printing

Custom Views allow saving a set of print options that are unique for each print area in the sheet, as well as creating a menu of views that lets you print any page at any time without redefining the **Page Setup** options for the page.

➢ **To add a new Custom View:**

1. Before defining the print area, hide the rows and columns you do not want to print.

2. Set the **Page Setup** options for the page to be printed.

3. Add a new **Custom View** by typing the **Custom View** name into the **Custom View** icon box (see *Tip #246*).

   OR

   From the *View* menu, select **Custom Views**.

4. Click **Add**.

5. In the *Add View* dialog box, type the name of the view in the **Name** box, and then click **OK**.

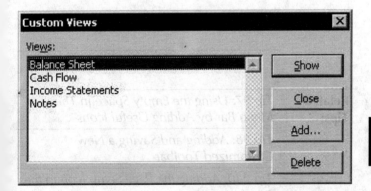

Notes:

My Tips/
Shortcuts:

Related Tips:	*Tip 97: Using the Empty Space in The Menu Bar by Adding Useful Icons*
	Tip 98: Adding and Saving a New Customized Toolbar
	Tip 230: Adding the Page Setup Icon to the Excel Menu Bar

Adding the Custom Views Icon to the Excel Menu Bar

➤ **To add the Custom Views box to the Excel Menu bar:**

1. Right-click one of the toolbars, and select **Customize** from the shortcut menu.

2. In the *Commands* dialog box, select **View** from **Categories**.

3. Drag the **Custom Views** box onto the Menu bar, and then close the *Commands* dialog box.

➤ **To add a new Custom View:**

1. Type the name of the **Custom View** straight into the **Custom View** box.

2. Click **OK** twice.

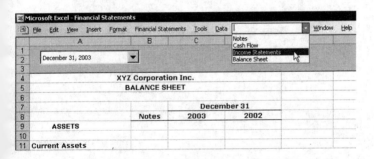

Notes:

**My Tips/
Shortcuts:**

| **Related
Tips:** | *Tip 245: Saving Defined Page Setups for
Future Printing* |
| | *Tip 246: Adding the Custom Views Icon to
the Excel Menu Bar* |

Quickly Printing a Page from the Workbook Using a Custom View

➤ **To print using a Custom View:**

1. From any sheet in the workbook, select the desired **Custom View** from the **Custom View** box.

2. Press **<Ctrl+ P>**.

3. In the *Print* dialog box, click **OK**.

Microsoft Excel - Financial Statements								
File	Edit	View	Insert	Format	Tools	Data		Window Help
	A	B	C	D	Notes			H	I

Notes
Cash Flow
Income Statements
Balance Sheet

Notes:

My Tips/
Shortcuts:

Related
Tips:

Tip 247: *Quickly Printing a Page from the*
Workbook Using a Custom View

Tip 249: *Creating a Custom Report*
Manager

Printing an Already Saved Report Using Report Manager

Excel lets you save pages with their page setup using **Custom Views**, and the **Report Manager** add-in allows creating and saving the pages in any number of reports.

Note: The **Office XP (2002)** and **Office 2003** CDs do not include the **Report Manager** add-in; **Excel 97** and **Excel 2000** CDs do. The name of the add-in file is **Reports.xla**.

➢ **To install the Report Manager add-in:**

1. Download the add-in from the Microsoft Web site: **http://office.microsoft.com/downloads/2002**.

2. From the *Tools* menu, select **Add-ins**.

3. If the **Report Manager** add-in appears in the list of available add-ins, there is no need to install it. Go to step 6.

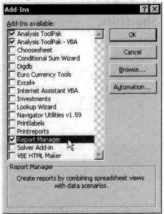

4. Click **Browse**.

5. Locate and select the file name **Reports.xla**, and then click **OK**.

6. In **Add-ins Available**, select **Report Manager**, and then click **OK**.

➢ **To add a report and save in Report Manager:**

1. From the *View* menu, select **Report Manager**.

2. Click **Add**.

continued...

Notes:

_____

_____

_____

_____

_____

_____

**My Tips/
Shortcuts:**

_____

_____

_____

_____

_____

_____

_____

_____

_____

_____

Printing an Already Saved Report Using Report Manager (cont.)

3. In the **Report Name** box, type the name of the report.

4. From **Section to Add**, open **View** or **Sheet**.

5. Select the first view to add to the report: **Income Statements**.

6. Click **Add**. The **Income Statement** view moves to the white list box at the bottom of the **Sections in this Report** box.

7. Repeat these steps to add other views, as necessary.

8. Select the **Use Continuous Page Number** box if you want to print continuous numbers at the bottom of the page.

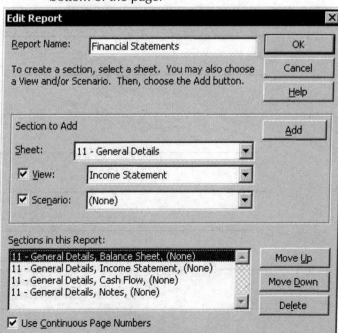

continued...

Notes:

My Tips/ Shortcuts:

Printing an Already Saved Report Using Report Manager (cont.)

Problem: When using the Use Continuous Page Number option:

There is no way to set the first page number, or to number additional pages (for example, a page added from Word) so that they will print in the report. The first page printed will be numbered **1**.

Solution:

Insert additional views into the report (for example, reinsert the **Income Statement** view), and use the report with the correct number in the footer (you may delete extra pages with incorrect numbers).

✦ **Using custom views to add pages to reports**

Using **Custom Views** to add pages to a report is like buying an insurance policy for safe printing. The pages are printed according to the print options defined and saved earlier.

➢ **To print a report:**
   1. From the *View* menu, select **Report Manager**.
   2. Select the report you want to print, and then click **Print**.

➢ **To change, add, or close a report, or arrange the printing of its pages:**
   ✦ Click **Edit**.

➢ **To delete a report:**
   ✦ Select the report and click **Delete**.

Notes:

_____

_____

_____

_____

_____

_____

_____

**My Tips/
Shortcuts:**

_____

_____

_____

_____

_____

_____

_____

Related Tips:	*Tip 245: Saving Defined Page Setups for Future Printing*
	Tip 247: Quickly Printing a Page from the Workbook Using a Custom View
	Tip 248: Print an Already Saved Report Using Report Manager

Creating a Custom Report Manager

You can create a custom **Print Reports** by adding **VBA** macro to a regular **Module** sheet (the macro can be downloaded from www.exceltip.com).

	A	B	C	D	E	F
	Microsoft Excel - Book1					
	File Edit View Insert Format Financial Statements Tools Data Window Help					
1	**Type Number**	**Name**	**Page Number**			
2	1	Balance Sheet	3		**Print Report**	
3	2	Income Statement	4			
4	3	Cash Flow	5			
5						
6						

Structure of the Custom Print Report:

✦ **Column A:** This column contains numbers between 1 and 3: **print from sheet**, **print by range name**, or **print from Custom View** (recommended).

✦ **Column B:** Type the sheet name, range **Name**, or **Custom View** name.

✦ **Column C:** Type the page number to be printed in the footer.

The macro on the next page will print from a sheet and automatically add the necessary information to the footer, including page number, workbook name, path address, and sheet name, as well as the date and time of printing.

Note: This macro can be downloaded from www.exceltip.com/f1toc.

continued...

7

Notes:

_____

_____

_____

_____

_____

_____

_____

_____

_____

My Tips/
Shortcuts:

_____

_____

_____

_____

_____

_____

_____

_____

_____

Creating a Custom Report Manager (cont.)

```
Sub PrintReports()
    Dim NumberPages As Integer, PageNumber As Integer, i As Integer
    Dim ActiveSh As Worksheet, ChooseShNameView As String
    Dim ShNameView As String, cell As Range

    Application.ScreenUpdating = False
    Set ActiveSh = ActiveSheet
    Range("a2").Select

    For Each cell In Range(Range("a2"), Range("a2").End(xlDown))
        ShNameView = ActiveCell.Offset(0, 1).Value
        PageNumber = ActiveCell.Offset(0, 2).Value

        Select Case cell.Value
        Case 1
            Sheets(ShNameView).Select
        Case 2
            Application.GoTo Reference:=ShNameView
        Case 3
            ActiveWorkbook.CustomViews(ShNameView).Show
        End Select

        With ActiveSheet.PageSetup
        .CenterFooter = PageNumber
        .LeftFooter = ActiveWorkbook.FullName & "   " & "&A &T  &D"
        End With

        ActiveWindow.SelectedSheets.PrintOut Copies:=1

    Next cell

    ActiveSh.Select
    Application.ScreenUpdating = True

End Sub
```

✦ The **For Each** loop in the macro causes a separate print for each cell in column **A** starting at **A2**.

✦ In the loop, the print area is selected using the **Select Case** technique.

✦ The information printed on the left side of the footer: **&08** = 8 point font, **&D** = Date, **&T** = Time.

✦ To run the macro from the sheet, press **<Alt+F8>**, select the macro and click **Run**.
  OR
  Add a button to the sheet and attach the macro to it (to add a button see *Tip #228*, instead of adding **Combo Box**, add a button to the **Forms** toolbar). •

Note: Use this technique to add an unlimited number of reports.

7

Notes:

_____

_____

_____

_____

_____

_____

My Tips/ Shortcuts:

_____

_____

_____

_____

Related Tips:

Tip 10: Selecting Special Cells

Tip 12: Selecting Cells from Any Cell to the Last Cell in the Sheet's Used Range

Tip 251: E-mailing an Excel Workbook, Sheet, Data or Chart

Reducing the Workbook Size for Quick Sending via E-Mail

➢ **To reduce the workbook size:**

1. Press **<Ctrl+End>** to find the last cell in the used area within the sheet. In the screenshot, the last cell is **E17**.

	A	B	C	D	E
1	1	2	3		
2	2	4	6		
3	3	6	9		
4	4	8	12		
5	5	10	15		
6	6	12	18		
7	7	14	21		
8	8	16	24		
9	9	18	27		
10	10	20	30		
11	11	22	33		
12					
13					
14					
15					
16					
17					

Microsoft Excel - Book1 — File, Edit, View, Insert, Format, Tools, Data, Window

2. Find the last cell containing data in the sheet. In the screenshot, the last cell containing data is cell **C11**.

3. Delete all the rows between the cells containing data to the row of the last cell in the used area. In the screenshot, the rows to delete are **12:17**.

4. Delete all columns to the right of the column of the last cell containing data, up to the column of the last cell in the area used. In the screenshot, the columns to delete are **D:E**.

5. To quickly delete the rows, select the first row to delete (row **12** in the screenshot), press **<Ctrl+Shift+Down Arrow>**. To quickly delete the columns, select the first column to delete (column **D** in the screenshot), and press **<Ctrl+Shift+Right Arrow>**, press **<Shift+F10>** and from the shortcut menu, press **<Delete>**.

6. Repeat the steps above for each sheet in the entire workbook.

7. Press **<Ctrl+S>** to save the file.

Notes:

**My Tips/
Shortcuts:**

Related Tips:	Tip 250: Reducing the Workbook Size for Quick Sending via E-Mail

E-mailing an Excel Workbook, Sheet, Data or Chart

➢ **To send an entire workbook as an attachment (supported by all four Excel versions):**

✦ From the *File* menu, select **Send To**, and then **Mail Recipient (as Attachment)**.

➢ **To send a sheet in the body of an e-mail message (supported from Excel 2000 and up):**

✦ From the *File* menu, select **Send To**, **Mail Recipient**, and then **Send the current sheet as the message body**.

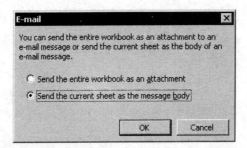

➢ **To send a workbook for review (supported from Excel 2002 and up):**

✦ From the *File* menu, select **Send To**, and then **Mail Recipient (for Review)**.

This new feature provides an easy way to circulate workbooks between your colleagues.

7

For Excel versions 97, 2000, 2002, 2003.

Sending an Excel Workbook, Sheet, Data or Chart

➤ To send an entire workbook as an attachment (supported by all four Excel versions):
  ◆ From the File menu, select Send To, and then Mail Recipient (as Attachment).

➤ To send a sheet in the body of an e-mail message (supported from Excel 2000 and later):
  ◆ From the File menu, select Send To, Mail Recipient, and then Send the current sheet as a message body.

➤ To send a workbook for review (supported from Excel 2002 and later):
  ◆ From the File menu, select Send To, and then Mail Recipient (for Review).

This new feature gives you an easy way to circulate workbooks before your publishing.

Part 8 — Lists, Analyzing Data

8

Notes:

_____

_____

_____

_____

_____

**My Tips/
Shortcuts:**

_____

_____

_____

_____

_____

Related Tips:	_Tip 1: What's New in Excel 2003?_
	Tip 2: What's New in Excel 2002/2003: Menu, Cell Shortcut Menu and Keyboard Shortcuts
	Tip 253: Sorting Rules & List Structure

Creating List Objects

New in **Excel 2003**!

✦ What are the advantages of creating a List Object?

You can **Sort**, **Print**, create **Charts**, **Insert** rows/columns, **Delete** rows/columns, add **Toggle Total Row**, import data to **XML** and publish the **List** to a **Share Point** site from the new **List** toolbar.

✦ What is the advantage of creating a Chart from a List Object?

When adding data to the **List Object**, the **Chart** automatically expands/updates itself.

➤ To create a List Object using Excel 2003:

✦ Select a cell in the **List** area and press **<Ctrl+L>**.

   OR

   From the *Data* menu, select **List**, and then **Create List**.

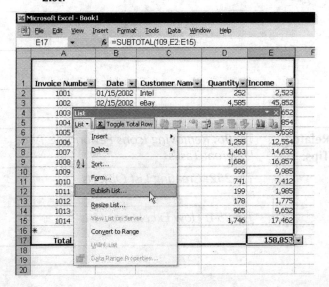

Notes:

_____

_____

_____

_____

_____

_____

**My Tips/
Shortcuts:**

_____

_____

_____

_____

_____

_____

_____

Related Tips:	*Tip 96: Removing Icons Performing Two Different Tasks*
	Tip 252: Creating List Objects
	Tip 254: How Excel Sorts Lists

Sorting Rules & List Structure

✦ **List structure**

 ❖ The **List** should have only one header row.

 ❖ Do not leave any empty cells in any cell of the header row.

 ❖ Do not leave empty rows in the data area.

✦ **Selecting ranges**

Do not select a column or a row in a **List** before sorting; instead, select only a single cell. Clicking the **Sort** icon automatically sorts the entire **List** and the data will be sorted according to the selected cell's field.

✦ **Formulas**

Be careful when sorting data if there are formulas in the cells. Sorting data linked by formulas to other cells, or to cells in other sheets, could distort the calculations. Be meticulous when sorting a **List** containing linked formulas and defined **Names** (which are defined with absolute references by default), or with formulas that have absolute references.

✦ **Inserting a sequence column to restore the original order**

Insert an additional column into the data **List** with ascending numbers (that is, **1**, **2**, **3**, and so on) before sorting the data (do **not** use a formula). If a **List** includes a column with consecutive dates, use this column as the first sorting column.

8

Notes:

_____

_____

_____

_____

_____

_____

_____

_____

_____

**My Tips/
Shortcuts:**

_____

_____

_____

_____

_____

_____

Related Tips:	*Tip 253: Sorting Rules & List Structure*
	Tip 255: Sorting by Columns
	Tip 256: Sorting by Custom Lists

How Excel Sorts Lists

Excel sorts Lists according to a defined order, as follows:

✦ **Numeric values**

❖ Numeric values, including date and time, are sorted from lowest (negative) to highest (positive). Excel does not consider the format of the cell, only its contents.

❖ Date and time are sorted by their numeric values.

✦ **Text**

Text is sorted first by ASCII characters, such as *, (,), $, and then by letters of the alphabet (also ASCII characters). Uppercase text is sorted before lowercase text.

➢ **To sort using case sensitivity:**

✦ From the *Data* menu, select **Sort**, then **Options**, and then select the **Case Sensitive** option.

✦ **Logical values**

FALSE is sorted before TRUE.

✦ **Errors**

Errors do not undergo internal sorting, and appear next to last.

✦ **Empty cells**

Empty cells are always sorted last. **Sort Descending** changes the sort order from the last to the first, except for empty cells, which are always last.

Notes:

My Tips/ Shortcuts:

Sorting by Columns

The default setting for sorting in **Ascending** or **Descending**
order is by row.

➢ **To sort by columns:**

1. From the *Data* menu, select **Sort**, and then
   Options.

2. Select the **Sort left to right** option button and click
   OK.

3. In the **Sort by option** of the *Sort* dialog box, select
   the row number by which the columns will be
   sorted and click **OK**.

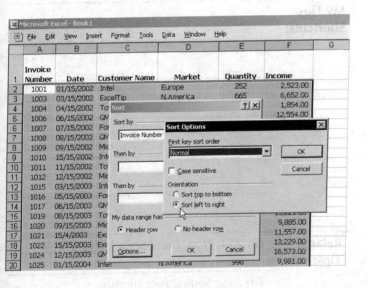

Notes:

_____

_____

_____

_____

_____

_____

**My Tips/
Shortcuts:**

_____

_____

_____

_____

_____

**Related
Tips:**

Tip 254: How Excel Sorts Lists

Tip 255: Sorting by Columns

_____

_____

Sorting by Custom Lists

➢ **To sort by Custom List:**

✦ **Step 1: Filter records to unique records**

1. Select the range containing records (column **C** in the screenshot).

2. From the *Data* menu, select **Filter**, and then **Advanced Filter**.

3. In the *Advanced Filter* dialog box, select **Copy to another location**.

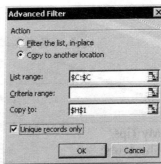

4. In the **Copy to** box, select a cell, select **Unique records only** and click **OK** (ensure that the **List range** is correct before clicking **OK**). The unique records are in cells **H2:H9** (see screenshot).

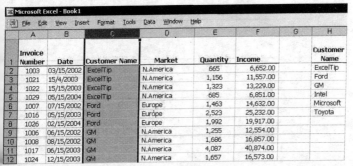

✦ **Step 2: Saving a Custom List**

1. Select the unique records **List** (cells **H2:H9** in the screenshot).

continued...

8

Notes:

_____

_____

_____

_____

_____

_____

My Tips/ Shortcuts:

_____

_____

_____

_____

_____

_____

_____

_____

Sorting by Custom Lists (cont.)

2. From the *Tools* menu, select **Options**, and then select the **Custom Lists** tab.

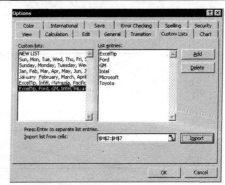

3. Click **Import**, and then click **OK**.

✦ Step 3: Sorting by a Custom List

1. Select one of the cells in the **List**.
2. From the *Data* menu, select **Sort**, and then **Options**.
3. From the **First key sort order** dropdown list, select the **Custom List** and click **OK**.
4. In the *Sort* dialog box, select **Sort by**, then **Customer Name**, and then click **OK**.

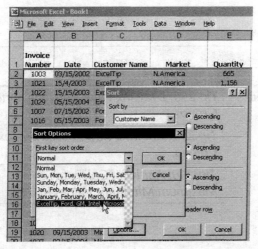

Notes:

_____

_____

_____

_____

_____

_____

**My Tips/
Shortcuts:**

_____

_____

_____

_____

_____

_____

Related Tips:	*Tip 258: Drawing Lines Between Sorted Groups*
	Tip 259: Coloring Rows Based on Text Criteria
	Tip 260: Applying Colors to Maximum/Minimum Values in a List

Deleting Empty Rows

➤ **To delete empty rows between data:**
  1. Select all columns containing data.
  2. Click the **Sort** icon (either **Ascending** or **Descending**).

Before:

	A	B	C	D	E	F
1	Invoice Number	Date	Customer Name	Market	Quantity	Income
2	1001	01/15/2002	Intel	Europe	252	2,523.00
3	1003	03/15/2002	ExcelTip	N.America	665	6,652.00
4	1004	04/15/2002	Toyota	Europe	185	1,854.00
5	1006	06/15/2002	GM	N.America	1,255	12,554.00
6	1007	07/15/2002	Ford	Europe	1,463	14,632.00
7	1008	08/15/2002	GM	N.America	1,686	16,857.00
8	1009	09/15/2002	Microsoft	Europe	999	9,985.00
9	1011	11/15/2002	Toyota	Europe	199	1,985.00
10						
11						
12	1012	12/15/2002	Microsoft	Europe	178	1,775.00
13	1015	03/15/2003	Intel	Europe	2,527	25,266.00

After

	A	B	C	D	E	F
1	Invoice Number	Date	Customer Name	Market	Quantity	Income
2	1001	01/15/2002	Intel	Europe	252	2,523.00
3	1003	03/15/2002	ExcelTip	N.America	665	6,652.00
4	1004	04/15/2002	Toyota	Europe	185	1,854.00
5	1006	06/15/2002	GM	N.America	1,255	12,554.00
6	1007	07/15/2002	Ford	Europe	1,463	14,632.00
7	1008	08/15/2002	GM	N.America	1,686	16,857.00
8	1009	09/15/2002	Microsoft	Europe	999	9,985.00
9	1010	15/15/2002	Intel	Africa	741	7,412.00
10	1011	11/15/2002	Toyota	Europe	199	1,985.00
11	1012	12/15/2002	Microsoft	Europe	178	1,775.00
12	1015	03/15/2003	Intel	Europe	2,527	25,266.00

8

Notes:

**My Tips/
Shortcuts:**

**Related
Tips:**

Drawing Lines Between Sorted Groups

➢ **To draw lines between sorted groups of data:**

1. Sort the **List** by **Customer Name** by selecting a cell in column **C** (see screenshot) and clicking the **Sort** icon.

2. Select cell **A1** in the **Current Region** and press **<Ctrl+Shift+*>** (in **Excel 2003**, press this or **<Ctrl+A>**).

3. From the *Format* menu, select **Conditional Formatting**.

4. In **Condition 1**, select **Formula Is**.

5. In the **Formula** box, enter the formula **=$C1<>$C2**. Be sure to enter the formula with absolute reference for the column and relative reference for the row.

6. In the *Conditional Formatting* dialog box, click the **Format** button, select the **Border** tab, in **Border** section click **Underline** and then choose a color.

7. Click **OK** twice.

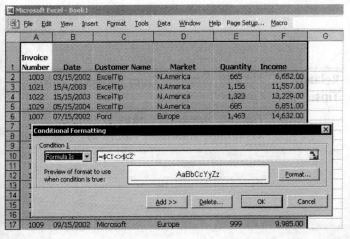

8

Notes:

_____

_____

_____

_____

_____

_____

_____

_____

**My Tips/
Shortcuts:**

_____

_____

_____

_____

_____

_____

_____

_____

Related Tips:	*Tip 258: Drawing Lines Between Sorted Groups*
	Tip 260: Applying Colors to Maximum/Minimum Values in a List

Coloring Rows Based on Text Criteria

➢ **To color rows based on text criteria:**

1. Select a cell in the region, and press **<Ctrl+Shift+*>** (in **Excel 2003**, press this or **<Ctrl+A>**) to select the **Current Region**.

2. From the *Format* menu, select **Conditional Formatting**.

3. In **Condition 1**, select **Formula Is**, and type **=$C1="Amazon"**.

4. Click **Format**, select the **Font** tab, select a color, and then click **OK**.

5. In **Condition 2**, select **Formula Is**, and type **=$C1="eBay"**.

6. Repeat step 4, select a different color than you selected for **Condition 1**, and then click **OK**.

7. In **Condition 3**, select **Formula Is**, and type **=$E1="ExcelTip"**.

8. Repeat step 4, select a different color than you selected for **Condition 1** and **Condition 2**, and then click **OK** twice.

Note: Be sure to distinguish between absolute reference and relative reference when entering the formulas.

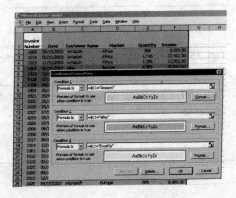

Notes:

**My Tips/
Shortcuts:**

| **Related
Tips:** | *Tip 258: Drawing Lines Between Sorted
Groups* |
| | *Tip 259: Coloring Rows Based on Text
Criteria* |

Applying Colors to Maximum/Minimum Values in a List

➤ **To apply colors to maximum and/or minimum values:**

1. Select a cell in the region, and press **<Ctrl+Shift+*>** (in **Excel 2003**, press this or **<Ctrl+A>**) to select the **Current Region**.

2. From the *Format* menu, select **Conditional Formatting**.

3. In **Condition 1**, select **Formula Is**, and type **=MAX($F:$F) =$F1**.

4. Click **Format**, select the **Font** tab, select a color, and then click **OK**.

5. In **Condition 2**, select **Formula Is**, and type **=MIN($F:$F) =$F1**.

6. Repeat step 4, select a different color than you selected for **Condition 1**, and then click **OK**.

Note: Be sure to distinguish between absolute reference and relative reference when entering the formulas.

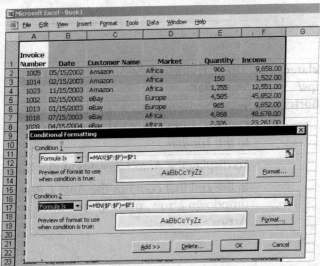

Notes:

_____

_____

_____

_____

_____

_____

**My Tips/
Shortcuts:**

_____

_____

_____

_____

Related Tips/ Shortcuts:	*Tip 271: Adding the Subtotals Icon to the Menu Bar*
	Tip 283: Adding the Auto Outline, Clear Outline, and Show Outline Symbols Icons to the Toolbar
	To display the *Auto Filter* dropdown list:
	In the cell that contains the *Auto Filter* dropdown arrow, press **<Alt+Down Arrow>**.

Quick Filtering Using the AutoFilter Icon

> **To quickly filter a List, add the AutoFilter and Show All icons to the Standard toolbar:**

1. Place the mouse arrow on one of the toolbars, right-click, and select **Customize** from the shortcut menu.

2. In the *Customize* dialog box, select the **Commands** tab.

3. From **Categories**, select **Data**, and from the **Commands** box, drag the **AutoFilter** and **Show All** icons to the **Standard** toolbar.

4. Click **Close**.

 Using keyboard shortcuts

After the **Show All** icon has been added, press **<Alt+S>** to show all items after filtering.

Note: The total number of unique items available for filtering is limited to 999.

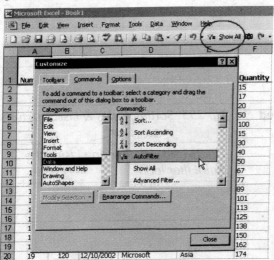

8

Notes:

**My Tips/
Shortcuts:**

| **Related
Tips:** | *Tip 253: Sorting Rules & List Structure* |
| | *Tip 261: Quick Filtering Using the AutoFilter Icon* |

Sort Ascending/Descending While Using AutoFilter

New in Excel 2003 — Sort Ascending/Descending with AutoFilter.

This new option allows you to sort straight from the **AutoFilter** dropdown list (identical to the Sort Ascending/Descending technique from the **Sort Ascending/Sort Descending** icons).

Using keyboard shortcuts

➢ **To display the Auto Filter dropdown list (in all Excel versions):**

✦ In the cell that contains the **Filter** dropdown arrow, (Blue arrow) press **<Alt+Down Arrow>**.

➢ **To display the Auto Filter dropdown list (in all Excel versions):**

✦ In the cell that contains the **Filter** dropdown arrow (Blue arrow), press **<Alt+Up Arrow>**.

	A	B	C	D	E	F
Microsoft Excel - Book1						
	File	Edit	View	Insert Format Tools Data Window Help		
1	Invoice Number ▾	Date ▾	Customer Nam ▾	Market ▾	Quantity ▾	Income ▾
2	1012	12/15/2002	Sort Ascending	Europe	178	1,775.00
3	1004	04/15/2002	Sort Descending	Europe	185	1,854.00
4	1011	11/15/2002	(All)	Europe	199	1,985.00
5	1001	01/15/2002	(Top 10...)	Europe	252	2,523.00
6	1003	03/15/2002	(Custom...)	N.America	665	6,652.00
7	1029	05/15/2004	Amazon	N.America	685	6,851.00
8	1010	15/15/2002	eBay	Africa	741	7,412.00
9	1013	01/15/2003	ExcelTip	Europe	965	9,652.00
10	1005	05/15/2002	Ford	Africa	966	9,658.00
11	1020	09/15/2003	GM	Europe	989	9,885.00
			Intel			
12	1025	01/15/2004	Microsoft	N.America	998	9,981.00
13	1009	09/15/2002	Toyota	Europe	999	9,985.00
			(Blanks)			
			(NonBlanks)			
14	1021	15/4/2003	ExcelTip	N.America	1,156	11,557.00

8

Notes:

**My Tips/
Shortcuts:**

Summing the Visible Filtered List

> **To total the values in the visible filtered rows, use the SUBTOTAL function:**

1. Filter the **List** by selecting any criteria.
2. Select a cell in the **List** area and press **<Ctrl+Shift+ *>** (in **Excel 2003**, press this or **<Ctrl+A>**) to select the **Current Region/List**.
3. Press **<Alt+=>**.

   OR

   Click the **AutoSum** icon (sigma).
4. The **SUBTOTAL** function is automatically entered below the values in each column.

	A	B	C	D	E	F
1	Invoice Numbe ▾	Date ▾	Customer Nam ▾	Market ▾	Quantity ▾	Income ▾
4	1003	03/15/2002	ExcelTip	N.America	665	6,652
22	1021	15/4/2003	ExcelTip	N.America	1,156	11,557
23	1022	15/15/2003	ExcelTip	N.America	1,323	13,229
30	1029	05/15/2004	ExcelTip	N.America	685	6,851
31					3,829	38,289
32						

E31 =SUBTOTAL(9,E2:E30)

continued...

Notes:

**My Tips/
Shortcuts:**

Summing the Visible Filtered List (cont.)

The SUBTOTAL function has been expanded in Excel 2003.

The digit **9** in the first argument of the **SUBTOTAL** function is for function number **9** (the **SUM** function) — see the table below for a list of the function numbers you may use.

The second column in the table below is new in **Excel 2003**. When using numbers from **1** to **11**, the **SUBTOTAL** function also returns values from hidden rows. When using the numbers from **101** to **111**, the **SUBTOTAL** function returns values from visible rows only.

Function_num (includes hidden values)	Function_num (ignores hidden values)	Function
1	101	AVERAGE
2	102	COUNT
3	103	COUNTA
4	104	MAX
5	105	MIN
6	106	PRODUCT
7	107	STDEV
8	108	STDEVP
9	109	SUM
10	110	VAR
11	111	VARP

Filtering

Notes:

**My Tips/
Shortcuts:**

Coloring and Filtering Lists According to Criteria

➤ **To color filtering results according to criteria:**

1. Filter the **List**.

2. Press **<Ctrl+Shift+*>** (in **Excel 2003**, press this or **<Ctrl+A>**) to select the **Current Region**.

3. From the **Formatting** toolbar, select **Fill Color**, and choose a color.

4. Repeat the steps above, choosing new criteria and different colors.

To quickly select a color, use the *"Tearing Off"* technique (see *Tip #52*).

	A	B	C	D	E	F
	Invoice Number	Date	Customer Name	Market	Quantity	Income
2	1001	01/15/2002	Intel	Europe	252	2,523.00
3	1003	03/15/2002	ExcelTip	Europe	665	6,652.00
4	1004	04/15/2002	Toyota	Europe	185	1,854.00
5	1006	06/15/2002	GM	N.America	1,255	12,554.00
6	1007	07/15/2002	Ford	Europe	1,463	14,632.00
7	1008	08/15/2002	GM	N.America	1,686	16,857.00
8	1009	09/15/2002	Microsoft	Europe	999	9,985.00
9	1010	10/15/2002	Intel	Africa	741	7,412.00
10	1011	11/15/2002	Toyota	Europe	199	1,985.00
11	1012	12/15/2002	Microsoft	Europe	178	1,775.00
12	1015	03/15/2003	Intel	Europe	2,527	25,266.00
13	1016	05/15/2003	Ford	Europe	2,523	25,232.00
14	1017	06/15/2003	GM	N.America	4,087	40,874.00
15	1019	08/15/2003	Toyota	N.America	1,522	15,221.00
16	1020	09/15/2003	Microsoft	Europe	989	9,885.00
17	1021	10/15/2003	ExcelTip	N.America	1,156	11,557.00
18	1022	11/15/2003	ExcelTip	Europe	1,323	13,229.00

Filtering

8

Notes:

**My Tips/
Shortcuts:**

Related Tips:	*Tip 261: Quick Filtering Using the AutoFilter Icon*
	Tip 264: Coloring and Filtering Lists According to Criteria
	Tip 267: Saving Filtering Criteria

Filtering by More Than Two Criteria

➤ **To filter a List using more than one criteria, use the Advanced Filter:**

1. Insert a few empty rows above the **List**.

2. Copy the heading row **List**, and paste it into row **1**.

3. In row **2**, under **Customer Name** (for example, see the screenshot), enter a **Customer Name**; under **Quantity**, enter the criteria.

4. From the *Data* menu, select **Filter**, and then **Advanced Filter**.

5. Select the **List range** box and insert the **List** range.

6. Select the **Criteria range** box and insert the criteria range.

7. Click **OK**.

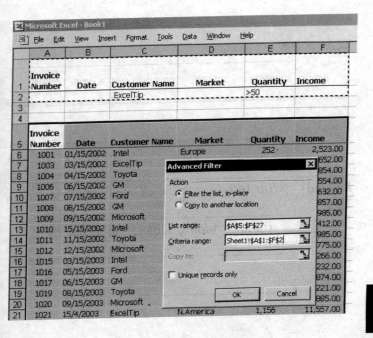

Notes:

**My Tips/
Shortcuts:**

| **Related
Tips:**	*Tip 149: Customizing Date Formatting*
	Tip 274: Adding Subtotals to a Date Field

Filtering by the Date Field

➤ **To filter by date:**

1. If the **List** is in **Filter** mode, turn it off by selecting **Filter**, and then **AutoFilter** from the *Data* menu.

2. Copy the **Date** column.

3. Select two columns to the right of the **Date** field.

4. Press **<Shift+F10>** and then press **<Ctrl++>** or right-click, and select **Insert Copied Cells** from the shortcut menu (pasting by inserting copied cells allows one to insert two columns, and paste the copied column into them).

5. Change the titles for the two columns to **Month** and **Year**.

6. Select the **Month** column and press **<Ctrl+1>** to format the cells.

7. In the **Number** tab, select **Custom**.

8. In the **Type** box, enter the format **mmmm** (full month format), and click **OK**.

9. Repeat steps 6 and 7 for the **Year** column.

10. In the **Type** box, enter the format **yyyy** (full year format), and click **OK**. You can now filter by any month or year.

11. The **List** is now ready to filter according to **Month** and **Year** criteria.

Filtering

	Invoice Number	Date	Month	Year	Customer Name	Market	Quantity	Income
2	1001	01/15/2002	January	2002	Intel	Europe	252	2,523.00
3	1003	03/15/2002	March	2002	ExcelTip	N.America	665	6,652.00
4	1004	04/15/2002	April	2002	Toyota	Europe	185	1,854.00
5	1006	06/15/2002	June	2002	GM	N.America	1,255	12,554.00
6	1007	07/15/2002	July	2002	Ford	Europe	1,463	14,632.00
7	1008	08/15/2002	August	2002	GM	N.America	1,686	16,857.00
8	1009	09/15/2002	September	2002	Microsoft	Europe	999	9,985.00
9	1010	10/15/2002	October	2002	Intel	Africa	741	7,412.00
10	1011	11/15/2002	November	2002	Toyota	Europe	199	1,985.00
11	1012	12/15/2002	December	2002	Microsoft	Europe	178	1,775.00

8

Notes:

**My Tips/
Shortcuts:**

8

Saving Filtering Criteria

➢ **To save filtering criteria, use Custom Views:**

✦ **Step 1: Add the Custom Views icon to the toolbar**

1. Place the mouse over one of the toolbars, right-click, and select **Customize** from the shortcut menu.

2. Select the **Commands** tab.

3. From **Categories**, select **View** and drag the **Custom Views** icon to the **Menu** bar.

✦ **Step 2: Save the filtering criteria**

1. Select a cell from the column containing the criteria you want to **Filter** with.

2. Click the **AutoFilter** icon (see *Tip #261*).

3. Type any text criteria you want into the **Custom Views** box and click twice to save.

4. Repeat the previous step and save as many filtering criteria as needed from any sheet within the workbook.

Note: Save as many filtering criteria in **Custom Views** as needed.

	A	B	C	D		Quantity	Income
1	Invoice Number	Date	Customer Nam	Market		Quantity	Income
3	1003	03/15/2002	ExcelTip	N.America		665	6,652.00
17	1021	15/4/2003	ExcelTip	N.America		1,156	11,557.00
18	1022	15/15/2003	ExcelTip	N.America		1,323	13,229.00
23	1029	05/15/2004	ExcelTip	N.America		685	6,851.00
24							

F
Filtering

8

Notes:

_____

_____

_____

_____

**My Tips/
Shortcuts:**

_____

_____

_____

_____

Related Tips:	*Tip 230:Add the Page Setup icon to Excel Menu Bar*
	Tip 261: Quick Filtering Using the AutoFilter Icon
	Tip 267: Saving Filtering Criteria

Printing a Filtered List

➤ **To print filtered Lists:**

1. Select a cell in the **Current Region** and press **<Ctrl+Shift+*>** (in **Excel 2003**, press this or **<Ctrl+A>**).

2. From the *File* menu, select **Print Area**, and then **Set Print Area**.

3. Filter the **List**, and print the filtered data area.

4. Filter the **List** again using new criteria, and print the new filtered data area.

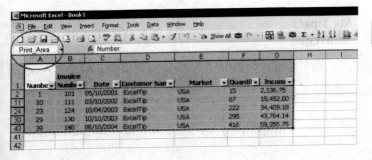

Notes:

**My Tips/
Shortcuts:**

Related Tips:	*Tip 261: Quick Filtering Using the AutoFilter Icon*
	Tip 264: Coloring and Filtering List According to Criteria
	Tip 294: Comparing Lists

Filtering a Range into a List of Unique Records

➢ **To filter a range into a List of unique records:**
1. Select a cell the range (see screenshot).
2. From the *Data* menu, select **Filter**, and then **Advanced Filter**.
3. Select **Copy to another location**.
4. In the **Copy to** box, insert a cell address.
5. Select the **Unique records only** checkbox, and then click **OK**.

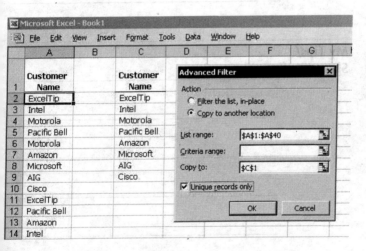

8

Notes:

**My Tips/
Shortcuts:**

**Related
Tips:**

Tip 183: COUNT Formulas

*Tip 295: Comparing Lists Using the
COUNTIF Formula*

8

Filtering a List into Unique Records Using the COUNTIF Formula

➢ **To filter a List into unique records using the COUNTIF formula:**

1. Select cell **B2**, and insert the formula =IF(COUNTIF($A$2:A2,A2)>1,1,0).

2. Copy the formula from cell **B2** downwards.

3. From the *Data* menu, select **Filter**, **AutoFilter**.

4. Select cell **B1** and press **<Alt+Down Arrow>** to open the filtering dropdown list or open it by clicking the dropdown arrow and then selecting **0**.

	A	B	C	D	E
	Customer Name ▾	Unique Record ▾			
1					
2	AIG	0			
3	AIG	1			
4	AIG	1			
5	Amazon	0			
6	Amazon	1			
7	Amazon	1			
8	Cisco	0			
9	Cisco	1			
10	Cisco	1			
11	ExcelTip	0			
12	ExcelTip	1			
13	ExcelTip	1			
14	ExcelTip	1			
15	ExcelTip	1			

Microsoft Excel - Book1

File Edit View Insert Format Tools Data Window Help

B2   ƒx =IF(COUNTIF($A$2:A2,A2)>1,1,0)

Filtering

8

Notes:

**My Tips/
Shortcuts:**

Related Tips:	Tip 230: Add the Page Setup icon to Excel Menu Bar
	Tip 261: Quick Filtering Using the AutoFilter Icon
	Tip 283: Adding the Auto Outline, Clear Outline, and Show Outline Symbols Icons to the Toolbar

Adding the Subtotals Icon to the Menu Bar

➢ **To add the Subtotals icon to the Excel Menu bar:**

1. Place the mouse over one of the toolbars, right-click, and select **Customize** from the shortcut menu.
2. Select the **Commands** tab.
3. From **Data**, drag the **Subtotals** icon to the **Menu** bar, and then click **Close**.

Using keyboard shortcuts

After the **Subtotals** icon has been added to the **Menu** bar, press **<Alt+b>** to open the *Subtotals* dialog box.

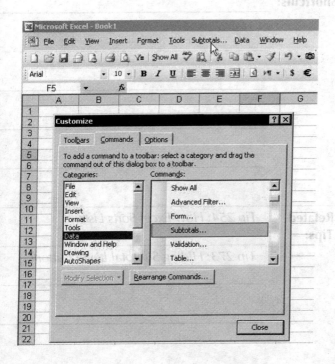

Notes:

**My Tips/
Shortcuts:**

**Related
Tips:**

Tip 254: How Excel Sorts Lists

Tip 273: Hiding Subtotal Level Buttons

Quickly Removing Subtotals

➤ **To quickly remove subtotals:**

1. Select any cell in the **List** and click **Sort Ascending** or **Sort Descending**.

2. Click **OK** in the dialog message box.

➤ **To remove subtotals by using the *Subtotals* dialog box:**

1. From the *Tools* menu, select **Data**, and then **Subtotals**.

   OR

   Press **<Alt+b>** (see *Tip #271*).

2. Click **Remove All**.

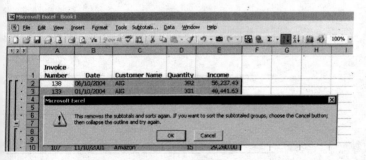

Notes:

**My Tips/
Shortcuts:**

**Related
Tips:**

Tip 272: Quickly Removing Subtotals

Tip 284: Hiding Outline Symbols

Hiding Subtotal Level Buttons

Using keyboard shortcuts

➢ **To hide the Subtotal level buttons:**
   ✦ Press **<Ctrl+8>**.

➢ **To redisplay the Subtotal level buttons:**
   ✦ Press **<Ctrl+8>** again.

Before:

	A	B	C	D	E
1	Invoice Number	Date	Customer Name	Quantity	Income
2	109	01/10/2002	AIG	40	8,040.00
3	118	10/10/2002	AIG	150	25,129.90
4	123	03/10/2003	AIG	210	32,850.02
5	133	01/10/2004	AIG	331	48,441.63
6	138	06/10/2004	AIG	392	56,237.43
7			**AIG Total**	1,122	170,698.97
8	107	11/10/2001	Amazon	15	29,280.00
9	113	05/10/2002	Amazon	89	13,095.00
10	122	02/10/2003	Amazon	198	31,290.86
11	131	11/10/2003	Amazon	307	45,323.30
12			**Amazon Total**	609	118,989.16
13	110	02/10/2002	Cisco	50	37,065.81
14	121	01/10/2003	Cisco	186	30,000.10
15	127	07/10/2003	Cisco	259	39,086.66

After:

	A	B	C	D	E
1	Invoice Number	Date	Customer Name	Quantity	Income
2	109	01/10/2002	AIG	40	8,040.00
3	118	10/10/2002	AIG	150	25,129.90
4	123	03/10/2003	AIG	210	32,850.02
5	133	01/10/2004	AIG	331	48,441.63
6	138	06/10/2004	AIG	392	56,237.43
7			**AIG Total**	1,122	170,698.97
8	107	11/10/2001	Amazon	15	29,280.00
9	113	05/10/2002	Amazon	89	13,095.00
10	122	02/10/2003	Amazon	198	31,290.86
11	131	11/10/2003	Amazon	307	45,323.30
12			**Amazon Total**	609	118,989.16
13	110	02/10/2002	Cisco	50	37,065.81
14	121	01/10/2003	Cisco	186	30,000.10
15	127	07/10/2003	Cisco	259	39,086.66

Subtotals

8

Notes:

My Tips/ Shortcuts:

Adding Subtotals to a Date Field

➤ **To add subtotals to a date field in a List:**

1. Copy the **Date** column and insert it twice (see *Tip #266*).

2. Change the titles for the two new columns to **Month** and **Year**.

3. Select the **Month** column, and press **<Ctrl+1>**.

4. Select the **Number** tab, select **Custom**, and in the **Type** box, type **MMMM**.

5. Repeat steps 3 and 4 for the **Year** column, and in the **Type** box, type **YYYY**.

6. Sort the **List** by the **Year** column.

7. Add **Subtotals** to the **List**.

	Invoice Number	Date	Month	Year	Customer Name	Market	Quantity	Income
2	101	05/10/2001	May	2001	ExcelTip	USA	15	2,136.75
3	102	06/10/2001	June	2001	Intel	Europe	17	2,270.94
4	103	07/10/2001	July	2001	Motorola	Asia	20	10,152.14
5	104	08/10/2001	August	2001	Pacific Bell	Europe	50	11,111.11
6	105	09/10/2001	September	2001	Motorola	Asia	100	8,717.95
7	107	11/10/2001	November	2001	Amazon	Asia	15	29,280.00
8	108	12/10/2001	December	2001	Microsoft	Europe	30	6,020.00
9				**2001 Total**			247	69,688.89
10	109	01/10/2002	January	2002	AIG	Asia	40	8,040.00
11	110	02/10/2002	February	2002	Cisco	Asia	50	37,065.81
12	111	03/10/2002	March	2002	ExcelTip	USA	67	15,452.00
13	112	04/10/2002	April	2002	Pacific Bell	Asia	77	13,032.00
14	113	05/10/2002	May	2002	Amazon	Africa	89	13,095.00
15	114	06/10/2002	June	2002	Intel	USA	101	23,084.00
16	115	07/10/2002	July	2002	Motorola	Asia	113	23,118.00
17	116	08/10/2002	August	2002	Intel	USA	125	18,495.00
18	117	09/10/2002	September	2002	Microsoft	Asia	138	23,506.50
19	118	10/10/2002	October	2002	AIG	Africa	150	25,129.90
20	119	11/10/2002	November	2002	Pacific Bell	Europe	162	26,753.30
21	120	12/10/2002	December	2002	Microsoft	Asia	174	28,376.70
22				**2002 Total**			1,286	255,148.21

Subtotals

8

Notes:

**My Tips/
Shortcuts:**

| **Related
Tips:** | *Tip 276: Adding Subtotals to Primary and
Secondary Fields* |
| --- | --- |
| | *Tip 301: Adding/Deleting Subtotals (in
PivotTable report).* |

Adding Additional Functions to Subtotals

➤ **To add additional functions to subtotals:**

1. Add **Subtotals** to the **List**.

2. Press **<Alt+b>**
   (see *Tip #271*).

   OR

   From the *Data*
   menu, select
   Subtotal.

3. From **Use
   function**, select
   a different
   function.

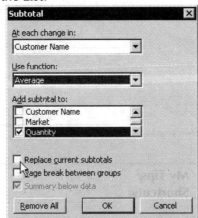

4. Deselect the **Replace current subtotals** checkbox,
   and then click **OK**.

5. Repeat the steps above to add more **Subtotals**
   functions to the **List**.

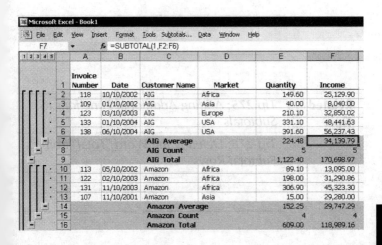

Notes:

**My Tips/
Shortcuts:**

| **Related
Tips:** | *Tip 275: Adding Additional Functions to
Subtotals* |
| | *Tip 278: Deleting the Word "Total" from
Subtotal Rows* |

Adding Subtotals to Primary and Secondary Fields

➢ **To add subtotals to primary and secondary fields:**

1. Sort, in ascending order, the field for which you want to have the secondary subtotal. In this example (see screenshot), **Customer Name** is the secondary field.

2. Sort, in ascending order, the field for which you want to have the primary subtotal. In this example (see screenshot), **Market** is the primary field.

3. Click the **Subtotals** box.

4. From the **At each change in** dropdown list, select **Market**.

5. In **Add Subtotal to**, select the **Quantity** and **Income** checkboxes.

6. Deselect the **Replace current subtotals** checkbox, and then click **OK**.

7. Repeat steps 3 and 4, and select **Customer Name**.

8. Click **OK**.

	Invoice Number	Date	Customer Name	Market	Quantity	Income
2	118	10/10/2002	AIG	Africa	149.60	25,129.90
3			**AIG Total**		**149.60**	**25,129.90**
4	113	05/10/2002	Amazon	Africa	89.10	13,095.00
5	122	02/10/2003	Amazon	Africa	198.00	31,290.86
6	131	11/10/2003	Amazon	Africa	306.90	45,323.30
7			**Amazon Total**		**594.00**	**89,709.16**
8	127	07/10/2003	Cisco	Africa	258.50	39,086.66
9	136	04/10/2004	Cisco	Africa	367.40	53,119.11
10	139	07/10/2004	Cisco	Africa	403.70	57,796.59
11			**Cisco Total**		1,029.60	150,002.36
12				**Africa Total**	**1,773.20**	**264,841.42**
13	109	01/10/2002	AIG	Asia	40.00	8,040.00
14			**AIG Total**		40.00	8,040.00
15	107	11/10/2001	Amazon	Asia	15.00	29,280.00
16			**Amazon Total**		15.00	29,280.00

F12 = =SUBTOTAL(9,F2:F10)

Notes:

My Tips/ Shortcuts:

Related Tips:	*Tip 230: Add the Page Setup icon to Excel Menu Bar*
	Tip 268: Printing a Filtered List
	Tip 271: Adding the Subtotals Icon to the Menu Bar

8

Printing Each Subtotal Group on a Separate Page

➢ **To print each subtotal group on a different page:**
  ✦ In the *Subtotals* dialog box, select the **Page break between groups** checkbox. Each group will be printed on a separate page.

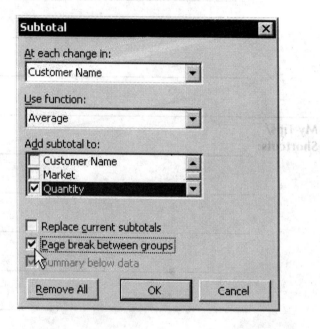

Notes:

**My Tips/
Shortcuts:**

Related Tips:	*Tip 271: Adding the Subtotals Icon to the Menu Bar*
	Tip 275: Adding Additional Functions to Subtotals
	Tip 276: Adding Subtotals to Primary and Secondary Fields

Deleting the Word "Total" from the Subtotal Rows

> ## To delete the word "Total" from the subtotal List:
> 1. Select the column in which the text appears.
> 2. Press **<Ctrl+H>**.
>
>   **OR**
>
>   From the *Edit* menu, select **Replace**.
> 3. In the **Find what** box, type the word **Total**.
> 4. Leave the **Replace with** box empty, and click **Replace All**.

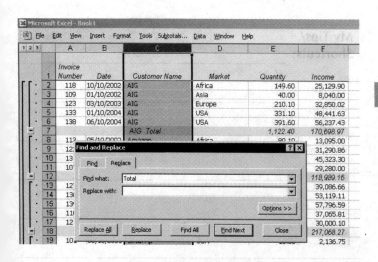

Notes:

**My Tips/
Shortcuts:**

Related Tips:	Tip 10: Selecting Special Cells
	Tip 286: Copying or Applying Color to Groups and Outlines
	Tip 290: Coloring and/or Copying Subtotals from Consolidated Lists Containing Links

Copying the Subtotals Summary

➢ **To copy the subtotals summary:**

1. Add **Subtotals** to the **List**.

2. In the **Subtotal** levels, click level **2**.

3. Select a cell in the **List**, and press **<Ctrl+Shift+*>** (in **Excel 2003**, press this or **<Ctrl+A>**).

4. To select visible cells, press **<Alt+;>**.

   OR

   Press **<F5>**, and in the *Go To* dialog box, click **Special**. In the *Go To Special* dialog box, select **Visible cells only** and click **OK**.

5. Copy and paste the summary of the subtotals into a different sheet.

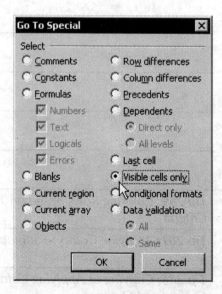

Notes:

**My Tips/
Shortcuts:**

Related Tips:	Tip 259: Coloring Rows Based on Text Criteria
	Tip 281: Applying Colors to Subtotal Rows
	Tip 286: Copying or Applying Color to Groups and Outlines

Applying Styles to Subtotal Rows

➢ **To apply styles to subtotal levels:**

1. Add **Subtotals** to the **List**.

2. Select a cell in the **List** area, and press
   <Ctrl+Shift+*> (in **Excel 2003**, press this or
   <Ctrl+A>) to select the **List**.

3. From the *Data* menu, select **Group and Outline**,
   and then **Settings**.

4. Click **Apply Styles**. The automatic style is applied
   to **Subtotal** lines level 2.

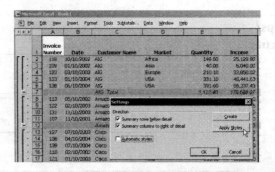

➢ **To modify the
   automatic style:**

1. From the
   Format menu,
   select **Style**.

2. From **Style name** in the *Style* dialog box, select
   RowLevel2 (the style **RowLevel2** & **RowLevel1** are
   automatically created upon clicking **Apply Styles**,
   as described above).

3. Click **Modify**, and select any desired format.

Notes:

**My Tips/
Shortcuts:**

Related Tips:	*Tip 10: Selecting Special Cells*
	Tip 259: Coloring Rows Based on Text Criteria
	Tip 280: Applying Styles to Subtotal Rows

Applying Colors to Subtotal Rows

Option 1: Permanent Colors

➤ **To apply colors to subtotal rows:**

1. Add **Subtotals** to the **List**.
2. Click **Level 2** of the **Subtotal** levels.
3. Select cell **A1**, and then press **<Ctrl+Shift+*>** (in **Excel 2003**, press this or **<Ctrl+A>**) to select the **List**.
4. Press **<Alt+;>** to select the visible cells.
5. Select a color from the **Fill Color** icon on the **Formatting** toolbar.
6. Click **Level 3** of the **Subtotal** levels to open the hidden rows.

continued...

8

Notes:

_____

_____

_____

_____

_____

_____

**My Tips/
Shortcuts:**

_____

_____

_____

_____

_____

_____

_____

_____

_____

Applying Colors to Subtotal Rows (cont.)

Option 2: Dynamic Coloring

➢ **To apply colors to subtotal rows using Conditional Formatting:**

1. Select cell **A1**, and then press **<Ctrl+Shift+*>** (in **Excel 2003**, press this or **<Ctrl+A>**) to select the **List**.

2. From the *Format* menu, select **Conditional Formatting**.

3. In **Condition 1**, select **Formula Is**.

4. In the formula box, enter the formula **=ISBLANK($B1)** (or use zero, see *Tip #282*).

5. Click **Format**, select the desired formatting, and then click **OK** twice.

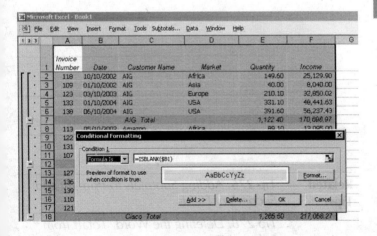

Notes:

**My Tips/
Shortcuts:**

| **Related
Tips:** | *Tip 276: Adding Subtotals to Primary and
Secondary Fields* |
| | *Tip 278: Deleting the Word "Total" from
Subtotal Rows* |

Coloring Two Subtotal Levels in Different Colors

Option 1: Permanent Coloring

➢ **To color each level in a different color by coloring visible cells:**

1. Add **Subtotals** with two totaling levels as in *Tip #276*.

2. Click **Level 3** of the **Subtotal** levels.

3. Select cell **A1**, and press **<Ctrl+Shift+*>** (in **Excel 2003**, press this or **<Ctrl+A>**) to select the **List**.

4. Press **<Ctrl+;>** to select the visible cells.

5. Select a color from the **Fill Color** icon on the **Formatting** toolbar.

6. Repeat steps 2 through 5 for **Level 2** of the **Subtotal** levels, using a different color

7. Click **Level 4** of the **Subtotal** levels to unhide all hidden rows in the **List**.

	A	B	C	D	E	F
1	Invoice Number	Date	Customer Name	Market	Quantity	Income
2	118	10/10/2002	AIG	Africa	149.60	25,129.90
3			AIG Total		149.60	25,129.90
4	113	05/10/2002	Amazon	Africa	89.10	13,095.00
5	122	02/10/2003	Amazon	Africa	198.00	31,290.86
6	131	11/10/2002	Amazon	Africa	306.90	45,323.30
7			Amazon Total		594.00	89,709.16
8	127	07/10/2003	Cisco	Africa	258.50	39,086.66
9	136	04/10/2004	Cisco	Africa	367.40	53,119.11
10	139	07/10/2004	Cisco	Africa	403.70	57,796.59
11			Cisco Total		1,029.60	150,002.36
12				Africa Total	1,773.20	264,841.42
13	109	01/10/2002	AIG	Asia	40.00	8,040.00
14			AIG Total		40.00	8,040.00
15	107	11/10/2001	Amazon	Asia	15.00	29,280.00

continued...

8

691

Notes:

**My Tips/
Shortcuts:**

Coloring Two Subtotal Levels in Different Colors (cont.)

Option 2: Dynamic Coloring

➤ **To color each level in a different color using Conditional Formatting:**

1. Select cell **A1**, and then press **<Ctrl+Shift+*>** (in **Excel 2003**, press this or **<Ctrl+A>**) to select the **List**.

2. From the *Format* menu, select **Conditional Formatting**.

3. In **Condition 1**, select **Formula Is**.

4. In the formula box, enter the formula **=$D1=0** (or insert **ISBLANK** formula, see *Tip #281*).

5. Click **Format**, select the desired formatting, and then click **OK**.

6. Repeat steps 3 and 4 for **Condition 2**, typing the formula **=$C1=0** into the formula box.

7. Repeat step 5, and click **OK** twice.

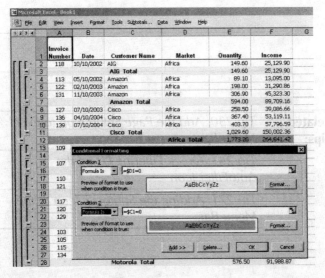

Subtotals

8

Notes:

**My Tips/
Shortcuts:**

| **Related
Tips:** | *Tip 230: Add the Page Setup icon to Excel
Menu Bar* |
| | *Tip 261: Quick Filtering Using the
AutoFilter Icon* |
| | *Tip 271: Adding the Subtotals Icon to the
Menu Bar* |

Adding the Auto Outline, Clear Outline, and Show Outline Symbols Icons to the Toolbar

➢ **To add the Auto Outline, Clear Outline, and Show Outline Symbols to the toolbar:**

1. Place the mouse arrow over one of the toolbars, right-click, and then select **Customize** from the shortcut menu.

2. Select the **Commands** tab.

3. From **Data**, drag the appropriate icons to the **Standard** toolbar.

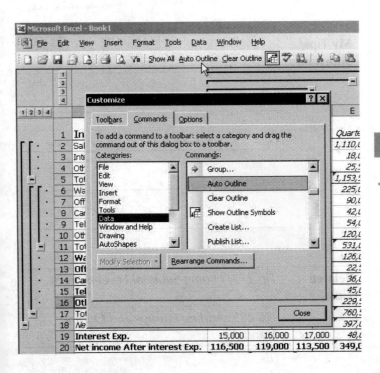

8

Notes:

**My Tips/
Shortcuts:**

**Related
Tips:**

Tip 273: Hiding Subtotal Level Buttons

*Tip 285: Adding Groups and Outlines
Manually*

Hiding Outline Symbols

Using keyboard shortcuts

➢ **To hide the outline symbols:**
 ✦ Press **<Ctrl+8>**.

➢ **To restore the outline symbols:**
 ✦ Press **<Ctrl+8>** again.

Before:

	A	B	C	D	E
1	Income	January	February	March	Quarter1
2	Sales	350,000	370,000	390,000	1,110,000
3	Interest	5,000	6,000	7,000	18,000
4	Other Income	7,500	8,500	9,500	25,500
5	Total Income	362,500	384,500	406,500	1,153,500
6	Wages Depart.1	70,000	75,000	80,000	225,000
7	Office Exp Depat.1	25,000	30,000	35,000	90,000
8	Car Exp. Depart.1	12,000	14,000	16,000	42,000
9	Telephone Depart1	16,000	18,000	20,000	54,000
10	Other Exp. Depart1	39,000	40,000	41,000	120,000
11	Total Exp. Depart1	162,000	177,000	192,000	531,000
12	Wages Depart.2	41,000	42,000	43,000	126,000
13	Office Exp Depat.2	5,000	7,500	10,000	22,500
14	Car Exp. Depart.2	10,000	12,000	14,000	36,000
15	Telephone Depart2	13,000	15,000	17,000	45,000
16	Other Exp. Depart2	69,000	76,500	84,000	229,500
17	Total Exp. Depart2	231,000	253,500	276,000	760,500
18	Net income	131,500	135,000	130,500	397,000

After:

	A	B	C	D	E
1	Income	January	February	March	Quarter1
2	Sales	350,000	370,000	390,000	1,110,000
3	Interest	5,000	6,000	7,000	18,000
4	Other Income	7,500	8,500	9,500	25,500
5	Total Income	362,500	384,500	406,500	1,153,500
6	Wages Depart.1	70,000	75,000	80,000	225,000
7	Office Exp Depat.1	25,000	30,000	35,000	90,000
8	Car Exp. Depart.1	12,000	14,000	16,000	42,000
9	Telephone Depart1	16,000	18,000	20,000	54,000
10	Other Exp. Depart1	39,000	40,000	41,000	120,000
11	Total Exp. Depart1	162,000	177,000	192,000	531,000
12	Wages Depart.2	41,000	42,000	43,000	126,000
13	Office Exp Depat.2	5,000	7,500	10,000	22,500
14	Car Exp. Depart.2	10,000	12,000	14,000	36,000
15	Telephone Depart2	13,000	15,000	17,000	45,000
16	Other Exp. Depart2	69,000	76,500	84,000	229,500
17	Total Exp. Depart2	231,000	253,500	276,000	760,500
18	Net income	131,500	135,000	130,500	397,000

Groups & Outlines

8

Notes:

**My Tips/
Shortcuts:**

**Related
Tips:**
*Tip 283: Adding the Auto Outline, Clear
Outline, and Show Outline Symbols Icons
to the Toolbar*

Adding Groups and Outlines Manually

➤ **To add groups and outlines manually:**

1. Select cells to group (cells **A2:A4** in the screenshot).

2. Press **<Alt+Shift+Right Arrow>**.

   OR

   From the *Data* menu, select **Group and Outline**, and then **Group**.

3. Repeat this technique for each group.

4. To clear the outlining, select the same rows or columns, and press **<Alt+Shift+Left Arrow>**.

Microsoft Excel - Book1

File Edit View Insert Format Tools Data Window Help

		A	B	C	D	E
	1	Income	January	February	March	Quarter1
	2	Sales	350,000	370,000	390,000	1,110,000
	3	Interest	5,000	6,000	7,000	18,000
	4	Other Income	7,500	8,500	9,500	25,500
	5	Total Income	362,500	384,500	406,500	1,153,500
	6	Wages Depart.1	70,000	75,000	80,000	225,000
	7	Office Exp Depat.1	25,000	30,000	35,000	90,000
	8	Car Exp. Depart.1	12,000	14,000	16,000	42,000
	9	Telephone Depart1	16,000	18,000	20,000	54,000
	10	Other Exp. Depart1	39,000	40,000	41,000	120,000
	11	Total Exp. Depart1	162,000	177,000	192,000	531,000
	12	**Wages Depart.2**	41,000	42,000	43,000	126,000
	13	**Office Exp Depat.2**	5,000	7,500	10,000	22,500
	14	**Car Exp. Depart.2**	10,000	12,000	14,000	36,000
	15	**Telephone Depart2**	13,000	15,000	17,000	45,000
	16	**Other Exp. Depart2**	69,000	76,500	84,000	229,500
	17	Total Exp. Depart2	231,000	253,500	276,000	760,500
	18	*Net income*	131,500	135,000	130,500	397,000

Notes:

**My Tips/
Shortcuts:**

**Related
Tips:**   *Tip 264: Coloring and Filtering List
          According to Criteria*

          Tip 280: Applying Styles to Subtotal Rows

          Tip 281: Applying Colors to Subtotal Rows

Copying or Applying Color to Groups and Outlines

➢ **To copy or apply colors to summary totals:**

1. Create the summary report using **Group and Outline**.

2. Select any cell in the **List**, and press **<Ctrl+Shift+*>** (in **Excel 2003**, press this or **<Ctrl+A>**) to select the **List**.

3. Press **<Alt+;>** to select the visible cells.

4. Copy and paste the data into a different sheet.

   OR

   Apply color to the visible cells by selecting a color from the **Fill Color** icon on the **Formatting** toolbar.

	A	E	I	M	Q	R	S
1	Income	Quarter1	Quarter2	Quarter3	Quarter4	YTD	
5	Total Income	1,153,500	1,351,500	1,153,500	1,351,500	5,010,000	
17	Total Exp. Depart2	760,500	963,000	760,500	963,000	3,447,000	
18	Net Income	397,000	394,000	397,000	394,000	1,582,000	
19	Interest Exp.	48,000	57,000	48,000	57,000	210,000	
20	Net Income After Interest Exp.	349,000	337,000	349,000	337,000	1,372,000	
21	Income Tax	125,640	121,320	125,640	121,320	493,920	
22	Net After Income Tax	223,360	215,680	223,360	215,680	878,080	
23							

Groups & Outlines

8

Notes:

My Tips/ Shortcuts:

Related Tips:	*Tip 288: Using Different Functions to Consolidate Lists*
	Tip 291: Summing Stock Lists
	Tip 292: Summing Sales Quantities and Amounts for Several Lists, or Presenting the Figures Side-by-Side

Consolidating Lists

The following rules allow the consolidation of Lists using Consolidate:

✦ The structure of the **Lists** must be identical.

✦ The headings of all rows and the leftmost columns in the **Lists** must contain the same topic.

✦ The number of columns and the number of rows do not have to be identical; nor does the internal order of the text.

✦ The **Lists** must have a single label row and a single column for labels.

✦ The cells in the **List**'s data range must contain only numeric data. Excel consolidates data by identifying corresponding text crossed between the header row and the leftmost column.

	A	B	C	D	E	F
	Microsoft Excel - Book1					
	File Edit View Insert Format Tools Data Window Help					
1	**Table1**	Eric	Nancy	Ana	Stephen	
2	Gross Salary	2,540	3,256	3,854	3,285	
3	Income Tax	381	488	578	493	
4	Social Security	127	163	193	164	
5	401K	76	98	116	99	
6						
7	**Table2**	Ana	Nancy	John	Eric	Lee
8	Gross Salary	3,758	3,125	3,526	2,758	1,552
9	Income Tax	564	469	529	414	233
10	Social Security	188	156	176	138	78
11	Other Deductions	100	50	25	35	25
12	401K	113	94	106	83	47
13						
14	**Table3**	John	Stephen	Eric	Nancy	
15	Gross Salary	3,541	2,985	2,999	3,125	
16	Income Tax	652	495	425	498	
17	Social Security	181	148	150	142	
18	401K	125	93	90	92	

Consolidating

8

continued...

Notes:

**My Tips/
Shortcuts:**

Consolidating Lists (cont.)

➢ **To consolidate Lists:**

1. Select a cell within **List1**, press **<Ctrl+Shift+*>** (in **Excel 2003**, press this or **<Ctrl+A>**) to select the **List**, and then press **<Ctrl+F3>** to define the **Name List1**, using the *Define Name* dialog box.

2. Repeat step 1 and define a **Name** for **List2** and a **Name** for **List3**.

3. Select a cell in any other sheet in the workbook, and from the *Data* menu, select **Consolidate**.

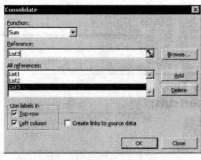

4. In the **Reference** box, press **<F3>**.

5. In the *Paste Name* dialog box, select **List1**, click **OK**, and then click **Add** to add **List1** to **All references**.

6. Repeat steps 4 and 5, and add **List2** and **List3** to **All references**.

7. In **Use Labels in**, select the **Top row** and **Left column** checkboxes, and then click **OK**.

The consolidated Lists:

	A	B	C	D	E	F	G
1		John	Eric	Nancy	Ana	Stephen	Lee
2	Gross Salary	7,067	8,297	9,506	7,612	6,270	1,552
3	Income Tax	1,181	1,220	1,455	1,142	988	233
4	Social Security	357	415	461	381	312	78
5	Other Deductions	25	35	50	100		25
6	401K	231	249	283	228	192	47
7							

Microsoft Excel - Book1

File   Edit   View   Insert   Format   Tools   Data   Window   Help

Consolidating

8

Notes:

**My Tips/
Shortcuts:**

Using Different Functions to Consolidate Lists

➤ **To consolidate Lists using different functions:**

1. Define **Names** for two **Lists**, and note the instructions on how to consolidate **Lists** (see *Tip #287*).

2. Select a cell in any other sheet in the workbook, and from the *Data* menu, select **Consolidate**.

3. In **Function**, choose **Sum**.

4. In the **Reference** box, press **<F3>**.

5. In the *Paste Name* dialog box, select **List1**, click **OK**, and then click **Add** to add **List1** to **All references**.

6. Repeat steps 4 and 5 and add **List2** and **List3** to **All references**.

7. In **Use Labels in**, select the **Top row** and **Left column** checkboxes, and then click **OK**.

8. Select a cell under the consolidated **Lists**, and repeat these steps twice, once with the **Count** function and then again with the **Average** function.

Microsoft Excel - Book1

File Edit View Insert Format Tools Data Window Help

	A	B	C	D	E	F	G	H	I
1		John	Eric	Nancy	Ana	Stephen	Lee		Consolidate using
2	Gross Salary	7,067	8,297	9,506	7,612	6,270	1,552		
3	Income Tax	1,181	1,220	1,455	1,142	988	233		
4	Social Security	357	415	461	381	312	78		Sum function
5	Other Deductions	25	35	50	100		25		
6	401K	231	249	283	228	192	47		
7									
8		John	Eric	Nancy	Ana	Stephen	Lee		
9	Gross Salary	2	3	3	2	2	1		
10	Income Tax	2	3	3	2	2	1		
11	Social Security	2	3	3	2	2	1		Count Function
12	Other Deductions	1	1	1	1		1		
13	401K	2	3	3	2	2	1		
14									
15		John	Eric	Nancy	Ana	Stephen	Lee		
16	Gross Salary	3,534	2,766	3,169	3,806	3,135	1,552		
17	Income Tax	590	407	485	571	494	233		
18	Social Security	179	138	154	190	156	78		Average function
19	Other Deductions	25	35	50	100		25		
20	401K	115	83	94	114	96	47		
21									

Consolidating

8

Notes:

My Tips/
Shortcuts:

Related Tips:	Tip 273: Hiding Subtotal Level Buttons
	Tip 291: Summing Stock Lists
	Tip 292: Summing Sales Quantities and Amounts for Several Lists, or Presenting the Figures Side-by-Side

Consolidating Lists While Adding Links to the Source Data

➢ **To consolidate Lists while adding links to the source data:**

1. Define **Names** for two **Lists**, and note the instructions on how to consolidate **Lists** (see *Tip #287*).

2. Select a cell in any other sheet in the workbook, and from the *Data* menu, select **Consolidate**.

3. In **Function**, choose **Sum**.

4. In the **Reference** box, press **<F3>**.

5. In the *Paste Name* dialog box, select **List1**, click **OK**, and then click **Add** to add **List1** to **All references**.

6. Repeat steps 4 and 5, and add **List2** and **List3** to **All references**.

7. In **Use Labels in**, select the **Top row**, **Left column** and **Create links to source data** checkboxes, and then click **OK**.

	A	B	C	D	E	F	G	H
			John	Eric	Nancy	Ana	Stephen	Lee
1								
2		Book1		2,540	3,256	3,854	3,285	
3		Book1	3,526	2,758	3,125	3,758		1,552
4		Book1	3,541	2,999	3,125		2,985	
5	Gross Salary		7,067	8,297	9,506	7,612	6,270	1,552
6		Book1		381	488	578	493	
7		Book1	529	414	469	564		233
8		Book1	652	425	498		495	
9	Income Tax		1,181	1,220	1,455	1,142	988	233
10		Book1		127	163	193	164	
11		Book1	176	138	156	188		78
12		Book1	181	150	142		148	
13	Social Security		357	415	461	381	312	78
14		Book1	25	35	50	100		25
15	Other Deductions		25	35	50	100		25
16		Book1		76	98	116	99	
17		Book1	106	83	94	113		47
18		Book1	125	90	92		93	
19	401K		231	249	283	228	192	47
20								

Microsoft Excel - Book1

File   Edit   View   Insert   Format   Tools   Data   Window   Help

C5   =SUM(C2:C4)

8

Notes:

**My Tips/
Shortcuts:**

**Related
Tips:**

Tip 279: Copying the Subtotals Summary

Tip 281: Applying Colors to Subtotal Rows

Tip 286: Copying or Applying Color to
Groups and Outlines

Coloring and/or Copying Subtotals from Consolidated Lists Containing Links

➤ **To color and/or copy subtotals summary from consolidated Lists:**

1. In the **Subtotal** levels, click level **1**.
2. Select a cell in the **List** and press **<Ctrl+Shift+*>** (in **Excel 2003**, press this or **<Ctrl+A>**).
3. Select visible cells, and press **<Alt+;>**.

   OR

   Press **<F5>** and in the *Go To* dialog box, click **Special**. In the *Go To Special* dialog box, select **Visible cells only** and click **OK**.

4. Copy and paste the subtotals summary into a different sheet or choose a color from the **Fill Color** icon in the **Formatting** toolbar.

	A	B	C	D	E	F	G	H
1			John	Eric	Nancy	Ana	Stephen	Lee
2		Book1	2,540	3,256	3,854	3,285		
3		Book1	3,526	2,758	3,125	3,758		1,552
4		Book1	3,541	2,999	3,125		2,985	
5	Gross Salary		7,067	8,297	9,506	7,612	6,270	1,552
6		Book1		381	488	578	493	
7		Book1	529	414	469	564		233
8		Book1	652	425	498		495	
9	Income Tax		1,181	1,220	1,455	1,142	988	233
10		Book1		127	163	193	164	
11		Book1	176	138	156	188		78
12		Book1	181	150	142		148	
13	Social Security		357	415	461	381	312	78
14		Book1	25	35	50	100		25
15	Other Deductions		25	35	50	100		25
16		Book1		76	98	116	99	
17		Book1	106	83	94	113		47
18		Book1	125	90	92		93	
19	401K		231	249	283	228	192	47
20								

C5 ▾ *fx* =SUM(C2:C4)

Notes:

My Tips/ Shortcuts:

Summing Stock Lists

➤ **To total stock List quantities:**

1. Define **Names** for two **Lists**, and note the instructions on how to consolidate **Lists** (see *Tip #287*).

2. Select a cell, and from the *Data* menu, select **Consolidate**.

3. In the **Reference** box, press **<F3>**.

4. In the *Paste Name* dialog box, select **List1**, click **OK**, and then click **Add** to add **List1** to **All references**.

5. Press **<F3>** again and add **List2** to **All references**.

6. In **Use Labels in**, select the **Top row** and **Left column** checkboxes, and then click **OK**.

	A	B	C
1	List 1- Stock Name	Quantities	Price Per Unit
2	Item1	5	5.00
3	Item2	7	6.00
4	Item3	4	3.00
5	Item4	3	3.50
6	Item5	2	4.50
7			
8			
9	List 2- Stock Name	Quantities	Price Per Unit
10	Item1	5	5.00
11	Item2	7	6.00
12	Item5	2	4.50
13	Item6	8	3.85
14	Item7	7	4.20
15			
16	Consolidate Lists		
17			
18		Quantities	Price Per Unit
19	Item1	10	10.00
20	Item2	14	12.00
21	Item3	4	3.00
22	Item4	3	3.50
23	Item5	4	9.00
24	Item6	8	3.85
25	Item7	7	4.20

Result:

Oops!!! The **Price per Unit** (see cells **C19:C25** in the screenshot) has also been totaled!!!

continued...

Consolidating

8

Notes:

**My Tips/
Shortcuts:**

Summing Stock Lists (cont.)

Solution:

1. For each **List**, change the heading above the **Price per unit** column to **Price per Unit L1** in cell **C1** and **Price per Unit L2** in cell **C9** (see screenshot).

2. Repeat steps 2 through 6 on the previous page to consolidate the **Lists**.

Result:

Microsoft Excel - Book1

File | Edit | View | Insert | Format | Tools | Data | Window | Help

	A	B	C	D
1	List 1- Stock Name	Quantities	Price Per Unit L1	
2	Item1	5	5.00	
3	Item2	7	6.00	
4	Item3	4	3.00	
5	Item4	3	3.50	
6	Item5	2	4.50	
7				
8				
9	List 2- Stock Name	Quantities	Price Per Unit L2	
10	Item1	5	5.00	
11	Item2	7	6.00	
12	Item5	2	4.50	
13	Item6	8	3.85	
14	Item7	7	4.20	
15				
16	Consolidate Lists			
17				
18		Quantities	Price Per Unit L1	Price Per Unit L2
19	Item1	10	5.00	5.00
20	Item2	14	6.00	6.00
21	Item3	4	3.00	
22	Item4	3	3.50	
23	Item5	4	4.50	4.50
24	Item6	8		3.85
25	Item7	7		4.20

Consolidating

8

Notes:

**My Tips/
Shortcuts:**

Summing Sales Quantities and Amounts for Several Lists, or Presenting the Figures Side-by-Side

➤ **To total the quantities and the amounts of monthly sales Lists:**

1. Define **Names** for two **Lists**, and note the instructions on how to consolidate **Lists**, see *Tip #287*.

2. Select a cell, and from the *Data* menu, select **Consolidate**.

3. In the **Reference** box, press **<F3>**.

4. In the *Paste Name* dialog box, select **List1**, click **OK**, and then click **Add** to add **List1** to **All references**.

5. Press **<F3>** again and add **List2** to **All references**.

6. In **Use Labels in**, select the **Top row** and **Left column** checkboxes, and then click **OK**.

	A	B	C
	Microsoft Excel - Book1		
	File Edit View Insert Format Tools Data Window Help		
	A	B	C
1	**January 2004- Item Name**	**Quantities**	**Total Sales**
2	Item1	5	25.00
3	Item2	7	42.00
4	Item3	4	12.00
5	Item4	3	10.50
6	Item5	2	9.00
7			
8			
9	**February 2004- Stock Name**	**Quantities**	**Total Sales**
10	Item1	5	25.00
11	Item2	7	42.00
12	Item5	2	9.00
13	Item6	8	30.80
14	Item7	7	29.40
15			
16	**Consolidate Lists**		
17			
18		Quantities	Total Sales
19	Item1	10	50.00
20	Item2	14	84.00
21	Item3	4	12.00
22	Item4	3	10.50
23	Item5	4	18.00
24	Item6	8	30.80
25	Item7	7	29.40
26			

Consolidating

continued...

Notes:

_____

_____

_____

_____

_____

_____

**My Tips/
Shortcuts:**

_____

_____

_____

_____

_____

_____

_____

_____

_____

_____

_____

Summing Sales Quantities and Amounts for Several Lists, or Presenting the Figures Side-by-Side (cont.)

➢ **To display total sales (quantities and amounts) by month, side-by-side:**

1. In **List1**, change the heading titles **Quantities** and **Total Sales** to **Quantities — Jan** and **Total Sales — Jan**, respectively.

2. In **List2**, change the heading titles **Quantities** and **Total Sales** to **Quantities — Feb** and **Total Sales — Feb**, respectively.

3. Repeat steps 2 through 6 on the previous page to consolidate the **Lists**.

Result:

Microsoft Excel - Book1

File Edit View Insert Format Tools Data Window Help

	A	B	C	D	E
1	January 2004- Item Name	Quantities - Jan	Total Sales - Jan		
2	Item1	5	25.00		
3	Item2	7	42.00		
4	Item3	4	12.00		
5	Item4	3	10.50		
6	Item5	2	9.00		
7					
8					
9	February 2004- Stock Name	Quantities - Feb	Total Sales - Feb		
10	Item1	5	25.00		
11	Item2	7	42.00		
12	Item5	2	9.00		
13	Item6	8	30.80		
14	Item7	7	29.40		
15					
16	Consolidate Lists				
17					
18		Quantities - Jan	Total Sales - Jan	Quantities - Feb	Total Sales - Feb
19	Item1	5	25.00	5	25.00
20	Item2	7	42.00	7	42.00
21	Item3	4	12.00		
22	Item4	3	10.50		
23	Item5	2	9.00	2	9.00
24	Item6			8	30.80
25	Item7			7	29.40
26					

C onsolidating

8

719

Notes:

**My Tips/
Shortcuts:**

Related Tips:	Tip 291: Summing Stock Lists
	Tip 292: Summing Sales Quantities and Amounts for Several Lists, or Presenting the Figures Side-by-Side
	Tip 294: Comparing Lists

Summing Monthly Trial Balance Figures

➢ **To total the figures of the monthly Trial Balances Lists:**

1. Define **Names** for each of the Trial Balances as follows: Select a cell within the January Trial Balance, press **<Ctrl+Shift+*>** (in **Excel 2003**, press this or **<Ctrl+A>**) to select the region, and then press **<Ctrl+F3>** to define the **Name TB_Jan**.

2. Repeat step 1 for the February Trial Balance and define a **Name** for **TB_Feb**.

3. Select a cell, and from the *Data* menu, select **Consolidate**.

4. In the **Reference** box, press **<F3>**.

5. In the *Paste Name* dialog box, select **TB_Jan**, click **OK**, and then click **Add** to add **TB_Jan** to **All references**.

	A	B	C
	Microsoft Excel - Book1		
	File Edit View Insert Format Tools Data Window H		
	A	B	C
1	**January**	**Debit**	**Credit**
2	Sales		10,000
3	Materials	1,252	
4	Subcontracted Costs	2,015	
5	Labor	1,953	
6	Rental	502	
7	Maintenance & Repairs	225	
8	Cleaning	152	
9	Insurance	303	
10	Utilities	175	
11			
12	**February**	**Debit**	**Credit**
13	Sales		12,856
14	Materials	1,442	
15	Subcontracted Costs	1,998	
16	Labor	2,023	
17	Rental	452	
18	Maintenance & Repairs	245	
19	Cleaning	172	
20	Insurance	297	
21	Utilities	166	
22	Property Taxes	283	
23	Travel	299	
24	Computer Software	99	
25			

Consolidating

continued...

8

Notes:

_____

_____

_____

_____

_____

_____

My Tips/
Shortcuts:

_____

_____

_____

_____

_____

_____

_____

_____

_____

_____

Summing Monthly Trial Balance Figures (cont.)

6. Press **<F3>** again and add **TB_Feb** to **All references**.

7. In **Use Labels in**, select the **Top row** and **Left column** checkboxes, and then click **OK**.

The Consolidated Trial Balances:

	A	B	C
		Debit	Credit
1		Debit	Credit
2	Sales		22,856
3	Materials	2,694	
4	Subcontracted Costs	4,013	
5	Labor	3,976	
6	Rental	954	
7	Maintenance & Repairs	470	
8	Cleaning	324	
9	Insurance	600	
10	Utilities	341	
11	Property Taxes	283	
12	Travel	299	
13	Computer Software	99	

Notes:

**My Tips/
Shortcuts:**

Comparing Lists

➤ **To compare Lists, use the Consolidate technique:**

1. The screenshot below shows two **Lists**, the first in column **A** and the second in column **D**. Add the text **List Number** as a heading in columns **B** and **E**, and then add the **List** numbers, as shown.

2. Define **Names** for two **Lists**, and note the instructions on how to consolidate **Lists** (see *Tip #287*).

3. Select a cell, and from the *Data* menu, select **Consolidate**.

4. In the **Reference** box, press **<F3>**.

5. In the *Paste Name* dialog box, select **List1**, click **OK**, and then click **Add** to add **List1** to **All references**.

6. Press **<F3>** again and add **List2** to **All references**.

7. In **Use Labels in**, select the **Top row** and **Left column** checkboxes, and then click **OK**.

The consolidation results are shown in cells **A10:B16**. The consolidation technique uses **SUM** to total the numbers in the **Lists** when the text at the top row and in the leftmost column matches for both **Lists**.

	A	B	C	D	E	F	G
	Microsoft Excel - Book1						
	File Edit View Insert Format Tools Data Window Help						
1	**List1**	**List Number**		**List2**	**List Number**		
2	Eric	1		Ana	2		
3	Nancy	1		Nancy	2		
4	Ana	1		John	2		
5	Stephen	1		Eric	2		
6				Lee	2		
7							
8	**Consolidate List**						
9							
10		List Number					
11	Stephen	1	1= the employee name appears in List1 only.				
12	John	2	2= the employee name appears in List2 only.				
13	Lee	2					
14	Eric	3	3= the employee name appears in both lists - 1+2=3				
15	Nancy	3					
16	Ana	3					

continued...

Notes:

_____

_____

_____

_____

_____

**My Tips/
Shortcuts:**

_____

_____

_____

_____

_____

_____

_____

_____

_____

_____

Comparing Lists (cont.)

➤ **To compare more than two Lists:**
  ✦ Use **2^** to add the **List** number, or any other
    combination that returns the same results. For
    List1, use the number **1**, for **List2**, use the number
    2, and for **List3**, use the number **4**.

The result of consolidating three **Lists**:

	A	B	C	D	E	F	G	H
	List1	**List Number**		**List2**	**List Number**		**List3**	**List Number**
1	List1	List Number		List2	List Number		List3	List Number
2	Eric	1		Ana	2		Ana	4
3	Nancy	1		Nancy	2		Nancy	4
4	Stephen	1		John	2		Lee	4
5	David	1		Eric	2		David	4
6								
7								
8	**Consolidate List**							
9								
10		List Number						
11	Stephen	1		Appears in List1 only				
12	John	2		Appears in List2 only				
13	Eric	3		Appears in List1 & List2				
14	Lee	4		Appears in List3 only				
15	David	5		Appears in List1 & List3				
16	Ana	6		Appears in List2 & List3				
17	Nancy	7		Appears in all three lists				
18								

C omparing Lists

8

Notes:

My Tips/
Shortcuts:

Related Tips:	*Tip 292: Summing Sales Quantities and Amounts for Several Lists, or Presenting the Figures Side-by-Side*
	Tip 293: Summing Monthly Trial Balance Figures
	Tip 294: Comparing Lists

8

Comparing Lists Using the COUNTIF Formula

➢ **To compare between two Lists:**

✦ **Step 1: Check each List**

1. For cells in column **B**, insert the formula
   =IF(COUNTIF(E:E,A2)>0,3,1).

2. For cells in column **F**, insert the formula
   =IF(COUNTIF(A:A,E2)>0,3,2).

✦ **Step 2: Merging the Lists into one List of unique names**

1. Select cell **B2**, and click the **Sort Ascending** icon on the **Standard** toolbar.

2. Repeat step 1 for cell **F2**.

3. In column **E**, beginning with cell **E2**, copy the names of those employees for whom the number **2** appears in column **F**, and then paste the names at the bottom of the first **List**.

	A	B	C	D	E	F	G
	List 1	Result	Function syntax		List 2	Result	Function syntax
2	Merrill	1	=IF(COUNTIF(E:E,A2)>0,3,1)		Joseph	2	=IF(COUNTIF(A:A,E2)>0,3,2)
3	Karen	1			Roy	2	
4	Julie	1			Patrick	2	
5	Trudy	1			Fred	2	
6	Woody	1			Mark	2	
7	Craig	1			Neil	3	
8	Neil	3			John	3	
9	Bonnie	3			Bonnie	3	
10	John	3			lee	3	
11	lee	3					

Comparing Lists

8

Notes:

**My Tips/
Shortcuts:**

**Related
Tips:**

Tip 297: PivotTable Report Terminology

Tip 298: Creating a PivotTable Report

Rules for Organizing the Source Data in Excel Sheets

The rules for organizing the List to create a PivotTable report are as follows:

✦ The **List** can have only one header row.

✦ All cells in the header row must contain unique text.

✦ The **List** cannot have subtotal rows, empty rows, empty columns, or a row containing totals under the **List**.

It is **highly recommended** that you define a **Name** that automatically updates its range reference for the **List** (see *Tip #193*).

	A	B	C	D	E	F
1	Invoice Number	Date	Customer Name	Market	Quantity	Income
2	1001	01/15/2002	Intel	Europe	252	2,523.00
3	1002	02/15/2002	eBay	Europe	4,585	45,852.00
4	1003	03/15/2002	ExcelTip	N.America	665	6,652.00
5	1004	04/15/2002	Toyota	Europe	185	1,854.00
6	1005	05/15/2002	Amazon	Africa	966	9,658.00
7	1006	06/15/2002	GM	N.America	1,255	12,554.00
8	1007	07/15/2002	Ford	Europe	1,463	14,632.00
9	1008	08/15/2002	GM	N.America	1,686	16,857.00
10	1009	09/15/2002	Microsoft	Europe	999	9,985.00
11	1010	15/15/2002	Intel	Africa	741	7,412.00
12	1011	11/15/2002	Toyota	Europe	199	1,985.00
13	1012	12/15/2002	Microsoft	Europe	178	1,775.00
14	1013	01/15/2003	eBay	Europe	965	9,652.00
15	1014	02/15/2003	Amazon	Africa	1,746	17,462.00

PivotTables

8

Notes:

**My Tips/
Shortcuts:**

Related Tips:	*Tip 296: Rules for Organizing the Source Data in Excel Sheets*
	Tip 298: Creating a PivotTable Report

PivotTable Report Terminology

The following terms are used in **PivotTable** reports:

✦ **Field:** The header at the top of a column in a **List** (data source table).

✦ **Item:** Numeric data or text in the **Field** column.

✦ **Data:** An area detailing the data in the lower part of the **PivotTable** report, including columns with numeric data.

✦ **Row Field:** A field that is positioned as a row in the lower left of the **PivotTable** report.

✦ **Column Field:** A field that is positioned as a column in the row above the data in the **PivotTable** report.

✦ **Page Field:** A field that is positioned in the upper left of the **PivotTable** report.

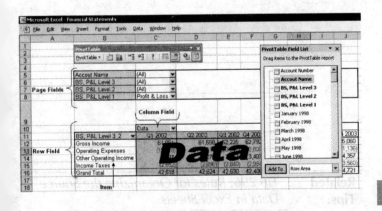

Notes:

My Tips/ Shortcuts:

Related Tips:

Tip 296: Rules for Organizing the Source Data in Excel Sheets

Tip 297: PivotTable Report Terminology

Creating a PivotTable Report

➢ **To create a PivotTable report:**

1. Select any cell in the source data, and press **<Ctrl+Shift+*>** (in **Excel 2003**, press this or **<Ctrl+A>**).

2. Press **<Ctrl+F3>**, and then type the defined **Name** for the source data.

3. From the *Data* menu, select **PivotTable and PivotChart Report**.

4. In **Step 1 of 3**, select **Microsoft Excel list or database**, and then click **Next**.

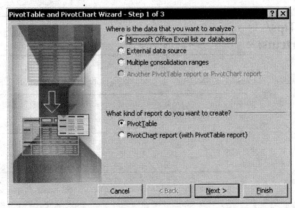

5. In **Step 2 of 3**, in the **Range** box, press **<F3>** to open the *Paste Name* dialog box, and paste the **Name** of the source data as defined in step 2.

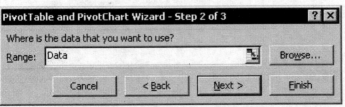

6. Click **Next**.

continued...

Notes:

**My Tips/
Shortcuts:**

Creating a PivotTable Report (cont.)

7. In **Step 3 of 3**, click **Layout** (in **Excel 97**, go to step 8).

In **Excel 2002** and **Excel 2003**, you can skip this step. Instead, click **Finish** in **Step 2 of 3** and then create the **PivotTable** report by dragging the fields from the *Pivot Table Field List* dialog box to the **PivotTable** report.

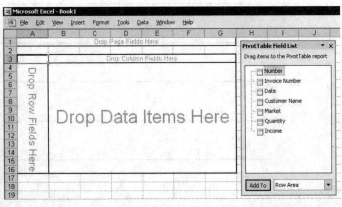

continued...

PivotTables

8

Notes:

**My Tips/
Shortcuts:**

Creating a PivotTable Report (cont.)

8. In the *Layout* dialog box, drag the **Data Fields** to the white **Data** area, and drag all other fields to the white **Page** area (except fields that are not going to be used in the **PivotTable** report), and then click **OK**.

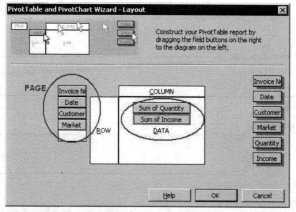

9. In **Step 3 of 3**, click **Finish**. The **PivotTable** report is created.

10. Drag **Data** (in cell **A5** in the screenshot) to the right of the **PivotTable** report to change the layout from horizontal to vertical.

	A	B	C	D	E	F
1	Date	(All) ▼				
2	Customer Name	(All) ▼				
3	Market	(All) ▼				
4						
5	Data ▼	Total				
6	Sum of Quantity	7549.6				
7	Sum of Income	1215979.969				
8						

continued...

PivotTables

8

Notes:

My Tips/ Shortcuts:

Creating a PivotTable Report (cont.)

11. The **PivotTable** report is now ready to be used. For more details on how to use the **PivotTable** report properly, see the other tips in this category.

	Microsoft Excel - Book1				
	File Edit View Insert Format Tools Data Window Help				
	A	B	C	D	E
1	Date	(All)			
2	Customer Name	(All)			
3	Market	(All)			
4					
5		Data			
6		Sum of Quantity	Sum of Income		
7	Total	7549.6	1215979.969		
8					

Related Tips: Tip 300: Automatically refreshing a PivotTable Report on

Tip 301: Adding/Deleting Subtotals

Tip 302: Hiding Items

PivotTables

8

Notes:

_____

_____

_____

_____

_____

_____

_____

**My Tips/
Shortcuts:**

_____

_____

_____

_____

_____

_____

_____

**Related
Tips:**

Tip 300: Automatically Refreshing a
PivotTable Report

Tip 301: Adding/Deleting Subtotals

Tip 302: Hiding Items

Setting the Number of Fields Displayed in the Page Layout

➢ **To set the number of fields displayed per column in the Page layout:**

1. Select a cell in the **PivotTable** report.
2. Press **<Alt+P>**.

    OR

    Right-click and then select **Table Options** from the shortcut menu.

3. Change the number in **Fields per column**, and then click **OK**.

Note: If the **PivotTable** toolbar is not visible, hover the mouse pointer on the toolbar, right-click and select the **PivotTable** toolbar.

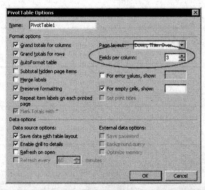

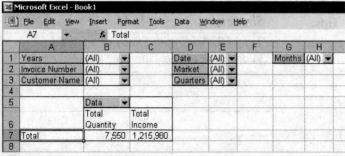

Notes:

**My Tips/
Shortcuts:**

| **Related
Tips:** | *Tip 19: Adding a Custom Keyboard
Shortcut* |
| | *Tip 118: Adding the Path of a Saved
Workbook to the Title Bar* |

Automatically Refreshing a PivotTable Report

➢ **To automatically refresh the data in a PivotTable Report:**

✦ **Step 1: Automatically update the source data range Name**

✦ See *Tip #193: Automatically Updating a Range Name Reference.*

✦ **Step 2: Add a VBA Event to automatically refresh the PivotTable report**

1. Press **<Alt+F11>**, and then double-click the sheet name in the **VBAProject** pane.

2. From the left dropdown list above the **Module** sheet, select **Worksheet**, and from the right dropdown list, select **Activate**.

3. Copy the code from the Macro Event **Activate** in the screenshot.

4. Press **<Ctrl+S>** to save the workbook, and then press **<Alt+F4>** to close the **VBE**. The **PivotTable** report is refreshed automatically upon selecting the sheet that contains it.

Note: To find the **PivotTable** report name (in this example, **PivotTable1**), select a cell in the **PivotTable** report, right-click, and then select **Table Options** from the shortcut menu.

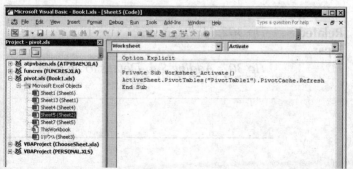

Notes:

_____

_____

_____

_____

_____

_____

_____

**My Tips/
Shortcuts:**

_____

_____

_____

_____

_____

_____

**Related
Tips:**

Tip 302: Hiding Items

Tip 307: Adding Sub-Details to an Item

_____

_____

Adding/Deleting Subtotals

➢ **To add subtotals to a PivotTable report:**

1. Drag at least two fields to the **Row** area that is left of the **Data** area).

2. Double-click the left **Row** field's gray title; see the mouse cursor in the screenshot.

The *PivotTable Field* dialog box has three option buttons:

✦ **Automatic:** Excel uses the **SUM** formula as the default when inserting subtotals.

✦ **Custom:** Selecting this option allows the insertion of one or more formulas.

✦ **None:** Displays the **PivotTable** report without subtotals.

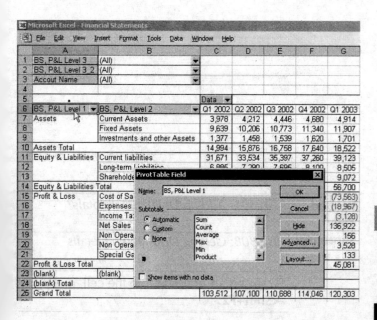

PivotTables

8

Notes:

**My Tips/
Shortcuts:**

Related Tips/ Shortcuts:	*Tip 301: Adding/Deleting Subtotals*
	Tip 308: Getting Drill-Down Details
	To insert a **Comment** into the cell, press **<Shift+F2>**

Hiding Items

➢ **To hide items in a PivotTable report:**

✦ In **Excel 97**, double-click the name of the leftmost **Row** field, and in **Hide Items**, select the item to hide, and then click **OK**.

✦ In all other Excel versions, open the dropdown list of any field and cancel the selection of the items you wish to hide. To open the dropdown list using a keyboard shortcut, press **<Alt+Down Arrow>** (or **<Up Arrow>**).

CAUTION! You must be very careful when reporting totals after hiding items in a **PivotTable** report. There is no indication in any field, page, row or column that one or more items are hidden (as opposed to other areas in Excel, for example, when using **Automatic Filter** in the **Filter** technique, the color of the dropdown list's arrow changes to blue). It is therefore **highly recommended** to insert a **Comment** in a cell to remind you of any hidden items.

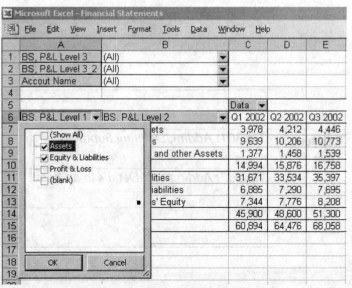

Notes:

**My Tips/
Shortcuts:**

Related Tips:	*Tip 301: Adding/Deleting Subtotals*
	Tip 307: Adding Sub-Details to an Item

Displaying the Top/Bottom Number of Items

➤ **To display the top 10 items:**

1. Select a cell in a row field and press **<Alt+P>** to display **PivotTable** shortcut menu from the **PivotTable** toolbar (if the **PivotTable** toolbar is not visible, see the **Note** in *Tip #299*).

2. Select **Sort and Top 10** (when using **Excel 2002** or **Excel 2003**).

   OR

   Right-click, and then select **Field Settings** from the shortcut menu.

3. Click **Advanced**.

4. In the **PivotTable** *Sort and Top 10* dialog box (when using Excel 2002 & Excel 2003), or in the *PivotTable Field Advanced Options* dialog box, select the **On** option button in the **Top 10 AutoShow** section.

5. Select **Top** (or **Bottom**) from the **Show** dropdown list, and then select the desired display number.

6. In **Using Field**, select the data field to filter for the **Top** (or **Bottom**) items, and then click **OK**.

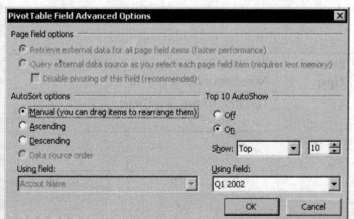

Notes:

**My Tips/
Shortcuts:**

Related Tips:	*Tip 303: Displaying the Top/Bottom Number of Items*
	Tip 305: Inserting a Chart

Formatting a PivotTable Report

➤ **To format a PivotTable report:**

1. Select a cell in the **PivotTable** report.
2. Click the **Format Report** icon on the **PivotTable** toolbar.

   OR

   Press **<Alt+P>** (if the **PivotTable** toolbar is not visible, see the **Note** in *Tip #299*).

   Select **Format Report and** select one of the format options, and then click **OK**.

In **Excel 97**, use **AutoFormat** (this exists in all Excel versions): From the *Format* menu, select **AutoFormat**.

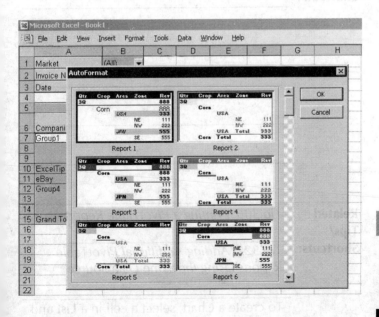

Notes:

_____

_____

_____

_____

_____

_____

**My Tips/
Shortcuts:**

_____

_____

_____

_____

_____

_____

Related Tips/ Shortcuts:	Tip 306: Printing a PivotTable Report
	Tip 322: Adding Additional PivotTable Reports Using the Same Data Source

To create a Chart, select a cell in a **List** and press **<F11>**.

Inserting a Chart

> **To insert a Chart while creating the PivotTable report:**

+ In **Excel 2000**, **2002** and **2003**, check the **PivotChart report** option button in **Step 1 of 3**. The **Chart** is automatically linked to the **PivotTable** report and displays the field structure.

> **To insert a Chart after the PivotTable report is created, in all Excel versions:**
+ Select a cell in the **PivotTable** report, and then press **<F11>**.

Note to Excel 97 users: In **Excel 97**, the **PivotTable** report is treated like a regular table. By changing the structure of the **PivotTable** report, you will cause undesired changes in the chart. To solve this problem, use only one **PivotTable** report per chart, and add more **PivotTables** for each chart (see *Tip #322*).

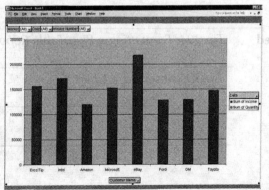

PivotTables

8

Notes:

_____

_____

_____

_____

_____

_____

My Tips/
Shortcuts:

_____

_____

_____

_____

_____

_____

Related Tips:	_Tip 304: Formatting a PivotTable Report_
	Tip 305: Inserting a Chart

Printing a PivotTable Report

➢ **To print a PivotTable report:**

1. Select one of the cells in the **PivotTable** report.
2. Press **<Ctrl+Shift+*>** (in **Excel 2003**, press this or **<Ctrl+A>**) to select the **PivotTable** report.
3. From the *File* menu, select **Set Print Area** (when using **Excel 97** and **Excel 2000**, pressing **<Ctrl+Shift+*>** selects the entire **PivotTable** report, including the fields in the page field).
4. To only print the itemization rows in the detailed lower section of the **PivotTable** report, select the rows without using the **<Ctrl+Shift+*>** shortcut and set the **Print Area**.

	B	C	D	E	F	G
1 Invoice Number	(All)					
2 Date	(All)					
3 Customer Name	(All)					
4						
5	Data					
6 Market	Total Quantity	% Quantity	Total Income	% Income	Invoices Number	Ave. Price Sold
7 Africa	1,773	23.49%	264,841	21.78%	7	149
8 Asia	1,538	20.38%	303,495	24.96%	12	197
9 USA	3,535	46.82%	532,670	43.81%	14	151
10 Europe	703	9.31%	114,974	9.46%	6	164
11 Grand Total	7,550	100.00%	1,215,980	100.00%	39	161
12						

Notes:

**My Tips/
Shortcuts:**

**Related
Tips:**

Tip 301: Adding/Deleting Subtotals

*Tip 303: Displaying the Top/Bottom
Number of Items*

Tip 310: Adding a Calculated Field

Adding Sub-Details to an Item

➢ **To add sub-details to an item:**

1. Select an item in the row field (in the screenshot, the selected item is **Cost of Sales**) and double-click.

2. In the *Show Detail* dialog box, select the name of the sub-detail field.

3. Click **OK**.

4. To hide the sub-detail **List**, double-click the selected item.

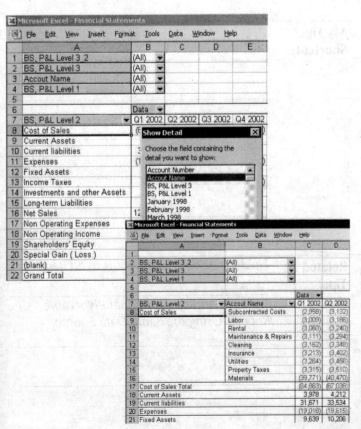

Notes:

**My Tips/
Shortcuts:**

| **Related
Tips:** | *Tip 307: Adding Sub-Details to an Item* |
| | *Tip 322: Adding Additional PivotTable
Reports Using the Same Data Source* |

Getting Drill-Down Details

➢ **To get full drill-down details:**

✦ In the **PivotTable** report, select a cell in the **Data**
area for which you want to get drill-down details
and double-click. A new sheet is automatically
inserted with an itemized data **List** showing all
rows included in the selected cell.

Example: Double-click cell **B7**.

	A	B	C	D
1	Invoice Number	(All) ▼		
2	Date	(All) ▼		
3	Market	(All) ▼		
4				
5		Data ▼		
6	Customer Name ▼	Sum of Quantity	Sum of Income	
7	ExcelTip	1,015	155,118	
8	Intel	809	128,260	

Result:

	A	B	C	D	E	F
1	Invoice Number	Date	Customer Name	Market	Quantity	Income
2	101	5/10/2001	ExcelTip	USA	15	2136.752137
3	140	8/10/2004	ExcelTip	USA	415.8	59355.75
4	130	10/10/2003	ExcelTip	USA	294.8	43764.14286
5	124	10/4/2003	ExcelTip	USA	222.2	34409.17857
6	111	3/10/2002	ExcelTip	USA	67	15452
7						

PivotTables

8

Notes:

**My Tips/
Shortcuts:**

Related Tips:	*Tip 311: Grouping the Date Field by Number of Days*
	Tip 312: Grouping the Date Field by Days, Months, Quarters, and Years

Grouping Text Fields

➤ **To group text fields:**

1. Select a few items in a row field. In the example, items are selected from **Customer Name**.

	A	B	C	D	E
	Microsoft Excel - Book1				
	File Edit View Insert Format Tools Data Window Hel				
	A	B	C	D	E
1	Market	(All) ▼			
2	Invoice Number	(All) ▼			
3	Date	(All) ▼			
4					
5		Data ▼			
6	Customer Name ▼	Total Quantity	% Quantity	Total Income	% Income
7	Amazon	609	8.07%	118,989	9.79%
8	Intel	1,122	14.87%	170,699	14.04%
9	Microsoft	979	12.97%	151,668	12.47%
10	ExcelTip	1,015	13.44%	155,118	12.76%
11	eBay	1,266	16.76%	217,068	17.85%
12	Toyota	939	12.44%	146,221	12.02%
13	GM	809	10.72%	128,260	10.55%
14	Ford	811	10.74%	127,957	10.52%
15	Grand Total	7,550	100.00%	1,215,980	100.00%

2. Press **<Alt+Shift+Right Arrow>**.

   OR

   Right-click, select **Group and Outline** from the shortcut menu, and then **Group**.

3. In the new field, change the text **Group1** by typing over it.

4. Repeat the steps above to add more groups and change the group text.

5. Type a new name for the new field on the gray title, and then click **OK**.

6. Drag the **Customer Name** field to **Page** (in the upper-left corner).

Note: Only one new group field can be created. If you want to add more group fields to the same field (for example, to group customers by salesperson name or product), you must copy and paste the **Customer Name** column into the source data, change the heading title, and then group each field in the **PivotTable** report.

PivotTables

8

Notes:

_____

_____

_____

_____

_____

_____

_____

My Tips/
Shortcuts:

_____

_____

_____

_____

_____

_____

| **Related** | *Tip 315: Adding a Calculated Percentage* |
| **Tips:** | *Field* |

Tip 317: Adding a Data Field That
Calculates Percentages from One Item of
the Row Field

_____

Adding a Calculated Field

➢ **To add a formula (Calculated Field) as a new column in a PivotTable report:**

1. Select a cell in the **PivotTable** report.

2. Press **<Alt+P>** to select **PivotTable** dropdown icon from **Pivot Table** toolbar, select **Formulas**, and then **Calculated Field**.

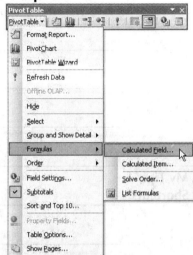

3. In the *Insert Calculated Field* dialog box, type the formula name in the **Name** box.

4. In the **Fields** list box, select the first field name to insert and click **Insert Field**. The field name is copied into the **Formula** box.

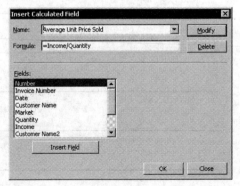

PivotTables

8

continued...

Notes:

_____

_____

_____

_____

_____

**My Tips/
Shortcuts:**

_____

_____

_____

_____

_____

_____

_____

_____

_____

Adding a Calculated Field (cont.)

5. Type **/** (in this example), repeat step 4 to insert the second field into the formula, and then click **OK**.

6. To format the new field, select a cell in the field and click the **Field Settings** icon on the **PivotTable** toolbar.

CAUTION! This option can some times return incorrect calculation results when using multiplying or dividing.

Notes:

_____

_____

_____

_____

_____

_____

My Tips/
Shortcuts:

_____

_____

_____

_____

_____

_____

Related Tips:	*Tip 312: Grouping the Date Field by Days, Months, Quarters, and Years*
	Tip 313: Grouping the Date Field by Week Number
	Tip 314: Grouping the Date Field by Quarters in a Fiscal Reporting Year

Grouping the Date Field by Number of Days

➢ **To group the Date field by number of days:**

1. Drag the **Date** field from **Page** (the fields in the top-left corner) to **Row** (to the left of the data area).

2. Select one of the dates in the **Date** field (cell **A8** in the screenshot).

3. Right-click, select **Group and Show Detail** from the shortcut menu, and then select **Group**.

4. In the *Grouping* dialog box, select **Days**, and in **Number of days**, set the desired number.

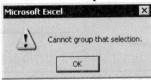

CAUTION!!! If the message **Cannot group that selection** appears, drag the **Date** field back to **Page**, and check the date column in the source data for empty cells or for dates that are not in date format, fix them all and then select the **PivotTable** report, click **Refresh**, drag the **Date** field to **Row** and try grouping again.

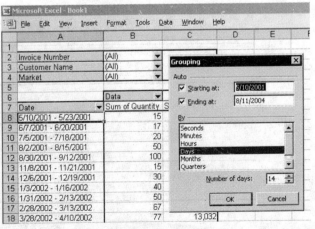

continued...

Notes:

**My Tips/
Shortcuts:**

Grouping the Date Field by Number of Days (cont.)

When displaying the *Grouping* dialog box, **Starting at** is the first date in the source data, which is **5/10/2001** in the above example.

➢ **To set the grouping starting date at the first working date in the week:**

1. Before opening the *Grouping* dialog box, type **5/10/2001** into any cell in the sheet, select the cell, and then press **<Ctrl+1>**.

2. In the *Format Cells* dialog box, select the **Number** tab, then **Custom**, and in the **Type** box, type **dddd**. The result is **Thursday**. The date for the first working day in the same week is therefore **5/7/2001**.

3. In the *Grouping* dialog box, type **5/7/2001** in **Starting at**, and then click **OK**.

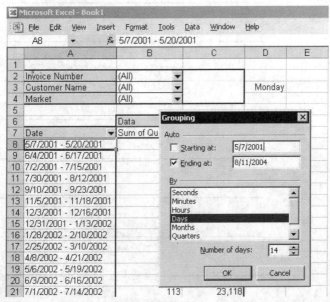

continued...

Notes:

_____

_____

_____

_____

_____

_____

_____

_____

My Tips/
Shortcuts:

_____

_____

_____

_____

_____

_____

_____

_____

_____

_____

Grouping the Date Field by Number of Days (cont.)

Grouping the Date Field by Number of Days and by Days, Months, Quarters, and Years

You can group a **Date** field only once, either by **Number of Days** or by **Days**, **Months**, **Quarters**, and **Years**, as explained in *Tip #312*.

If you want to group the **Date** field by both **Number of Days** or by **Days**, **Months**, **Quarters**, and **Years**:

1. Copy and insert the **Date** column in the source data so that there are two **Date** columns.
2. Change the heading title of the new **Date** column.
3. Add the new field to the **PivotTable** report, and then group each one of the **Date** fields, one by **Number of Days** and the other by **Days**, **Months**, **Quarters, and Years**.

Notes:

_____

_____

_____

_____

_____

_____

**My Tips/
Shortcuts:**

_____

_____

_____

_____

_____

_____

Related Tips:	*Tip 311: Grouping the Date Field by Number of Days*
	Tip 313: Grouping the Date Field by Week Number
	Tip 314: Grouping the Date Field by Quarters in a Fiscal Reporting Year

Grouping the Date Field by Days, Months, Quarters, and Years

➢ **To group the Date field by days, months, quarters, and years:**

1. Drag the **Date** field from **Page** (the fields in the top-left corner) to **Row** (to the left of the data area).

2. Select one of the dates in the **Date** field (cell **A9** in the screenshot).

3. Right-click, select **Group and Show Detail** from the shortcut menu, and then select **Group**.

4. In the *Grouping* dialog box, select **Days**, **Months**, **Quarters**, and **Years**, then click **OK**. Three fields have been added to the **PivotTable** report: **Years**, **Quarters**, and **Months**.

5. Click and drag each of the three new fields from **Row** to **Page**

CAUTION!!! If the message **Cannot group that selection** appears, drag the **Date** field back to **Page**, and check the date column in the source data for empty cells or for dates that are not in date format, fix them all and then select the **PivotTable** report, drag the **Date** field to **Row**, click **Refresh** and try grouping again.

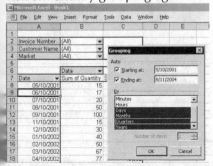

continued...

PivotTables

8

Notes:

_____

_____

_____

_____

_____

_____

_____

**My Tips/
Shortcuts:**

_____

_____

_____

_____

_____

_____

_____

_____

_____

_____

Grouping the Date Field by Days, Months, Quarters, and Years (cont.)

Grouping the Date Field by Number of Days and by Days, Months, Quarters, and Years

You can group a **Date** field only once, either by **Number of Days** or by **Days**, **Months**, **Quarters**, and **Years**, as explained in *Tip #311*.

If you want to group the **Date** field by both **Number of Days** or by **Days**, **Months**, **Quarters**, and **Years**:

1. Copy and insert the **Date** column in the source data so that there are two **Date** columns.
2. Change the heading title of the new **Date** column.
3. Add the new field to the **PivotTable** report, and then group each one of the **Date** fields, one by **Number of Days** and the other by **Days**, **Months**, **Quarters**, and **Years**.

PivotTables

8

Notes:

**My Tips/
Shortcuts:**

**Related
Tips:**

*Tip 311: Grouping the Date Field by
Number of Days*

*Tip 312: Grouping the Date Field by Days,
Months, Quarters, and Years*

*Tip 314: Grouping the Date Field by
Quarters in a Fiscal Reporting Year*

Grouping the Date Field by Week Number

➢ **To group by week number, add a column to the source data containing the formula WEEKNUM:**

1. In the source data, insert new column and enter the **WEEKNUM** formula into it.

2. In the second argument of the formula, set **Return Type** to **2** (**1** = Sunday, **2** = Monday, and so on).

Microsoft Excel - Book1

File Edit View Insert Format Tools Data Window Help

B2 =WEEKNUM(A2,2)

	Date	Week Number	Details	Ck #	Debit	Credit	Balance
2	01/01/2003	1	Openning Balance			9,852.00	9,852.00
3	01/02/2003	1	Credit Card pmts.		2,713.14		7,138.86
4	01/03/2003	1	Bank Charges		13.09		7,125.77
5	01/03/2003	1	Bank Charges		7.50		7,118.27
6	01/03/2003	1	CK	45	1,889.48		5,228.79
7	01/09/2003	2	Bank Charges		7.00		5,221.79
8	01/09/2003	2	Car Lease		319.00		4,902.79
9	01/09/2003	2	CK	54	5,600.00		-697.21
10	01/09/2003	2	CK	55	4,000.00		-4,697.21

Microsoft Excel - Book1

File Edit View Insert Format Tools Data Window Help

	A	B	C	D
1	Ck #	(All)		
2	Details	(All)		
3	Date	(All)		
4				
5		Data		
6	Week Number	Total Debit	Total Credit	Running Balance
7	1	4,623	9,852	5,229
8	2	9,926	15,000	10,303
9	3	4,163		6,140
10	4	537	5,852	11,455
11	5	4,016	1,313	8,752
12	6	1,047	20,000	27,705
13	7	2,412		25,293
14	8	38	3,589	28,844
15	9	539		28,305
16	10	1,518		26,787

PivotTables

8

Notes:

_____

_____

_____

_____

_____

_____

_____

**My Tips/
Shortcuts:**

_____

_____

_____

_____

_____

_____

Related Tips:	*Tip 311: Grouping the Date Field by Number of Days*
	Tip 312: Grouping the Date Field by Days, Months, Quarters, and Years
	Tip 313: Grouping the Date Field by Week Number

Grouping the Date Field by Quarters in a Fiscal Reporting Year

> **To group by quarters when reporting on a fiscal year basis:**

1. Add a new column to the source data (column **G** in the screenshot), and enter the formula below to calculate the quarter number for the fiscal year:

   ="Q"&(MOD(CEILING(22+MONTH(F2)-9-1,3)/3,4)+1)

2. Add a new column to the source data (column **H** in the screenshot), and insert the formula below to calculate the fiscal year number:

   =IF(MONTH(F2)<=9,YEAR(F2),YEAR(F2)+1)

Note: The number **9** in the formulas is the fiscal year month end (September).

Account Number	Account Name	BS, P&L Level 3	BS, P&L Level 2	BS, P&L Level 1	Month	Quarters by Fiscal Year	Fiscal Year	Sum
1011	Checking Account #1	Cash	Current Assets	Assets	January 2002	Q2	2002	1,483,475
1012	Checking Account #2	Cash	Current Assets	Assets	January 2002	Q2	2002	
1021	Payroll Checking Account	Cash	Current Assets	Assets	January 2002	Q2	2002	
1051	Savings Account #1	Cash	Current Assets	Assets	January 2002	Q2	2002	
1061	Money Market Account #1	Cash	Current Assets	Assets	January 2002	Q2	2002	

	A	B	C	D
1	BS, P&L Level 3	(All)		
2	BS, P&L Level 1	(All)		
3	BS, P&L Level 2	(All)		
4	Account Name	(All)		
5	Account Number	(All)		
6				
7	Balance	Fiscal Year		
8	Quarters by Fiscal Year	2002	2003	2004
9	Q1		47,419	54,986
10	Q2	1,209,890	1,216,609	
11	Q3	63,427	77,255	
12	Q4	13,549	58,291	
13	Grand Total	1,286,867	1,399,574	54,986
14				

PivotTables

8

781

Notes:

**My Tips/
Shortcuts:**

Adding a Calculated Percentage Field

➢ **To add a calculated percentage field:**

1. Select any cell in the **Pivot Table** report.

2. In **Excel 2002 & Excel 2003**: In the *PivotTable Field List* dialog box, drag one of the data fields to the **Data** area in the **PivotTable** report.

   In **Excel 2000**: Drag the data field from the bottom of the **PivotTable** toolbar.

   In **Excel 97**: Right-click any cell in the **PivotTable** report, select **Wizard** from the shortcut menu, and then **Layout**. Drag the data field to the **Data** area, and then click **Finish**.

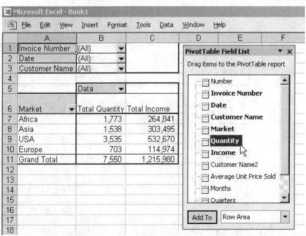

3. Select any cell in the new data field, and from the **PivotTable** toolbar, select **Field Settings** (in **Excel 97**, select **PivotTable Field**).

4. In the **Name** box, type the new heading text: **% Quantity**.

continued...

PivotTables

8

Notes:

_____

_____

_____

_____

_____

_____

_____

_____

My Tips/
Shortcuts:

_____

_____

_____

_____

_____

_____

_____

_____

_____

_____

_____

Adding a Calculated Percentage Field (cont.)

5. From **Show Data as**, choose **% of Total** and click **OK**.

6. To move the new field, select the column in the **PivotTable** report and drag to a new position.

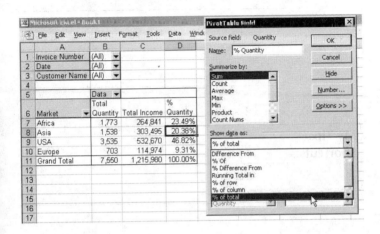

Notes:

_____

_____

_____

_____

_____

**My Tips/
Shortcuts:**

_____

_____

_____

_____

Related Tips:	*Tip 315: Adding a Calculated Percentage Field*
	Tip 318: Adding a Data Field That Calculates Percentage Difference from the Previous Item
	Tip 319: Adding a Data Field That Calculates Difference from the Previous Item

Adding a Data Field That Calculates the Difference Between Two Data Fields

➢ **To add data fields that calculate the difference between two data fields (columns H and I in the screenshot on the next page):**

1. Select a cell in the **PivotTable** report, and from the **PivotTable** toolbar, click the **PivotTable** icon and select **Formulas**, and then **Calculated Field**.

2. In the *Insert Calculated Field* dialog box, type the field title in the **Name** box.

3. In the **Fields** box, select **December 2003**.

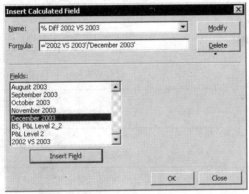

4. Click **Insert Field**, and then type the minus (-) sign in the **Formula** box.

5. In the **Fields** box, select **December 2002**, click **Insert Field**, and then click **OK**.

6. Insert the new calculated field into the **Data area** by dragging the new calculated field from the **PivotTable Field List** to the **Data** area.

   In **Excel 97** and **Excel 2000**, use the *Layout* dialog box (**Step 3** of the **PivotTable** Wizard in **Excel 97**, and **Step 4** in **Excel 2000**) to drag it to the **Data** area.

continued...

PivotTables

8

Notes:

**My Tips/
Shortcuts:**

Adding a Data Field That Calculates the Difference Between Two Data Fields (cont.)

7. Select a cell in the first calculated field (cell **H7** for example) and click the **Field Setting** icon on the **PivotTable** toolbar.

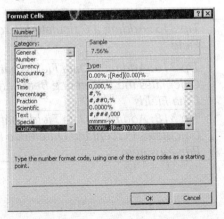

BS, P&L Level 3	2003	Running Balance 2003	% of Sales 2003	2002	Running Balance 2002	% of Sales 2002	Diff 2002 VS 2003	Diff in % 2002 VS 2003
Sales	145,148	145,148	100.00%	134,180	134,180	100.00%	10,968	7.56%
Cost of goods sold	(80,088)	(80,088)	(55.18)%	(71,388)	(71,388)	(53.20)%	(8,700)	10.86%
General & Administration	(10,255)	(10,255)	(7.07)%	(9,367)	(9,367)	(6.98)%	(888)	8.66%
Marketing	(6,550)	(6,550)	(4.51)%	(5,950)	(5,950)	(4.43)%	(600)	9.16%
Research & Development	(2,891)	(2,891)	(1.86)%	(3,980)	(3,980)	(2.95)%	1,269	(47.16)%
Amortization	(1,640)	(1,640)	(1.13)%	(1,532)	(1,532)	(1.14)%	(108)	6.59%
Non Operating Expenses	183	183	0.13%	147	147	0.11%	36	19.67%
Non Operating Income	4,032	4,032	2.76%	3,360	3,360	2.50%	672	16.67%
Special Gain (Loss)	142	142	0.10%	(100)	(100)	(0.07)%	242	170.42%
Income Taxes	(3,560)	(3,560)	(2.45)%	(2,984)	(2,984)	(2.22)%	(576)	16.18%
Grand Total	44,721	44,721		42,406	42,406		2,315	5.18%

8. Click **Number**, and then change the field formatting.

9. Select a cell in the second calculated field (cell **I7** for example) and click the **Field Setting** icon on the **PivotTable** toolbar.

10. Click **Number**, select **Custom**, and in the **Type** box change the field formatting to "**0.00% ;[Red](0.00%)**".

Notes:

_____

_____

_____

_____

_____

**My Tips/
Shortcuts:**

_____

_____

_____

_____

Adding a Data Field That Calculates Percentages from One Item of the Row Field

➢ **To add a data field that calculates % from one item of the row field:**

1. From the **PivotTable Field List**, drag a field to the **Data** area. In the example below, the field is **December 2003**.

    In **Excel 97** and **Excel 2000**, use the *Layout* dialog box (**Step 3** of the **PivotTable** Wizard in **Excel 97**, and **Step 4** in **Excel 2000**) to drag the extra field to the **Data** area.

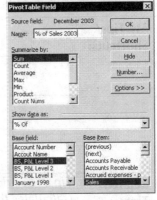

2. Select a cell in the new field and click the **Field Setting** icon.

3. Change the title of the field in the **Name** box.

4. Click **Options**, and from the **Show data as** dropdown list, select **% of**.

5. In **Base field**, select the detailed **Row** field.

6. In **Base item**, select first item of the **Base field**, and then click **OK**.

	A	B	C	D	E	F	G	H	I
1	BS, P&L Level 1	Profit & Loss ▼							
2	Accout Name	(All) ▼							
3	BS, P&L Level 2	(All) ▼							
4									
5		Data ▼							
6	BS, P&L Level 3 ▼	2003	Running Balance 2003	% of Sales 2003	2002	Running Balance 2002	% of Sales 2002	Diff 2002 VS 2003	Diff in % 2002 VS 2003
7	Sales	145,148	145,148	100.00%	134,180	134,180	100.00%	10,968	7.56%
8	Cost of goods sold	(80,088)	(80,088)	(55.18)%	(71,388)	(71,388)	(53.20)%	(8,700)	10.86%
9	General & Administration	(10,255)	(10,255)	(7.07)%	(9,367)	(9,367)	(6.98)%	(888)	8.66%
10	Marketing	(6,550)	(6,550)	(4.51)%	(5,950)	(5,950)	(4.43)%	(600)	9.16%
11	Research & Development	(2,691)	(2,691)	(1.85)%	(3,960)	(3,960)	(2.95)%	1,269	(47.16)%
12	Amortization	(1,640)	(1,640)	(1.13)%	(1,532)	(1,532)	(1.14)%	(108)	6.59%
13	Non Operating Expenses	183	183	0.13%	147	147	0.11%	36	19.67%
14	Non Operating Income	4,032	4,032	2.78%	3,360	3,360	2.50%	672	16.67%
15	Special Gain (Loss)	142	142	0.10%	(100)	(100)	(0.07)%	242	170.42%
16	Income Taxes	(3,560)	(3,560)	(2.45)%	(2,984)	(2,984)	(2.22)%	(576)	16.18%
17	Grand Total	44,721	44,721		42,406	42,406		2,315	5.18%
18									

Notes:

_____

_____

_____

_____

_____

**My Tips/
Shortcuts:**

_____

_____

_____

**Related
Tips:**

*Tip 316: Adding a Data Field That
Calculates the Difference Between Two
Data Fields*

*Tip 317: Adding a Data Field That
Calculates Percentages from One Item of
the Row Field*

*Tip 319: Adding a Data Field That
Calculates Difference from the Previous
Item*

Adding a Data Field That Calculates Percentage Difference from the Previous Item

➢ **To add a data field that calculates the % difference from the previous item:**

1. From the **PivotTable Field List**, drag a field to the **Data** area. In the example below, the field is **Quantity**.

   In **Excel 97** and **Excel 2000**, use the *Layout* dialog box (**Step 3** of the **PivotTable** Wizard in **Excel 97**, and **Step 4** in **Excel 2000**) to drag the extra field to the **Data** area.

2. Select a cell in the new field and click the **Field Setting** icon.

3. Change the title of the field in the **Name** box.

4. Click **Options**, and from the **Show data as** dropdown list, select % **Difference From**.

5. In **Base field**, select the detailed **Row** field.

6. In **Base item**, select first item of the **Base field**, and then click **OK**.

Result: See column **D** in the **Pivot Table** report.

Notes:

**My Tips/
Shortcuts:**

Adding a Data Field That Calculates the Difference from the Previous Item

➢ **To add a data field that calculates the difference from the previous item:**

1. From the **PivotTable Field List**, drag a field to the **Data** area. In the example below, the field is **Quantity**.

   In **Excel 97** and **Excel 2000**, use the *Layout* dialog box (**Step 3** of the **PivotTable** Wizard in **Excel 97**, and **Step 4** in **Excel 2000**) to drag the extra field to the **Data** area.

2. Select a cell in the new field and click the **Field Setting** icon.

3. Change the title of the field in the **Name** box.

4. Click **Options**, and from the **Show data as** dropdown list, select **Difference From**.

5. In **Base field**, select the detailed **Row** field.

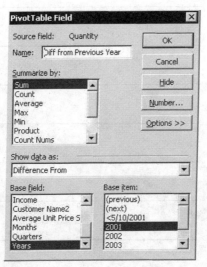

continued...

795

Notes:

_____

_____

_____

_____

_____

**My Tips/
Shortcuts:**

_____

_____

_____

_____

_____

_____

_____

_____

_____

Adding a Data Field That Calculates the Difference from the Previous Item (cont.)

6. In **Base item**, select first item of the **Base field**, and then click **OK**.

Result: See column **C** in the **Pivot Table** report

Microsoft Excel - Book1							
File Edit View Insert Format Tools Data Window Help							
	A	B	C	D	E	F	G	H
1	Invoice Number	(All)		Months	(All)			
2	Market	(All)		Customer	(All)			
3	Quarters	(All)		Customer Nar	(All)			
4	Date	(All)						
5								
6		Data						
7	Years	Total Quantity	Diff from Previous Year	% Diff from Previous Year	% Quantity	Invoices Number	Total Income	
8	2001	247			3.27%	7	69,689	
9	2002	1,286	1,039	420.49%	17.03%	12	255,148	
10	2003	3,029	2,782	1126.48%	40.13%	12	459,953	
11	2004	2,988	2,741	1109.55%	39.57%	8	431,190	
12	Grand Total	7,550			100.00%	39	1,215,980	
13								

PivotTables

8

Notes:

_____

_____

_____

_____

_____

_____

**My Tips/
Shortcuts:**

_____

_____

_____

Related Tips:	*Tip 316: Adding a Data Field That Calculates the Difference Between Two Data Fields*
	Tip 318: Adding a Data Field That Calculates Percentage Difference from the Previous Item
	Tip 319: Adding a Data Field That Calculates Difference from the Previous Item

Adding a Running Balance Calculation Column

➤ **To add a Running Balance Calculation Column:**

✦ **Step 1: Add a New Calculated Field**

1. Select a cell in the **PivotTable Report**, press **<Alt+P>** and from the **PivotTable** icon on the **PivotTable** toolbar, select **Formula**, and then **Calculated Field**.

2. In the **Name** box, type **Running Balance Field** as the name of the calculated field.

3. From **Fields** select the **Credit** field, and then click **Insert Field**.

4. In **Formula**, type the minus (-) sign.

5. In **Fields**, select the **Debit** field, and then click **Insert Field**.

6. Click **OK**.

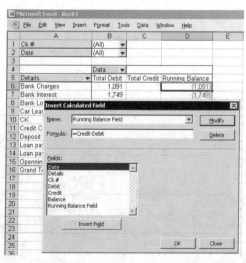

continued...

PivotTables

8

Notes:

_____

_____

_____

_____

_____

_____

**My Tips/
Shortcuts:**

_____

_____

_____

_____

_____

_____

_____

_____

_____

_____

Adding a *Running Balance* Calculation Column (cont.)

✦ **Step 2: Calculate the Running Balance**

1. Select a cell in the new calculated field and click the **Field Settings** icon on the **PivotTable** toolbar.

2. In the *PivotTable Field* dialog box, change the field name in the **Name** box.

3. Click **Options**.

4. From the **Show Data as** dropdown list, select **Running Total in**.

5. In **Base field**, select **Details**, and then click **OK**.

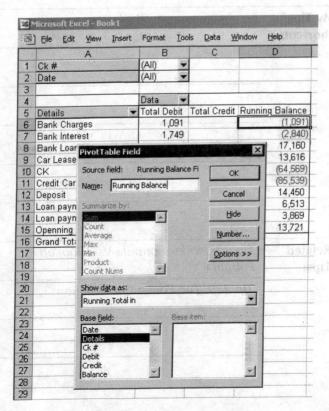

Notes:

My Tips/
Shortcuts:

Related
Tips:

Tip 227: Index Formula Vs. Vlookup
Formula

Tip 229: The Power Combination

Retrieving Data from a PivotTable Report

The **GETPIVOTDATA** formula allows the retrieval of data from a **PivotTable** report while its structure is being changed.

➤ **To retrieve data, use the GETPIVOTDATA formula:**

✦ In **Excel 2002** and **Excel 2003**, it is much easier to use the **GETPIVOTDATA** formula. Simply select any cell outside the **PivotTable** report, press the equals (=) sign and select a cell in the **PivotTable** report's **Data** area.

In **Excel 97** and **Excel 2000**, insert the formula by manually typing the data field name and the fields.

Result:

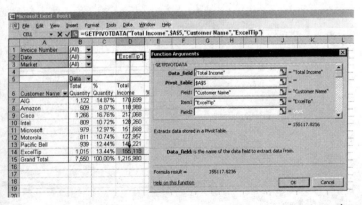

continued...

PivotTables

8

Notes:

_____

_____

_____

_____

_____

_____

_____

**My Tips/
Shortcuts:**

_____

_____

_____

_____

_____

_____

_____

_____

_____

_____

_____

Retrieving Data from a PivotTable Report (cont.)

➢ **To retrieve data when the structure of the PivotTable Report is stable, use either:**

✦ The **INDEX** formula combined with the **MATCH** formula. The defined **Names** used in the formulas are:

❖ **PivotTableSheet:** The name of the entire sheet.

❖ **ColA:** Column A.

Note: The number **4** in the **MATCH** formula stands for column **D**, which is column **4** in the sheet.

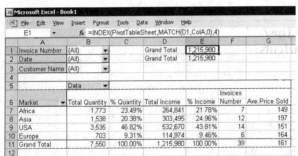

Microsoft Excel - Book1

File Edit View Insert Format Tools Data Window Help

E1 ▾ =INDEX(PivotTableSheet,MATCH(D1,ColA,0),4)

	A	B	C	D	E	F	G
1	Invoice Number	(All)		Grand Total	1,215,980		
2	Date	(All)		Grand Total	1,215,980		
3	Customer Name	(All)					
4							
5		Data					
6	Market	Total Quantity	% Quantity	Total Income	% Income	Invoices Number	Ave.Price Sold
7	Africa	1,773	23.49%	264,841	21.78%	7	149
8	Asia	1,538	20.38%	303,495	24.96%	12	197
9	USA	3,535	46.82%	532,670	43.81%	14	151
10	Europe	703	9.31%	114,974	9.46%	6	164
11	Grand Total	7,550	100.00%	1,215,980	100.00%	39	161
12							

✦ The **SUMIF** formula combined with the **OFFSET** formula.

Note: The number **3** in the **OFFSET** formula stands for the three columns from reference, which is column **A**.

Microsoft Excel - Book1

File Edit View Insert Format Tools Data Window Help

E2 ▾ =SUMIF(ColA,D2,OFFSET(ColA,0,3))

	A	B	C	D	E	F	G
1	Invoice Number	(All)		Grand Total	1,215,980		
2	Date	(All)		Grand Total	1,215,980		
3	Customer Name	(All)					
4							
5		Data					
6	Market	Total Quantity	% Quantity	Total Income	% Income	Invoices Number	Ave.Price Sold
7	Africa	1,773	23.49%	264,841	21.78%	7	149
8	Asia	1,538	20.38%	303,495	24.96%	12	197
9	USA	3,535	46.82%	532,670	43.81%	14	151
10	Europe	703	9.31%	114,974	9.46%	6	164
11	Grand Total	7,550	100.00%	1,215,980	100.00%	39	161
12							

PivotTables

8

Notes:

_____

_____

_____

_____

_____

_____

**My Tips/
Shortcuts:**

_____

_____

_____

_____

_____

_____

**Related
Tips:**

Tip 305: Inserting a Chart

*Tip 321: Retrieving Data from a PivotTable
Report*

Adding Additional PivotTable Reports Using the Same Data Source

➤ **To create several PivotTable reports with different structures from one data source:**

✦ **Option 1: Assuming a PivotTable report has already been created**

1. Select a cell in another sheet.

2. From the *Data* menu, select **PivotTable and PivotChart Report**.

3. In **Step 1 of 3**, select **Another PivotTable or PivotChart**, and then click **Next**.

4. Select the name of the **PivotTable** report already created in the workbook, and then click **Next**.

5. Continue building the **PivotTable** report.

✦ **Option 2: The fastest method**

Quickly create several **PivotTable** reports from a single one by copying and pasting the existing **PivotTable** report.

1. Right-click a cell in the existing **PivotTable** report, select **Select** from the shortcut menu, and then **Entire Table**.

2. Press **<Ctrl+C>** to copy it.

3. Press **<Shift+F11>** to insert new sheet, and then press **<Ctrl+V>** to paste the **PivotTable** report.

4. Repeat step 3 to add more **PivotTable** reports. You can now change the field structures of each **PivotTable** report to analyze the data and present it differently.

Note: Refreshing one **PivotTable** report refreshes each of the additional **PivotTable** reports, as they all use the same source data stored in the cache memory.

PivotTables

8

Index

X

Z

We'd Like to Hear from You!

Our goal is to publish a book that will help you to **Get the Most Out of Excel**, upgrade your working level, and bring to your desk the best solutions needed for everyday tasks — all this while using this book **F1- Get the Most Out of Excel! The Ultimate Excel Tip Help Guide**.

I would appreciate it if you could find a few moments and share with us your thoughts, comments, suggestions, ideas, tips, areas to cover, helpful solutions that other Excel users might need, and how we can improve and make this book better.

Looking forward to hear from you,

Joseph Rubin, CPA

Author

jrubin@exceltip.com

www.exceltip.com

Joseph Rubin's Excel books:

✦ **F1 — Get the Most out of Excel! The Ultimate Excel Help Tip Guide** (print & e-Book)

✦ **Financial Statements.xls** (print & e-Book)

✦ **Mr Excel On Excel** (print)

For more information and ordering: www.exceltip.com